IMPERIAL WAR MUSEUM REVIEW

ARTICLES ON ASPECTS OF
TWENTIETH CENTURY HISTORY
PRINCIPALLY BY THE STAFF OF
THE IMPERIAL WAR MUSEUM

PUBLISHED BY
THE TRUSTEES OF
THE IMPERIAL WAR MUSEUM
1989
GENERAL EDITOR:
SUZANNE BARDGETT
HISTORICAL EDITOR:
PETER SIMKINS
DESIGNED BY
GRUNDY & NORTHEDGE DESIGNERS
DISTRIBUTED BY LEO COOPER IN ASSOCIATION
WITH WILLIAM HEINEMANN LTD.
PRINTED BY
BAS PRINTERS LTD
© TRUSTEES OF THE IMPERIAL
WAR MUSEUM AND THE AUTHORS
BRITISH LIBRARY CATALOGUING IN PUBLICATION DATA
IMPERIAL WAR MUSEUM REVIEW.—NO. 4-
1. WARFARE. HISTORY. SERIALS
I. IMPERIAL WAR MUSEUM. *TRUSTEES*
355′.02′09
ISBN 0-901627-52-6

Cover illustration: Bill Brandt: Shelterers at Elephant and Castle underground station, November 1940.

Contents

Unless otherwise stated, all photographs and historical sources cited are from the Imperial War Museum's archives.

Olive Edis: Imperial War Museum Photographer in France and Belgium, March 1919

Jane Carmichael

Jane Carmichael is Keeper of the Department of Photographs.

In the first months after its foundation in March 1917, the various specialist committees of the National War Museum, as it was then known, set about their task of collecting with enormous vigour and determination; none more so than the Women's Work Committee.[1] It was the daughter of the Museum's first Director General, Miss Agnes Conway, who was asked by her father, Sir Martin Conway, to draw up the original scheme for a women's work committee in April 1917. Her ideas for the creation of a comprehensive record of women's work through the collection of as many artefacts, documents and photographs as possible were endorsed by the committee's first chairman, Lady Priscilla Norman. The daughter of Lord Aberconway, a coal mining and shipping magnate, and wife of a liberal Member of Parliament, Sir Henry Norman, she was capable, imaginative and well-connected. Supported by half a dozen other prominent ladies, Lady Norman and Miss Conway were a formidable combination and set to with a will to make up for the relatively late start in collecting for the national record of the war.

They quickly recognised that photographs would be important in providing the necessary retrospective. During 1917 and 1918, the committee corresponded with innumerable kinds of organisations, industrial, medical and military, asking them for material with which to put on record the role that women had played in the war. It also sought the cooperation of the Ministry of Information in providing a directly commissioned photographic record of war work, and the two MOI photographers then active on the home front were instructed to concentrate on the new roles of women with a view to their work being lodged in the newly established archive. In October and November 1918 the first fruits of the Women's Work Committee's collecting activities were shown in a resoundingly successful exhibition at the Whitechapel Gallery.

Lady Norman was eager to organise a tour of the Western Front in order to make a photographic record of the women's organisations there. The journey was planned to allow coverage of the main military women's services; the Women's Royal Naval Service, the Women's Army Auxiliary Corps (still referred to familiarly as Queen Mary's Army Auxiliary Corps), and the various nursing organisations; Queen Alexandra's Imperial Military Nursing Service, the First Aid Nursing Yeomanry and the Voluntary Aid Detachment, and to look at least briefly at some of the American and French organisations. The scheme was approved by the main Imperial War Museum Committee and it seems to have been taken for granted that a woman photographer would be appropriate to record 'a woman's point of view'.[2] Agnes

Dame Rachel Crowdy,
Commandant of the VAD, and her
assistant, Miss Monica
Glazebrook, in their office at the
Hotel Christol, Boulogne.
Q 7978

A group of senior nurses
taking tea at the American
Hospital at Toul.
Q 8075

FANY drivers with their vehicles at Commercy. Q 8074

QMAAC telegraphists in the Signals Office at Boulogne. Q 7972

An Officers Expeditionary Force Canteen staffed by QMAAC. Q 8106

Conway first approached Olive Edis in October 1918.

The fifth daughter of a Norfolk architect, at forty two Olive Edis was firmly established as a professional portraitist, and prided herself on her excellent presentation and technical abilities. She had opened a studio near her home in Sheringham, Norfolk, and another in Farnham, Surrey. A pioneer of the use of natural light for interior shots and also an exponent of the autochrome, an early form of colour photography, she was admitted to membership of the Royal Photographic Society in 1914. Surviving records do not unfortunately show whether other candidates were considered, or whether Miss Edis was especially recommended, but it is unlikely that the field of choice for professional women photographers was very large. The war had given a tremendous boost to the reporting of news in photographs, but the profession of news photographer remained very much a male preserve – on the whole associated with the cheaper type of newspaper. The basis of most photographers' business remained the studio and as there were few professional women photographers, it was inevitable that they would be primarily studio portraitists. There is also a suggestion in the correspondence surrounding the commission that the photographer chosen should be as like-minded and of a similar class as possible to her well-connected companions in order to minimise the difficulties of travelling and working together.

In any case, Olive Edis responded to Miss Conway's invitation to join her and Lady Norman on a month long tour of France with enthusiasm, and was quite prepared to carry out the commission on an expenses only basis for the benefit of the newly-formed national collection. For the whole of October letters flew back and forth between London and Norfolk. Miss Edis had clear ideas about her methods of work. In her first letter to Miss Conway she expressed her preference for natural light although she was prepared if necessary to use some of the primitive flash equipment of the period:

> I have always avoided flash exposures – and managed to get results under the most difficult conditions by daylight – but you may be right about the necessity in November for taking flash exposures. There is an apparatus which I believe only costs about a sovereign for producing two flashes at opposite ends of the room connected by an electric cord and fired by a pocket flash lamp.[3]

She proposed to travel with one large field camera which could take the large format 10 × 8 inch plates she preferred and a smaller 7 × 5 inch one as back up. As a last resort she also had one of the popular small format amateur cameras, a Folding Kodak. She would take all the glass plates required with her and it was agreed that she should aim to produce

Olive Edis (1876–1955), wearing the Museum's badge in her cap and carrying a folding plate camera similar to the one she used in France. National Portrait Gallery 30015

about two hundred prints for the Museum.

The correspondence was not only concerned with photography: sartorial matters were also discussed at length. Miss Edis was anxious that her official position should be recognised, and although a uniform was clearly impractical for such a short trip, she very much wanted to wear a badge of some sort. The Museum had been founded as the 'National War Museum' until the Dominions' request that they too should participate, and the only badges available showed the original initials. Gratified to have something so unique, Miss Edis sewed one into her cap, and when trying it on, was amused to be asked whether the initials stood for 'New Women's Movement'.[4] She was also reminded by Miss Conway that as they would be visiting large bases where they would be received in some style there might be occasions when she would need a smart dress.

The Museum now had a representative at General Headquarters, but the authorities were less than helpful, preoccupied as they were with the final stages of the war. The women's organisations themselves, however, when contacted directly, responded favourably. Lady Norman had

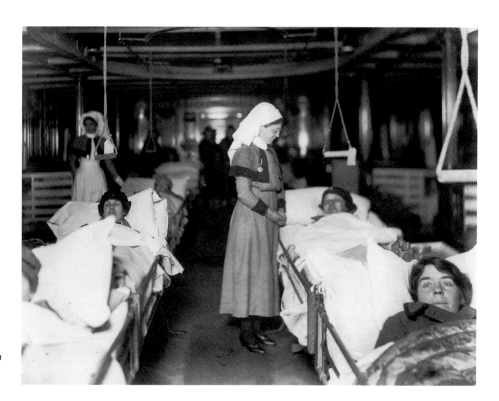

The women's ward on board the hospital ship, *St Andrew*.
Q 7997

The hairdressers' shop, for the QMAAC at Pont de l'Arche, which enjoyed the reputation of being 'a regular Bond Street establishment'.
Q 8108

hoped to make a start in November but plans were swept aside in the flurry of arrangements for the Armistice. The postponement was disappointing but more setbacks were to come. Lady Norman fell ill with a bad case of the influenza epidemic that was raging in late 1918, and by the time she recovered, was committed to working in her husband's constituency for the forthcoming General Election.

In January 1919, finding that the Museum's representative at General Headquarters had achieved nothing, she decided to plead her case in the highest quarter, and wrote to her fellow committee member and wife of the Commander in Chief of the British Army, Lady Haig, protesting at the apparent exclusion and arguing that it was vital to obtain the records before the women's organisations, already beginning to be run down, were further dismantled.[5] This ploy seems to have worked, because by the middle of February, she was writing jubilantly to Olive Edis to say that all was well and that arrangements were definitely in hand. They would start from Victoria on 2 March and their four week tour in a car lent by the British Red Cross Society would include bases at or near Boulogne, Calais, Brussels, Amiens, Abbeville, Etaples, Le Havre, Rouen, Tours, Bourges, Nancy, Bar le Duc, Lille and Arras.

The diary which Olive Edis kept of their travels shows how strenuous the schedule was and how demanding for a photographer whose reflective style needed careful preparation and checking of the proposed subjects in the available light. Her lively prose describes their various adventures. Of her encounter at Beaumarais with the officer responsible for photography on the Western Front, Colonel J. Lee, she wrote:

> He was a little inclined to challenge the need of my coming, and showed us volumes of 5 × 4 photos, many taken in the women's camps, by the official photographers. However, I explained that the Imperial War Museum thought that a woman photographer, living among the girls in their camps, was likely to achieve more intimate pictures, more descriptive of their everyday life, than a man press photographer. He quite saw the point . . .[6]

Colonel Lee had little interest in photography in fact, for his prime concern was the operation of the war artists scheme, but at the same time he was wary of any apparent encroachment on his preserves. The price of food and the general standard of sanitation in France appalled Miss Edis, though in Belgium matters improved. Plagued by a throat infection and subjected to long car journeys frequently in cold, snow and a bitter wind, she sometimes found the vigour of her two companions daunting. After a particularly tortuous day in and around Lille, with poor opportunities for photography, a broken car spring, a missed road, and miserable weather, the ladies finally arrived at their destination. Miss Edis wilted when she heard Lady Norman pronounce firmly; 'I propose that we photograph the Canteen first and have tea afterwards.' Nevertheless, 'to this superhuman suggestion, frozen and miserable, I did my best to rise, but I did not enjoy it.'[7] Miss Edis also had to cope with various accidents to her cameras; a hospital orderly dropped one and on the penultimate day, the focussing screen on her large camera was shattered. This was ingeniously overcome by the substitution of an X-ray plate covered with a piece of oiled tissue paper.

Their stalwart Ford, driven by an aged but indefatigable Quaker nicknamed 'Daddy Blow', rattled along the French and Belgian highways, across the war-torn terrain. The sights were unforgettable:

> The Menin road to Ypres impressed us tremendously. The indescribable wrack of war was to be seen as nowhere else. The remnants of tanks lay everywhere in shell-holes. We could see eight from one point of view. Cartridges, bombs, grenades of every kind lay strewn upon the ground. One could pick up 'trophies' by the hundred had one cared, accoutrements, helmets, bayonets, shell cases. The sun was beginning to gleam after a long morning of rain. . . . The whole land lay in water – shell-hole after shell-hole – . . . The cemetery at Hooge was a swamp, on a sloping ground, the tiny white crosses packed close together, two men in every grave, and a path of duck-boards to slide on, one's boots coated with slimy yellow mud.[8]

Despite their tribulations the three ladies seem to have found a comradeship in their shared experiences. With the help of Lady Norman's organisational ability and unexpected and much-appreciated willingness to act as photographer's assistant, the travelling was accomplished and the photographs taken.

Miss Edis tried to show something of the duties expected and the skills acquired in the women's organisations, by the telephone operators, the enormous number of clerks, drivers, cooks and canteen workers, besides the more familiar nurses and medical attendants. She demonstrated over and over her capacity for taking interiors using the available light, particularly in her charming studies of recreational pastimes such as taking tea and reading newspapers. In some cases her use of long exposures resulted in blurred figures, but the sense of depth and the clarity of textures are remarkable. Her well-

A French Red Cross Canteen with
British staff.
Q 8086

WAAC gardeners tending the
graves of the war dead, Etaples
1919. The wooden crosses would
later be replaced by white
headstones.
Q 8027

developed sense of composition was strongly apparent; she in fact deliberately arranged groups to give the most pleasing effect. In her more familiar role as a portraitist, she produced some memorable work, such as her candid picture of Dame Rachel Crowdy, showing the redoubtable characters of those in command.

The ladies returned exhausted but pleased with their efforts at the end of March and Miss Edis set to work to produce a set of prints. In the end the Museum accepted 171 prints from Miss Edis and professed itself very pleased with them although there were one or two quibbles about the number which had been issued as gifts in thanks for cooperation.

After her trip, Olive Edis lost contact with the Museum. She remained a professional photographer all her life until her death aged 79 in 1955. Sheringham in Norfolk remained her base but her London studio in Ladbroke Grove allowed her to run a lucrative portrait business. Occasionally she portrayed the famous but the backbone of her work was the professional middle class. In 1928, she married a solicitor, Edwin Henry Galsworthy, a cousin of the famous novelist of the middle classes, John Galsworthy. A representative sample of her photographs survives at the National Portrait Gallery but it was not until recently when greater information about the provenance of the First World War collection was discovered that it became possible to identify once again Olive Edis's work within the Imperial War Museum collection.

Although the 171 photographs may seem a modest output for such a well-prepared expedition, they are nevertheless an unusual and attractive set. Miss Edis could allow herself little room for wastage, as even on a good day, given the need for careful arrangement of her subject and her cumbersome equipment, she would not expect to expose more than about a dozen plates and there were clearly no second chances on such a journey. Her style was more serious and intimate than that of the official photographers who had previously covered the role of women on the Western Front. They worked in a smaller format which allowed a degree of spontaneity in contrast to Miss Edis's posed figures. Their photographs, destined for publication in the popular press, frequently emphasised the appeal of pretty, smiling girls in contrast to Miss Edis's rather solemn figures. Her work remains what her commissioners asked: a dignified and visually pleasing series of studies of women's roles in what had been the main theatre of war. The sense of decorum, propriety and good manners is powerful throughout, and difficulties are minimised in the portrayal of the communal working and living for the same cause. Naturally in the time available it was bound to be an incomplete record, but it is a record that throws interesting light on the assumptions and values of this accomplished photographer and her commissioners.

Notes

1. In the first two years of the Museum's existence, various committees such as the War Office, the Admiralty, Munitions, etc organised its collecting activities. There were usually about eight in existence at any one time. A detailed account of the Museum's foundation and early years may be read in Diana Condell, *The Imperial War Museum, 1917–1920: a study of the institution and its presentation of the First World War*, CNAA unpublished M Phil thesis, June 1984.
2. Women's Work Committee file, Report of 1918/19.
3. WWC file, *Tour in France by Miss Conway, Lady Norman and Miss Edis to obtain a photographic record of Women's War Work March 1919*, letter from Olive Edis to Agnes Conway 20 October 1918.
4. Ibid, Olive Edis to Agnes Conway, 24 October 1918.
5. Ibid, Lady Norman to Lady Haig, 16 January 1919.
6. Olive Edis's Diary, *The Record of a Journey to Photograph the British Women's Services Overseas begun on Sunday March 2 1919*, held by the Royal Photographic Society, p 3.
7. Ibid, p 77.
8. Ibid, pp 15 and 16.

Acknowledgements

Special thanks are due to Brian Coe of the Royal Photographic Society, for making Olive Edis's diary available, to Terry Pepper of the National Portrait Gallery, for her photograph and additional biographical information, and to Diana Condell of the Imperial War Museum, for information on the Museum's early history.

Further Reading

Diana Condell and Jean Liddiard, *Working for Victory? Images of Women in the First World War*, Routledge, London, 1987.
Val Williams, *Women Photographers*, Virago, London, 1986.

An introduction to the papers of Field Marshal Sir Henry Wilson

Keith Jeffery

Dr Keith Jeffery is a lecturer in history at the University of Ulster.

Field Marshal Sir Henry Wilson was one of the most controversial British soldiers of the modern age. Today, however, he is perhaps remembered more for the circumstances of his death than for the achievements of his career. On 22 June 1922, five months after he had retired from the army, Wilson was assassinated by two Irish Republicans on his doorstep in Eaton Place, London. A lifelong Unionist from southern Ireland (though with Ulster forbears), by 1922 he had become a symbol of British 'repression' in Ireland and as Chief Security Advisor to the relatively new Northern Ireland government, he was identified with the uncompromisingly Unionist administration in Belfast. As a retired senior officer who had refused the offer of police protection he was also a comparatively 'soft' target. Wilson was accorded a State funeral and was buried in St Paul's Cathedral. He was celebrated as one of the greatest British soldiers ever, and a man who had played a crucial role in the Allied victory in the Great War. Five years later his reputation was ruined by the publication of his official biography, *Field Marshal Sir Henry Wilson, His Life and Diaries*, by Sir C E Callwell.[1]

Callwell's biographical method was to quote very extensively from Wilson's diaries. The impression given by these quotations was almost that of an overambitious, self-serving monster, with such violent passions and prejudices as to appear at times actually unbalanced. 'Relying upon the book alone', wrote Sir Andrew MacPhail, 'the inevitable judgment is that he [Wilson] and the editor have created a figure and not a man, an inhuman figure, calculating, callous, without a single generous sentiment or kind word.'[2] But Wilson's diary entries cannot simply be dismissed as 'just his Irish way of letting off steam and high spirits',[3] for they contain much of value for the historian, military and political. Together with the correspondence and other material preserved in the Imperial War Museum, they comprise one of the most remarkable and important twentieth-century British military archives.

The Wilson papers are outstanding for their range and quality as historical source material. The forty-one volumes of manuscript diaries covering the years 1893 – when Wilson was a student at the Staff College – to 1922[4] cover a very important period of British history in considerable detail. Wilson appears to have written up his diary every evening, sometimes writing several hundred words. Thus we have an immediate and vivid record of his own activities, which over the years become steadily more and more significant in broader military and political terms. His diaries are a major, and in some cases the only source, for many military affairs in the 1910–22 period. This is especially true regarding

Sir Henry Wilson, from a portrait by Oswald Birley, 1922. HU55860

Sir Henry Wilson, from an etching by John Day, 1921. HU55859

Anglo–French liaison and for Wilson's time as Chief of the Imperial General Staff (CIGS) in 1918–22. It seems, for example, that minutes were not kept – at least none are available in the War Office papers – during the regular meetings of the Military members of the Army Council, a crucial policy-making and policy-implementing group. Wilson's diary goes some way towards filling this gap.

The Wilson diaries are a comparatively well-known historical source, if only through the medium of Callwell's haphazardly-edited selection. But the collection in the Imperial War Museum also contains a large quantity of correspondence and other papers which, although they are not so well known, provide much very valuable evidence. The largest single part of this material is a series of 130 numbered files containing correspondence with some 65 individuals. The original numbering of these files has been retained in the War Museum catalogue.[5] These papers cover the period from November 1917, when Wilson became British Military Representative at the Supreme War Council, to February 1922, although there are a few letters dating from after he left the War Office. The great bulk of this material dates from Wilson's time as CIGS and, in effect, they comprise virtually all his official and semi-official correspondence while he was professional head of the British army. It seems that Wilson, who at the time of his death was planning to write his memoirs, simply took all these letters away with him when he retired.

Apart from this correspondence, which was all carefully filed and catalogued by Wilson's own office staff, there are another 24 files of letters from 1908 to 1922, most of which were saved by Wilson in a number of different categories. There are letters of congratulation on his promotion, or receipt of official honours;[6] correspondence with particular individuals;[7] and chronologically-arranged miscellaneous letters. Scarcely used by historians, and only now being catalogued, this material illustrates the breadth of Wilson's contacts, particularly his closeness to Conservative and Unionist politicians. It also demonstrates that the intemperance and frustration expressed in Wilson's diary was quite widely shared among other soldiers and politicians. Indeed, since the pre-1918 correspondence mostly includes only 'in' letters, the archive is of especial value for political historians. An outstanding theme of the correspondence from the beginning of the First World War until Lloyd George became Prime Minister, for example, is the growing political opposition to Asquith's administration. Much of this opposition depended on specifically military criticisms of the government's war policy, and in the Wilson Papers we find ample documentation of one of the vital links between soldiers and politicians.

The political richness of the Wilson archive is not wholly balanced by a corresponding depth of evidence concerning Wilson personally. One of the gaps in the collection is the absence of any letters from Wilson to his mother or to his wife, both of whom outlived him. Callwell in the official biography quotes extensively from such personal letters, but these do not seem to have survived. There are, nevertheless, a few family letters, mostly to and from Wilson's elder brother, James Mackay Wilson, which help to fill in some of the personal background.

The final major part of the archive is made up of miscellaneous papers mostly relating to Wilson's professional career.[8] These include subject files kept by Sir Henry concerning the South African War, Staff College papers from 1909, and documents from the 'Petrograd Mission' to Russia in 1917. There is also a file containing notes for what appears to be most of the lectures he gave at the Staff College when he was Commandant, together with various other talks and speeches delivered in the period 1907–14. In addition there are many official papers, including a set of the minutes Wilson wrote while he was Director of Military Operations (1910–14) and a large number of documents relating to the Supreme War Council (1917–18).

The arrangement of the Wilson collection catalogue reflects the papers' provenance. Wilson died childless and his literary estate was divided up. The first part of the collection to come to the Museum was the diaries, which were deposited by Sir Henry's nephew, Major Cyril Wilson, in

1972. Major Wilson subsequently gave some other miscellaneous letters and papers. The numbered correspondence files from Wilson's time as CIGS arrived by a different route. They had come into the possession of Mrs Marjorie Stevenson, a first cousin once removed of the Field Marshal, and had been left for safekeeping in the vault of Coutts Bank, London. Mrs Stevenson, having been alerted to the historical significance of the documents, consulted with Major Wilson and in 1973 gave the material to the Museum.

The significance of the collection also clearly stems from the important and influential positions which Wilson occupied. Wilson joined the army in 1882. In 1885–6 he served with the 1st Battalion of the Rifle Brigade in India, where he was quite seriously wounded in a fight with Burmese bandits. Most of his career, however, was spent in staff appointments. Indeed, he emerged as one of the ablest staff officers ever to serve in the British army. In the 1890s he served in the Intelligence Department of the War Office as the youngest staff officer in the army. During the South African War of 1899–1902 he served first as brigade-major of the 4th 'Light' Brigade and saw action at the disastrous Battle of Colenso during 'Black Week' in December 1899, and also the British defeat at Spion Kop on 24 January 1900. The following month he was present at the relief of Ladysmith. After the South African War ended Wilson collected together a considerable number of papers relating to the war in order to assist Leopold Amery who was editing *The Times History of the South African War*. Among these documents are nearly five hundred telegrams relating to his service as brigade-major. From the very beginning of the war, they indicated that the campaign was not necessarily going to be very easy. For one thing the Boers were exceptionally good shots and their unsportsmanlike habit of picking off officers prompted a message from the British headquarters in late November 1899: 'There is no objection to officers carrying rifles or sticks or in fact doing anything that they think will make them less conspicuous. Officers should remove any badges that would make them distinguishable from the men.'[9] At Colenso Wilson wrote to his wife that although 'I was under fire for 5 hours, and sometimes brisk fire, I can only swear to having seen 5 Boers'.[10] In his diary he was critical of the high command, a feeling he shared with his brigade commander, Major-General Neville Lyttleton. Early in January 1900:

> Lyttleton and I went to headquarters to have a chat about things which are eminently unsatisfactory. There is no go or spirit about Redvers Buller [the British CinC]. It's most curious. Constant chopping and changing and no scheming to throw the Dutchmen off their guard . . . à Court [Repington], who is an alarmist and has a per-

fervid imagination, thinks very badly of things, and it's certainly difficult for anyone to be hopeful.[11]

But Buller also had his virtues. During the unsuccessful attempt to occupy Vaalkranz Spur in February 1900, Wilson wrote:

> We had a very disagreeable night. At 5.30 a.m. the Boers opened a very sharp fire, which was practically kept up till 7 p.m. when darkness stopped it. At 4 p.m. they had a try at our extreme left flank, but were driven back after about 10 minutes. Hildyard relieved us at 9 p.m., our men having been under fire for 33 hours. Our loss was 16 officers and 253 killed and wounded. We were glad to get back, and Buller gave us each a horn of champagne, than which I never drank anything I liked so much.[12]

Buller, however, was replaced as Commander-in-Chief by Lord Roberts, who took Wilson on to his staff, eventually as assistant military secretary.

From 1903 to 1906 Wilson returned to the War Office where he served as Assistant Adjutant-General and Deputy Director of Staff Duties with important responsibilities for the Staff College, the training and appointment of Staff Officers, together with Sandhurst and Woolwich. This fitted him well for his next appointment, as Commandant of the Staff College. From 1907 to 1910 Wilson was an inspiring and notably successful Commandant. The post admirably suited his gifts as a teacher: his infectious enthusiasm, his ready wit and his genius for lecturing. The lecture notes which Wilson kept indicate the wide range of topics he covered: 'Efficiency', 'Intelligence', 'Scheme for the defence of Egypt', 'N.W. Frontier Scheme', 'Is Conscription Necessary?', 'Lecture on French–Belgian–German Frontiers', and so on.[13] He also laid special emphasis on practical exercises, such as staff tours and battlefield visits.

One of Wilson's greatest concerns during these years was to prepare the British army for what he regarded as the inevitable war between France and Germany. A lifelong Francophile, Wilson believed – like many other soldiers – that Britain's place was at France's side in this conflict, and he laboured to ensure that this came to pass. His unusually close friendship with the French general Ferdinand Foch, whom he first met in 1909, did much to facilitate close Anglo–French co-operation, then and later. We find Foch writing to Wilson at the beginning of 1912 inviting him to his daughter's wedding.[14] As a child, Wilson had gained a useful knowledge of the French language from a series of

French governesses. His fluency in the language greatly assisted relations with French colleagues. As the following notes for an after dinner speech at the French XXth Army Corps Manoeuvres in 1913 indicate, Wilson's French was not always absolutely accurate, but he spoke it with a characteristic and engaging enthusiasm:

M. Général et Messieurs je vous remercie de pleine cour [*sic*] pour l'acceuil si bienfaisant que vous m'avez faites. J'ai souvant vu les soldats français en campagne, et chaque fois que je les ai vu, je les aime et je les admire le [*sic*] plus. L'année dernière à vos Grands Manoeuvres j'ai dit que 'je prefererai [*sic*] infiniment [*sic*] me battre avec eux que contre eux'. En causant un jour avec Le Général Lanzac je lui ai demandé s'il parlait Anglais. Il m'a dit que oui – un peu – c'est à dire qu'il savait l'Anglais pour 'beautiful woman' (Dame charmante), 'Kiss me quick' (Embrassez moi vite) ['Donnez moi un baiser vite' crossed out], et 'Beef steak and potatoes' (Bifsteak et pommes de terre) – et il ajouta qu'avec ces brefs ['trois' crossed out] mots 'on peut faire le tour du monde'. Je crois, mon Général, qu'avec quelques Corps d'Armée comme le Vingtième vous pourriez faire sinon le tour du monde au moins le tour d'Europe.
Je lève mon verre à la Vingtième Corps d'Armée et à l'Armée glorieuse de la France.[15]

As Director of Military Operations (DMO) between 1910 and 1914 Wilson was responsible for making the detailed arrangements to deploy the British Expeditionary Force (BEF) in Northern France. This, the 'W.F.' ('With France') scheme, was sometimes even known as the 'Wilson–Foch' scheme.[16] In a 'Minute to the CIGS reporting progress on scheme of E[xpeditionary]. F[orce].' in April 1913 Wilson clearly indicated his priorities. He observed that his two immediate predecessors as DMO had secured permission 'to "work out all the details" of a scheme of combined operations with the French against the Germans. When I became D.M.O. I conceived it to be my most important duty to continue this work and so far as human foresight was possible to complete a scheme which would be at once useful and practical'.[17]

There is much material in the Wilson papers concerning Wilson's involvement with Ireland during the Home Rule crisis immediately before the First World War. Early in 1913 Asquith's Liberal government decided to introduce a measure for Irish Home Rule. Unionists in Ireland responded vigorously, mobilising under Sir Edward Carson

powerful support in Westminster and organising armed resistance, if necessary, in Ulster. In March 1913 Wilson dined with Lord Roberts, who was very sympathetic to the Unionist cause. 'He told me', wrote Wilson in his diary, 'he had been approached to know if he would take command of the Army of Ulster and if he could get me as his Chief of Staff, & he wanted to know if I would. I said that if the alternatives were to go & shoot down Ulster or shoot for Ulster I would join him if he took Command. Imagine our having come to such a state'.[18] A year later matters came to a head with the 'Curragh Incident' when fifty-eight officers of the 3rd Cavalry Brigade at the Curragh Camp in county Kildare resigned their commissions rather than obey orders which they believed were aimed at coercing Ulster Unionists into a united Home Rule Ireland. Throughout the crisis Wilson worked behind the scenes in support of the Ulster cause, and he kept leading Opposition politicians fully informed of developments. Wilson's own file of correspondence relating to the affair and containing over fifty letters is one of the best single sources for the army side of the affair.[19] He was also frequently in contact with Unionist politicians and journalists. Letters survive from Lord Milner, H A Gwynne (editor of the *Morning Post*), Leopold Amery, F S Oliver, Lord Derby, Geoffrey Robinson (editor of *The Times*) and Sir Charles Hunter. Hunter, a Conservative MP, carried messages between Wilson, Carson and Bonar Law, the Leader of the Opposition. In May Hunter reported that Bonar Law preferred not to meet Wilson personally because 'they watch him closely'.[20]

The rapid deterioration in international relations which followed the assassination of the Austrian Archduke Franz Ferdinand at Sarajevo on 28 June 1914 soon overshadowed Irish affairs. But many Unionists and those who like Wilson were committed to supporting France against Germany began to worry about the Liberal government's resolve. Lord Milner was particularly vehement. Writing to Wilson in late July he noted that the 'nightmare' of British troops being used against Ulstermen 'seems to be vanishing', but 'everything else is as black as possible . . . The Army may have to take charge yet, to prevent a general relapse into anarchy'. A few days later he returned to his ominous criticism of the government: 'Sooner or later we have got to tell these Radical "pacifists" to go to hell, or go there ourselves. So why not do it at once?'[21] We can see the tension also building up in others while it seemed as if the government might not finally side with France from a handwritten note Wilson made on a copy of a telegram from the British Ambassador in St Petersburg reporting a general mobilisation in Russia:

Eyre Crowe [assistant under-secretary at the Foreign Office] brought this over at 5.45 p.m. 31.7.14. He told me that he had had $\frac{3}{4}$ of an hour

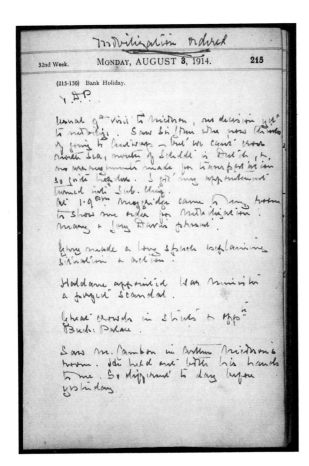

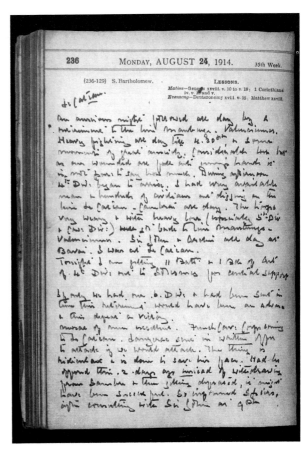

Wilson's diary entry of the day before war was declared. Among others mentioned are Sir Arthur Nicolson (Permanent Secretary at the Foreign Office), Sir John French, Sir Edward Grey, Lord Haldane and M Paul Cambon (French Ambassador in London). HU55853

A page from Wilson's diary on the second day of the retreat from Mons. '. . . Heavy fighting all day till 4.30 pm & some moments of great anxiety . . .' HU55854

with Grey [the Foreign Secretary] & he thought the case was hopeless. Grey spoke of the ruin of commerce, etc, & in spite of all Crowe's arguments appeared determined to act the coward. Crowe begged me to see Asquith or Grey, but of course they would not see me. Crowe was in despair.[22]

In the end the government, of course, did declare war and Wilson's work over the past seven years was vindicated. 'You have laid the foundation', wrote Lord Roberts, 'for the success which – with God's help – we firmly believe will be achieved by our troops'.[23]

Wilson became Sub-Chief of the General Staff of the BEF under Sir Archibald Murray. The successful mobilisation of the Expeditionary Force and its deployment to France was perhaps his greatest military achievement. Murray's health soon broke down and Wilson effectively took charge of the BEF headquarters staff. His diaries provide a

detailed and dramatic record of the nightmare retreat from Mons when, by all accounts, Wilson's cheerfulness and good spirits played a crucial role in keeping up morale at the British headquarters. He also maintained very close communication with Foch, who by this time was deputy to the French Commander-in-Chief. Although Sir John French was keen to replace Murray with Wilson, both Lord Kitchener (Secretary for War) and Asquith objected to the move. Wilson's activities during the Curragh Incident had earned him a deserved reputation for intrigue which blackened him in the eyes of some army colleagues (including Sir Douglas Haig) and Liberal politicians. In effect this contributed to his exclusion from really important jobs after the first four months of the war.

In 1915–16 Wilson served successively as Chief Liaison Officer to the French Headquarters and in command of IV Corps, a formation which saw little action under his command. Yet he remained in close touch with many military colleagues and also with politicians at home. His surviving

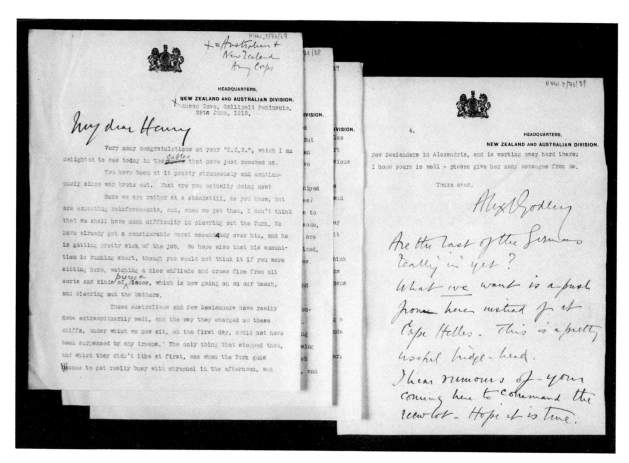

Letter to Wilson from Maj-Gen Alexander Godley, a divisional commander
at Gallipoli, 28 June 1915. HU55857

correspondence for 1914 and 1915 (some four hundred items) contains many letters from Conservative politicians. Again, Sir Charles Hunter acted as a conduit for Wilson's opinions: 'Any of your letters which contain information I may think advisable for Bonar Law to know I always send on to Edmund Talbot [Conservative Chief Whip] ... I take it Austen [Chamberlain] and Curzon get to know their contents also'.[24] A quotation from the diary in the spring of 1916 – just after the Easter Rising had broken out in Dublin – gives a flavour of Wilson's political contacts:

> Spent an hour with [Lord] Esher. He was very pessimistic, thought the war was lost, thought Robertson much too narrow in his outlook; said there were still 13 Divisions at home though some had only 5000 men, & a total of 440,000 rifles; thought there were about 1,200,000 in uniform at home. France was calling for help in money & men & was rather unreasonable, but was get-

ting suspicious of us. Russia was calling for help in their Asian campaign; affairs in Ireland bad; Kut [Mesopotamia] would fall for certain etc. etc. I insisted on necessity of getting rid of Squiff [Asquith]. He entirely agreed but said it was impossible ...

Lunched with Duncannon [Conservative MP] ... who told me that Bonar Law had told him I was perhaps 'the cleverest man in England'. At lunch B.L. telephoned to ask me to go to Colonial Office to see him. I went down & he told me Irish thing was serious. Conkie [General Sir John] Maxwell had been given command & went over tonight. He, B.L., & some others wanted me to go, but agreed my Ulster record made it impossible.[25]

Wilson's critical comments on the conduct of the war were undoubtedly welcome to those who were becoming increasingly dissatisfied with Asquith. This group was not restricted to Conservatives. Lloyd George also began to develop a high opinion of Wilson's abilities. The two men had much in common, although not their politics. They were both quick-witted, articulate and jesting, and found each other good company. They also shared a low opinion of Douglas Haig, who succeeded Sir John French as British Commander-in-Chief in France in December 1915. During 1916 Wilson came to believe that the war could only be won by a 'real fighting Government' under Lloyd George.[26]

Wilson's correspondence is not just confined to matters of high policy, although it does give an extraordinarily vivid picture of the politico-military currents of criticism which existed in the first two years of the war. The files of correspondence with the French Generals Joffre and Foch demonstrate the extent and, in the case of the Wilson–Foch relationship, the warmth of Anglo–French liaison. There are letters from many other quarters. Clive Wigram, Assistant Private Secretary to The King, wrote with news from England. Some of Wilson's former colleagues in the War Office also wrote from London. These include the Major-Generals Dick Stuart-Wortley (Director of Movements) and Charles Callwell (Wilson's successor as DMO). News, too, comes from friends on active service, both in Gallipoli and France. George Harper wrote in September 1915: 'I arrived at Poperinghe to find that poor Sparrow had died on Wednesday from collapse. He apparently had diabetes v. badly & when told that he was really bad – He said "righto – I have had a very good time. I only wish I had drunk more port".'[27]

But after Lloyd George became Prime Minister in December 1916 Wilson's fortunes rose. Lloyd George thought Wilson had 'undoubtedly the nimblest intelligence amongst the soldiers of high degree'.[28] He enjoyed discussing policy with him and used him as an alternative source of military advice to either Haig or Sir William Robertson, the then CIGS. In February 1917 he made Wilson the British military representative on a full-scale Anglo–French Mission to Russia. Wilson's diary provides a series of sharp impressions of Russia on the eve of the 1917 Revolutions. On first being presented at the Imperial Court:

> The Emperor was most affable, and talked to every single one of us. I was astonished to find much more character in his face than I had imagined, and quite a twinkle in his eye. We were received in a charming suite of rooms, with court officers in quaint uniforms, and some servants in marvellous Catherine clothes and feathers in bonnets. What a murderous pity that the Emperor is so weak and so under the Empress's thumb, for, according to all the accounts I get, he and the Empress are heading straight for ruin.[29]

Sir Henry nursed higher hopes for the Russian war effort in general. Despite the chaotic administration which held up military supplies, he was impressed with some of the troops he saw, and the generals, at least, seemed confident. 'Even if the Tsar and Tsarina are assassinated', he wrote, 'it will not make for a separate peace'.[30] In effect, Wilson anticipated the February Revolution, but not the October one which finally took Russia out of the war.

On his return, Wilson did a variety of jobs, including a brief resumption of liaison duties between the British

The Allied Mission to Russia at the Imperial Palace in Tsarskoe Selo (now Pushkin) outside Leningrad, 3 February 1917. The Emperor Nicholas II is sitting in the middle of the front row, with Sir Henry Wilson standing just behind his left shoulder.
HU52750

and French armies. All through 1917, as is documented in his diary and correspondence, he pressed Lloyd George – and any other politicians and generals he could buttonhole – to improve the co-ordination of Allied policy-making. In early November the Prime Minister secured French and Italian consent to the creation of a Supreme War Council which would supervise policy at a high level. Wilson became the British Permanent Military Representative, a position in which he now challenged Robertson as the government's chief military adviser. In February 1918 Lloyd George succeeded in manoeuvring Robertson out of the CIGS-ship and replaced him with Sir Henry. Among the first people to write and congratulate him was General Foch.[31]

For the next year or so Wilson was at the centre of British military and strategic policy-making. He saw the Prime Minister virtually every day, and attended Cabinet meetings where he had effectively equal status with the politicians. He corresponded with other senior generals: there is a comparatively cordial series of letters between Wilson and Haig, for example.[32] There is also an interesting file of correspondence with Brigadier-General L A E Price-Davies, his brother-in-law, who in 1918 was liaison officer at the Italian headquarters.[33] Wilson's diary provides a lively record of events at the top level, together with merciless snap judgement on his colleagues. During the great German spring offensive in March 1918:

> An anxious day. The 5th Army seems to be beaten & has fallen back beyond the Somme.
> I was about 5 hours with L[loyd] G[eorge] . . .
> For hours I insisted on the importance of taking a long, broad view of the future of conscription on *everyone* up to 50 & of course on Ireland. I think I did good & Winston helped like a man. Smuts was good but more cautious. Milner disappointing, B.L. ditto, A J B[alfour] rather uninterested. Curzon not there.[34]

Eight months later, when the war had been won, there were problems now about dividing the spoils:

> Imperial War Cabinet discussion about captured German Colonies etc. Much discussion about what we could – or ought to – give up. I was opposed giving up anything on the double ground of the safety of the Empire and of the good Government of the people concerned. Curzon & Hughes [the Australian Prime Minister] excellent, Austen not bad; Milner wobbly. L.G. very poor.[35]

Wilson's position as an intimate and influential prime ministerial adviser, however, did not very long survive the end of the war. Once Lloyd George turned to wider questions of domestic and foreign reconstruction, Wilson's value as a confidante began to decline. Sir Henry's uncompromising strategic vision, which had so impressed Lloyd George during the war, and which rather suited the single-minded quest for victory over Germany, was not so appropriate for peacetime conditions. Faced with an over-extended empire in the aftermath of the war, and an upsurge of internal discontent, all Wilson could recommend was 'govern or get out'. He became, moreover, increasingly gloomy about the prospects for Britain and the Empire. 'And so we are off into the New Year', he wrote on 1 January 1920, '& if L.G. & his wretched Cabinet do not take up the reins and *whip* of Government we shall be in a worse mess this day year'.[36]

There are over three thousand letters in the 'numbered correspondence files' dating from Wilson's time as CIGS. Although most of these are 'out' letters, there is also a substantial number of 'in' letters from politicians, including Lloyd George, Winston Churchill, Lord Curzon and Lord Milner.[37] He also corresponded with all the principal British Army commanders throughout the world. This provides a series of accounts of military policy and operations during the last year of the Great War and its aftermath. Where the correspondent is a close friend of Wilson these letters can be extremely full. General Lord Rawlinson (C in C in India from November 1920 to March 1925), a very old regimental colleague, regularly wrote at length about the situation in India, at a time when the nationalist Non-Co-operation Movement of Mahatma Gandhi was getting off the ground. This correspondence, moreover, provides an interesting supplement to Rawlinson's own private journal.[38] Similarly Wilson's voluminous correspondence with Lord Allenby and Sir Walter Congreve, respectively High Commissioner and GOC in Egypt, illuminates another corner of the Empire in which nationalism was beginning to become a significant force.[39]

One of the most striking features of this 1918–22 material is the enormous range of subjects covered, which itself reflects not only the world-wide nature of Britain's imperial commitments but also the unusually extensive post-war responsibilities in Europe. There are, for example, letters from British commanders in North Russia and the Baltic,[40] Danzig,[41] and the occupation forces in Germany.[42] In the summer of 1920 an Anglo-French Mission was sent to Warsaw to assist the Poles in their war against the Soviet Red Army. Major-General Sir Percy Radcliffe was the senior British officer in the Mission.

> This is a great life [he wrote to Wilson] and especially the last week intensely interesting. Now

that the front is so close one can get out to the front line every day, between breakfast and lunch, or go out after lunch and be back for dinner and the local 'Travellers' [Club] is full of excited individuals every evening, who come back with tales of desperate adventures. The Italian Staff are specially graphic in their account, but as I happened to see the effect of a single spent bullet on them, (and all the other crowd who were watching the start of yesterday's attack) I take their stories with a great deal of salt.[43]

Not far away, the following year an Anglo–French peacekeeping force was deployed in Upper Silesia to police a League of Nations' plebiscite which was to decide whether the area would be part of Poland or Germany. Inevitably, the British GOC, Sir William Heneker, corresponded with Wilson. He had a particularly high proportion of Irish battalions in his force, since with the 'troubles' in Ireland hotting up the War Office preferred to send them to Eastern Europe. But problems arose there also, as Heneker reported to the CIGS: 'I find some of our Irishmen have been egging the Germans on to attack the Poles in order to watch a good fight. I have had to issue a strict reminder to the troops pointing out to them why we are here.' [44]

More than anywhere else, Wilson was exercised about the fate of his native country. He would contemplate no policy in Ireland beyond the forcible crushing of Sinn Fein and the IRA. He was disgusted when Lloyd George decided to negotiate with the Irish nationalists in mid-1921 and he simply refused to speak to the Prime Minister for the rest of his time as CIGS. After the Anglo–Irish Treaty of 6 December 1921 his disillusionment was complete. In his diary:

I could not help recalling my advice to the Cabinet given repeatedly ever since Nov. 11th 1918. 'Come out of those places that don't belong to us & hang on like hell to those places that do' and contrasting that with L.G.'s performances which have been, & are, the exact opposite – for he is coming out of those places that *do* belong to us viz. Ireland, Egypt & India, & he is hanging on to those places that do *not* belong to us viz. Silesia, Constantinople, Palestine and Mesopotamia. Wonderful.[45]

When Sir Henry retired in February 1922 he became an MP at Westminster for a constituency in Northern Ireland, but had scarcely begun his new political career when he was assassinated. While Irish affairs suffuse all Wilson's correspondence during the last year or so of his life, there are a few letters from the end of his career exclusively concerned with security matters in Northern Ireland. For all his militant Unionism these reflect his strongly-held opinion that the maintenance of security in the province should be as non-sectarian and as disciplined as possible.[46]

At the end of his career Sir Henry Wilson was a disappointed man. In the Army he had, perhaps, been a frustrated politician and yet in the end he had little chance to prove himself in the House of Commons. Reporting on Wilson speaking in parliament, Austen Chamberlain noted that the Field Marshal, 'as always, was incisive, dangerous and mischievous'.[47] It seems that these qualities, which undoubtedly contributed to his achievements, were also his undoing. He was too mercurial – and too obsessed with Irish affairs – to inspire wholehearted trust among all his military and political colleagues. But this mercurial quality also drove him to pour out his arguments, views and opinions on paper in great quantity. Throughout his career he never stopped writing. (Indeed, in his diary he scarcely stopped to think *before* writing.) For the historian the voluminous records he has left additionally have the priceless quality of immediacy. Not only do his papers tell us a lot about Wilson himself, but they also reveal much of the age he lived in, its politics, its military problems and its personalities. No student of early twentieth-century Britain can afford to neglect the archive.

Sir William Robertson and Winston Churchill, followed by Sir Henry Wilson, during a visit of the Army Council to Cologne in August 1919. Q34706

Summary of the Papers of Sir Henry Wilson

Section One: Diaries

Section Two: Correspondence

Section Three: General Papers

Section Four: Printed Material

Notes

1. 2 vols, Cassell, London, 1927. Other biographical sources for Wilson are: H de Watteville's essay in the *Dictionary of National Biography*; Basil Collier, *Brasshat*, Secker & Warburg, London, 1961; and Bernard Ash, *The Lost Dictator*, Cassell, London, 1968.
2. Sir Andrew Macphail, *Three Persons*, Louis Carrier, New York, 1929, p 143.
3. Sir Charles Harington, *Tim Harington Looks Back*, John Murray, London, p 89.
4. The diaries may be read on microfilm by application to the Museum's Department of Documents.
5. HHW 2/1–2/65. These files were used extensively in Keith Jeffery (ed), *The Military Correspondence of Field Marshal Sir Henry Wilson, 1918–1922*, Army Records Society/The Bodley Head, London, 1985.
6. For example, 'Letters about my C.B. July 1908', HHW 2/69.
7. For example with General C Callwell, or General Joffre, HHW 2/75, 2/80.
8. Catalogued as HHW 3.
9. 24 November 1899, AAG, Pietermaritzburg to GOC Mooi [*sic* – ?Modder] River, HHW 3/1/2a, no 11.
10. Quoted in Callwell, *Sir Henry Wilson*, op cit, vol 1, p 29.
11. Wilson Diary, 3 January 1900. Also in Typescript extracts from Diary, HHW 3/1/5.
12. Wilson Diary, 5 February 1900.
13. HHW 3/3.
14. Foch to Wilson, 14 January 1912, HHW 2/71/3.
15. Handwritten notes for a speech, September 1913, HHW 3/7/5. 'General and gentleman, I thank you from the bottom of my heart for the warm welcome you have given to me. I have often looked at French soldiers in the field, and each time that I have seen them, I like and admire them more. Last year at your Grand Manoeuvres, I remarked that 'I would infinitely prefer to fight with them than against them'. Chatting one day with General Lanzac, I asked him if he spoke English. He told me yes – a little – that is to say he knew the English for 'beautiful woman', 'kiss me quick' and 'beef steak and potatoes' – and he added that with these few words 'one could go round the world'. I believe, General, that with several Army Corps like the Twentieth you would be able to go round Europe, if not the world. I lift my glass to the Twentieth Army Corps and to the glorious French Army.'
16. See 'The "W.F." Plan and the genesis of the Western Front: a previously unpublished account by General Sir Percy Radcliffe', *Stand To*, No 10, Spring 1984, pp 6–13.
17. HHW 3/7/2.
18. Wilson Diary, 16 March 1913.
19. HHW 2/74. These letters were used extensively in the standard work on the affair: I F W Beckett, *The Curragh Incident, 1914*, Army Records Society/The Bodley Head, London, 1986.
20. Hunter to Wilson, 8 May 1914, HHW 2/73/8
21. Milner to Wilson, 27 July and 3 August 1914, HHW 2/73/32 and 39.
22. Notes on telegram from Sir George Buchanan to Foreign Office, 31 July 1914, HHW 3/8/4.
23. Roberts to Wilson, 7 August 1914, HHW 2/73/45.
24. Hunter to Wilson, 14 June 1915, HHW 2/76/25.
25. Wilson Diary, 27 April 1916.
26. Ibid, 27 November 1916.
27. Harper to Wilson, 3 September 1915, HHW 2/77/54.
28. David Lloyd George, *War Memoirs*, Odhams edn, London, nd, vol 2, p 1687.
29. Wilson Diary, 31 January 1917.
30. Ibid, 18 February 1917.
31. 20 February 1918, HHW 2/24A/1.
32. HHW 2/7A–C.
33. HHW 2/32A–C.
34. Wilson Diary, 23 March 1918.
35. Ibid, 20 December 1918.
36. Ibid, 1 January 1921.
37. Lloyd George (HHW 2/10A–B), Churchill (HHW 2/18A–C), Curzon (HHW 2/20A–B), Milner (HHW 2/11).
38. Rawlinson's Indian Journal is preserved in the National Army Museum, reference 5201/33/23. The correspondence with Wilson is in HHW 2/13A–G.
39. The Allenby and Congreve letters are in HHW 2/33A–E and 2/52A–B.
40. For example Generals Poole (HHW $\frac{2}{3}$8), Rawlinson (HHW 2/13B/14–20), and Gough (HHW 2/49).
41. General Haking, HHW 2/48A–B.
42. Generals Robertson (HHW 2/1A/19–43) and Morland (HHW 2/57), and Mr Arnold Robertson (HHW 2/23).
43. 18 August 1920, HHW 2/44A/29.
44. 12 June 1921, HHW 2/60/3.
45. Wilson Diary, 10 December 1921.
46. See correspondence with Sir James Craig (HHW 2/63) and Sir Percy Radcliffe (HHW 2/44B/4–5).
47. 11 May 1922, Chamberlain to Winston Churchill, Chamberlain Papers (Birmingham University Library) AC 35/1/11.

Images of war in Italy: the record made by the Army Film and Photographic Unit in Emilia Romagna, 1944–1945

Gianfranco Casadio

Dott Gianfranco Casadio is an Italian historian who has written extensively on the history of film.

Translated, edited and introduced by Kay Gladstone

The Army Film and Photographic Unit (AFPU)[1] was set up in October 1941 under the British Army's Directorate of Public Relations. The Unit amalgamated the cine cameramen of the Army Film Unit and the Army's Official Photographers who, following the outbreak of war, had been recruited from civilians with professional experience of film production and photographic journalism. The task of these cameramen and photographers in uniform was to document the activities of the British Army at home and overseas, both for the immediate needs of publicity and the long term record. By November 1944 the AFPU had been greatly expanded by the intake of serving soldiers. After an eight weeks' training course in cinematography and photography at Pinewood Film Studios in Buckinghamshire, they were posted as sergeants to one of the overseas Army Film and Photographic Sections: No. 1 based in Cairo, No. 2 in Italy (though originally formed to record the North African campaign), No. 5 in North West Europe and No. 9 in South East Asia Command. These four Sections also supplied the greater part of the film footage for the four campaign documentaries on their respective theatres of operations ('Desert Victory' 1943, 'Tunisian Victory' 1944, 'The True Glory' 1945, 'Burma Victory' 1945). Only the Allied campaign in Italy, though filmed in detail by cameramen of the British, Indian, Free French, New Zealand, Polish and United States Film Units, was denied its own celebratory documentary.

The material taken in Italy by the cameramen of No. 2 AFPS, especially after June 1944 when British public attention increasingly focused on the Allied offensive in North West Europe and the Russian advances on the Eastern Front, is consequently less well-known than combat film of the same period from the other fronts.

The following article by an Italian historian seeks to right this imbalance and provides an illuminating perspective on film customarily viewed as a British record of British operations.[1]

The appearance in recent years of hundreds of books and articles, not to mention considerable local press interest, is a measure of the extraordinary interest which persists to this day in events in Emilia Romagna during the Second World War. Enthusiasm for the subject is stronger perhaps than that for the wartime history of any other region in Italy, a testimony, in my view, to the closely-woven political and social fabric of the region which has kept alive the memory of the civilian population's active involvement with the partisan struggle alongside the 'official' war of the fighting forces.

It is indeed difficult to separate the 'real war' from that fought by the Resistance: for the Allied armies and the Partisan brigades in Emilia, but even more so in Romagna, the war was very much a shared experience. Unlike elsewhere in Italy, the Allies did not disarm the partisans, but allowed them to form their own unit, the 1,800-strong 28th Garibaldi Brigade 'Mario Gordini' commanded by the partisan leader Bulow. Placed under the command of the British Army's V Corps on 12 January 1945 as an 'autonomous fighting unit', the unit later passed under the 2nd Commando Brigade's command, and was finally demobilised on 20 May 1945. As a result the battles fought by the British in Romagna were closely involved with those fought by the Resistance, especially during the closing months of 1944, when the partisans of Southern Romagna joined up with Popski's Private Army and with the various Allied missions parachuted into the hilly districts near Forli and Ravenna.

Following the collapse of German resistance on the Gothic Line, the British Army crossed the River Metauro into Emilia Romagna in September 1944. The terrain here was very different from that through which the troops had passed in Umbria and Tuscany. The province occupies the southern part of Italy's northern plain, and its landscape has a distinctive character. A narrow strip of coastline, some twenty miles across, runs the length of the region: gently sloping dunes are bordered in some places by pinewoods, elsewhere the flat, fertile land is cultivated, watered by irrigation channels. Inland numerous rivers intersect the plateau which rises to meet the foothills of the Apennines. Much of the region's land has been reclaimed, and a prominent feature are the so-called 'larghe', flatlands originally submerged in water which stretch from Cervia to Alfonsine and Bondeno at the northern edge of the province. It was this last region which most often formed the backdrop for the British cameramen – plains dominated by endless horizon broken only by banks some three to ten metres high. These banks, built to prevent the rivers and canals flooding the surrounding countryside, have always had great tactical significance, and the British cameramen managed to convey in their film how German and Allied armies alike made tactical use of these earthworks during the six months of fighting in the region.

The films taken by the AFPU show how the British maintained their advance, building hundreds of Bailey bridges across the rivers and impassable low-lying roads, drowned in the winter mud. The region's valleys posed problems too, in particular the vast expanse of the Commachio

The British advance through Emilia Romagna

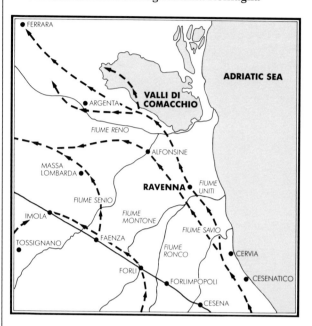

Eighth Army area of operations in Emilia Romagna.

German Dragons Teeth anti-tank obstacles north of Cervia, 9 November 1944. NA20025 (Sgt Meyer)

Canal north of Cervia, 9 November 1944. NA20026 (Sgt Meyer)

The plain south of Ravenna, flooded after the Germans blew the banks of the River Savio, 16 November 1944. NA20152 (Sgt Bowman)

'One of the many German tanks knocked out during the advance towards Ravenna', 9 November 1944. NA20030 (Sgt Meyer)

'Gunner Strange of Lambeth filling in his greetings card to the people back home', 18 November 1944. NA20174 (Sgt Palmer)

'Lt General Sir R L McCreery talking over the battle situation with Brigadier S Shoosmith (centre) and Colonel W Liardet (left) at 10th Infantry Brigade HQ', 24 November 1944. NA20229 (Sgt Lupson)

'Probably the only person to find any use for the flood waters is this old woman, washing clothing in her garden, Savio, south of Ravenna', 16 November 1944. NA20157 (Sgt Bowman)

Sherman passing 'an interested audience of Italian children, north west of Forli', 11 November 1944. NA20093 (Sgt Palmer)

Lagoon and the marshland of the Ravenna region where even Fantails and other amphibious vehicles got bogged down. In these conditions the local knowledge of the partisans from the 'Bassa' (the part of Romagna between the foot of the Apennines and the sea) with their light, flat-bottomed boats was a decisive factor both in the winter skirmishes and later in the battles of the spring.

When I began this research in 1980, a number of the photographs taken by the Allies in Emilia Romagna were already known in Italy, but only two very brief sequences of British film of the region had been screened. Some short sequences covering the investiture of the partisan commander Bulow (now Senator Arrigo Boldrini) in Ravenna in February 1945, and some clips showing partisans of the 28th Garibaldi Brigade in the winter of 1944/45 had appeared in two film documentaries: *Lotta Partigiana* (Partisan Struggle) (1975) by Paolo Gobetti and Giuseppe Risso, and *Resistenza: Una Nazione che Risorge* (Resistance: A Nation which Rises Again) (1975) by Ansano Giannarelli. Starting from these few clues, and in the certainty that there was more material in London, I began a systematic search for photographs, films and other documents about the Second World War in Emilia Romagna.

My researches, carried out in 1982 and 1983, led to the discovery at the Imperial War Museum of more than 4,000 photographs and 127 reels of mute film (30,000 feet) covering the work of the AFPU cameramen and photographers in the province from November 1944 to April 1945. A further useful research tool came to light at the Public Record Office in the form of the War Diaries for this period of the 5th and 8th Armies.

For the purposes of this essay I have divided the subject matter of the film coverage into four sections: the British and Allied Armies, liberation and devastation, the new Italian Army, and the Italian partisans. I was interested to see how attention was divided between each of these areas. Approximately four-fifths of the coverage relates to the activity of the British Army and its allies; the remaining fifth shows Italian military, civilian and partisan subjects.

The British Army in Action

Watching the film, the most immediately striking images are those which show the panorama of desolation wrought by the war on the towns and countryside of Emilia Romagna. The power of the advancing army is suggested by a close-up of a destroyed German tank, once the pride of the Nazi armies but now an abandoned wreck at the side of a road along which pass an unending line of troop transports, Sherman tanks, ambulances, jeeps, and bulldozers on transporters; all this against the bleak November backdrop of flooded land (the Germans had blown the banks of the rivers).

The camera dwells on the remains of the bridges destroyed by the retreating Germans and other trappings of war: anti-tank 'dragons teeth', minefields and noticeboards left behind by the Germans bearing a skull and the inscription 'Achtung Minen'. And so the images continue: half-sunk boats in the canal port of Cervia, abandoned German gun positions in the middle of pine woods, barbed-wire and anti-tank obstacles which cut the landscape – beach, forests, fields and roads – in two. All these obstacles are rapidly overcome by the Allied war machine. The bulldozers raise earth ramps for crossing anti-tank devices; Sherman flail tanks detonate mines on the roads; Bailey bridges take the place of bridges destroyed by the Germans.

And thus the 'great Allied circus' continues its march, pausing only to remove obstructions; what remain are the desolation and injuries to a land, Romagna, which will take years to heal. But the cameraman also focuses his lens on the inhabitants of this region, symbolised by the family with their few possessions loaded on a horse-drawn cart, the only treasures salvaged from the fury of war and the demands of requisitioning; trudging along the road against the path of the Allied columns, they seem to embody the hard fate and suffering which has always been, and which will remain, their lot in life.

The cameramen and photographers of the AFPU took pictures of every variety of subject, often of scenes far removed from the accepted notions of war: soldiers feeling homesick, thinking of Christmas; the High Command who have had the forethought five weeks before the festivities to have designed and printed Christmas airgraph greetings cards bearing a picture of St George, patron saint of the Eighth Army, leaving the soldier only to sign and address the card. A stern-looking sergeant turned Father Christmas distributes the cards to the gunners of the 58th Medium Regiment of Royal Artillery as they busily pile up shells beside their guns.

But the ordinary soldiers are not the only players in this drama; the scene changes to the generals who command this great army and who are shown at work, studying a battle plan, on a day like any other. The impression comes over that the generals too have faces. In this case it is the Eighth Army commander, Lieutenant-General McCreery, and the commander of V Corps, Lieutenant-General Keightley, visiting 46 Division HQ, where they are seen in a caravan with Major-General Weir examining a map on a table; the rest of the sequence is shot outside: the Army commander emerges from the caravan, salutes his officers, gets into his jeep and departs. The sequence leaves one with the impression that McCreery and his colleagues are not very good actors, but of course the sergeant cameraman would not have been able to film the generals' private discussions.

Continuing in his capacity as director, the AFPU

cameraman, on this occasion Sergeant French who shot much of the Ravenna material, stages some action by the 1st Battalion, Kings Royal Rifle Corps. The exercise is set in a farmhouse courtyard, four kilometres from the occupied town of Alfonsine, where some soldiers have constructed mortar positions from sand bags and bundles of wood. The sequences show, with monotonous repetition, the laying of the mortar, the passing of the shells, the gunner firing, and then again passing the ammunition, reloading and firing. A simple exercise filmed from different angles. What is interesting though is the curiously unreal, almost illogical setting in which the event takes place: the farmer's house to the right, the barn to the left and fields beyond; hens running across the threshing-floor as the mortar fires. Near the house, some chicks flutter beneath an upturned basket, while by the porchway, thinking perhaps that he is not in frame, the farmer stands leaning against a shovel. One is left wondering which is out of place in this film, the farmyard in which the action takes place or the presence of the 1st Battalion of the Kings Royal Rifle Corps in these strange surroundings?

The cameramen also recorded actual fighting, an example being the action on 2 March 1945 when the Cremona Division launched an attack to clear the Germans from their positions on the south-eastern shore of the Laguna di Commachio and in the pine woods south of the River Reno. Even though Sergeants Herbert and French filmed the artillery rather than the infantry in the front line the feeling of 'real battle' is just as strong. The film of the guns repeatedly opening up in sequence down the line of the battery, conveys a sense of live action, which is heightened as the camera pans across the enemy lines. It is plain that these are true images of war, not effects achieved by editing. The same can be said of the shots taken on the wharf of the Marina at Ravenna where French, from his vantage point in the ruins of the lighthouse, filmed the 70th Artillery Regiment's guns in action, their shells bursting beyond the mouth of the River Reno.

Liberation and Destruction

The film goes on to show the first pictures of Allied liberation – the entry into Ravenna on 5 December 1944. The main obstacle separating the Eighth Army from this large town was, yet again, water, in this case the *Fiumi Uniti*, which channel the Montone and the Ronco down to the coast. The destroyed bridge was no hindrance to the South African sappers, who built a Bailey bridge on the remains of the stone one blown up by the Germans, at the same time operating a ferry service for the jeeps and other vehicles of the 27th Lancers to cross to the other side. Once across, the cameraman accompanies the column of vehicles through the deserted suburb of Portanuova, where a few people emerge timidly at their doorsteps or windows. The scene moves to the main

square, renamed the Piazza del Popolo; the camera frames the Town Hall, its balcony draped with the Allied and Italian flags. A group of twelve German prisoners comes marching across the piazza, guarded by four armed and wretchedly clothed partisans: members of the 28th Garibaldi Brigade, they have been fighting for two days to liberate the town. Among them is a South African pilot shot down by the Germans a month before. Sergeant French does some close-ups of the pilot who like his companions in arms is somewhat strangely attired. These pictures lack the wild enthusiasm which greets the liberators on other occasions, as we shall see later; all we see here are desolation and sadness.

Moving around the city, the cameraman records successive scenes of devastation: the destroyed railway station, the bomb-wrecked avenue and piazza, the toppled monument to Luigi Carlo Farini,[2] the uprooted railway tracks, the water tank for supplying railway engines which has been ripped open and the wreckage of overturned goods wagons. Ironically still intact is the signboard 'Ravenna' hanging under the station's roof: the station will stay out of use for another year. The panorama shifts to the port. The docking quays blown up by the Germans, the Customs House, the harbour master's office and the Callegari and Montecatini factories – the now mere skeletons of buildings; in the water lurks the wreckage of ships and barges sunk to prevent the Allies entering the port.

Back in the town the camera picks out signs in English indicating the danger of mines and warning against looting the wrecked homes of people who have fled north: 'Do not loot, the streets of the town are being watched', or 'All vehicles subject to anti-looting inspection. You have been warned!'

The New Italian Army

On 14 January 1945 the Cremona Combat Group, one of the four Italian Combat Groups (the others were 'Friuli', 'Legnano' and 'Folgore'), reached the front line in the Ravenna–Alfonsine Sector and lined up on the left of the 2nd Canadian Brigade along the River Reno.

Sergeant Frost's film of the Italians patrolling the forward areas, from the pine woods to the mouth of the River Reno towards Casalborsetti and the sea, was taken a few days later. The men advancing along the road which borders the canal in Destra Reno and crossing the pine woods and beach towards the north backed up by Churchill tanks, are Italian soldiers. Italian too are the soldiers manoeuvering their 17 and 25-pounder guns into position beside a haystack, and more are seen under the banks of the Reno in the neighbourhood of Sant'Alberto, aiming and firing mortars, while their officers survey the river with binoculars. From trenches on

The Entry into Ravenna

'The first obstacle outside Ravenna – the blown bridge over the *Fiumi Uniti*', 5 December 1944. NA20454 (Sgt Bowman)

'Outside the decorated Town Hall, the few civilians in the town gather to welcome the troops', 5 December 1944. NA20458 (Sgt Bowman)

'Notices that speak for themselves are placed at the entrances to Ravenna', 7 December 1944. NA20577 (Sgt Bowman)

'A lone civilian stands among the wreckage of the railway station which was once so busy', 7 December 1944. NA20578 (Sgt Bowman)

Bailey Bridge 'almost completed after eighteen hours' hard work by South African Engineers', 7 December 1944. NA20572 (Sgt Bowman)

Statue of Luigi Carlo Farini outside Ravenna railway station, 12 December 1944. NA20682 (Sgt Bowman)

The Partisans

'Home and headquarters of the Partisans of the *Distaccamento* 'Garavini', two miles south of Ravenna', 18 November 1944. NA20183 (Sgt Bowman)

Partisans using a small rowing boat to cross the Fosso Ghiaia canal in the pine forests of Classe. NA20199

'Bread, of which the Italians eat a lot, is baked on the spot. A young Italian woman prepares the moulded loaf for the oven', 18 November 1944. NA20197 (Sgt Bowman)

'All work is shared by the women. A partisan woman hangs out the washing', 18 November 1944. NA20195 (Sgt Bowman)

the top of the embankment the expanse of the Commachio Valley is regularly 'swept' by the Bren guns of Italian infantry.

Public ceremonies were staged by the Allies as a means to gain the support of their Italian co-belligerents and that of the civilian population. Thus the film records General Keightley, accompanied by the commander of the 'Friuli' Group, General Scattini, inspecting the newly equipped Italian troops at Forli on 4 February 1945, and making a short speech, which is translated by an Italian officer. Then follows a marchpast by Italian soldiers who, a few days later, will join the 2nd Polish Corps in the front line in the Senio Valley. The film follows a much-used formula: the arrival by car of high-ranking officers, inspection, speech, marchpast, parade, and departure. The whole scene is a local public relations

'Partisans crossing the River Reno in a punt, with some sheep they had shot on the German-held side of the river, under cover of the mist', 27 January 1945. NA21865 (Sgt Levy)

General McCreery decorates Major Bulow, alias Senator Arrigo Boldrini, with the *Medaglia d'Oro* in the Piazza Garibaldi, Ravenna, 4 February 1945. NA22058 (Sgt Bowman)

The Italian Partisans

The partisan base of the *Distaccamento* 'Garavini'[3] of the 28th Garibaldi Brigade, hidden in pine trees along the coast, was filmed in some detail. The house, the home of the forest keeper, is a low building of one storey, around which men and women of the unit are busily engaged in what might best be described as logistical tasks. Women with revolvers in their belts are doing the laundry and kneading dough for baking in a wood-fired oven; men are chopping wood for the fire; sheets and clothes are spread out to dry under the pale November sun; and in the distance armed figures can be seen standing guard over the base. In the following sequence an instructor drills a group of men in the use of a mortar. Another detachment returns and a close-up shows a group of people among whom is Major Peniakoff, Popski[4] of 'Popski's Private Army', wearing a white duffle-coat and black beret. The partisans peer at a map, then one presents the Major with a double-barrelled shot-gun which he studies with interest while those around him stand laughing.

By the time the next reel was taken, Ravenna had already been liberated and the partisans appear as a fighting unit alongside the Allies. In fields adjoining the banks of the Reno, shielded by undergrowth, they train with rifles and a Bren gun, under the watchful eye of their commander, 'Major Bulow'. From the banks, a partisan gives sharp bursts of covering machine-gun fire across the river, as a small boat makes it way against the strong current of the Reno, bringing two partisans back from a patrol.

The following reels record the investiture of the commander of the 28th Garibaldi Brigade. It was unusual, to say the least, for an Italian soldier (Boldrini was a Lieutenant in the Army), to receive Italy's highest award for bravery, the *Medaglia d'Oro*, not from a compatriot – in this case it would have been General Clemente Primieri – but from the commander of the British Eighth Army, General McCreery. The ceremony was just one of several such well-publicised gestures and is evidence of the Allies' policy to appease and thereby control the partisan movement, which was thought to be a volatile force in the province, particularly in Romagna where there was a strong communist following.

Summary

As has been seen, partisan activity and the role of the Italian Army is documented in some detail in these reels of record film, but it is likely that this interest was due less to any political calculation than to the mere fact that the Allied armies ended up stranded on the banks of the Senio and Reno rivers in a winter standstill during which many thousands of feet of film and several thousand photographs were taken.

The results are certainly not exceptional and

exercise, from the close-ups of the columns of soldiers and the faces of the British and Italian generals to the panning shots of the troops and the cheering crowds. Judging by the film coverage, apart from the brief episode of the battle of Torre di Primaro, the Allies viewed the Italian troops more as a show army than as a fighting force. In any event, none of these films appeared in the British newsreels.

The New Italian Army

Soldiers of 3rd Battalion, 22nd Infantry Regiment, Cremona Division, shelter behind Churchill tanks firing on German forces, 22 January 1945. NA21726 (Sgt Levy)

Italians of 21st Infantry Regiment, Cremona Division with a 17 pdr anti-tank gun near the village of Sant' Alberto, 20 January 1945. NA21647 (Sgt Bowman)

reflect what the campaign in Northern Italy essentially was: a secondary front where practically nothing was ever risked, where the generals only moved when all their reinforcements were securely in place and the enemy's collapse certain. But the long drawn out war effort in Italy had still to be recorded by the sergeants of the Army Film and Photographic Unit, even after Allied public interest, and the cameramen of the commercial newsreel companies, had been switched to the campaign in North West Europe.

But if the formal activities of the 8th Army (official visits and ceremonies) and their military operations take place according to a routine formula, it is the cameramen's absorption with the scenery, and their curiosity in the Italian people which brings a spontaneity and vividness to this journey up the peninsula, whose great variety of observed situ-

ations brings to mind the anthological quality of Rossellini's *Paisà*.[5] In particular the attention given to the landscape throws the seasons into sharp relief, lending a structure to this day by day narrative, so that viewed as a whole the record acquires an almost epic quality.

In November 1944 the south of Romagna had already been liberated by the Allied armies and the offensive which would finally bring an end to operations in Italy was flagging. The pictures show columns of vehicles, tanks and men advancing along the roads of Romagna. Despite the technology and the power of the forces displayed, these pictures do not convey an atmosphere of war. There are no direct engagements nor indication of the huge losses suffered by both sides in the struggle. (Casualties in the Gothic Line had numbered over 123,000 on the German and nearly 160,000 on the Allied side.) The enemy appears here only in the role of defeated, never as a combatant, which is why the images seem weak and sanitised versions of those cruder and more dramatically violent images of the war shown elsewhere. On the other hand this practice of taking pictures of everything which happened (or did not happen) in the armies' lines of communication allows us to grasp more vividly the atmosphere of the territory where the war was being fought. In these autumn months the floods deluged the Ravenna Plain, causing the heavy mechanised vehicles to become bogged down, and this, together with torrential rain, forced the powerful and well-organised Allied machine of war to halt for the whole winter in Romagna.

The months of this halt are characterised by detailed scenes of preparations for the final advance, but also as a pause in which the soldiers had time for recreation and for contact with the people of the region. For the military they are straightforward records, but records which frequently cover, as well as the great parades, the folklore, ceremonies and reality of the atmosphere of the Romagna, and it is this which makes the film's visual record so precious.

When the offensive recommences in the spring, the record quickens pace; little time is spent on the background – instead the camera recounts successive entries into liberated towns. Unlike the earlier bleak scenes, these final pictures, taken in the spring, capture the landscape of a countryside in flower, and of towns which, though scarred by bombing, are bursting with wild joy at the end of the war and its nightmares. Happiness is captured for all time on the faces and in the gestures of the men and women of our country who have just appeared in this cinema epic in which the British soldier is the lead performer and the Italian soldiers and partisans are the bit-players. It is a great film which will not appear in any cinema, but which will remain a unique document of a people and a place at a precise time, preserved in the archives of the Imperial War Museum.

Liberation

Top: **Eighth Army passes through Castel San Pietro, 23 April 1945. NA24415 (Sgt Menzies)**

Middle: **'British infantryman gets a welcome kiss from an Italian girl as Eighth Army enters Ferrara', 24 April 1945. NA24439 (Sgt Wooldridge)**

Bottom: **'Under the protection of the Red Cross flag a medical orderly brings in a batch of Italian civilian refugees returning to their homes now that the Germans have left', near Argenta, 16 April 1945. NA24134 (Sgt Currey)**

Biographical notes

Gianfranco Casadio, awarded a doctorate from the University of Bologna for his thesis on Documentary Cinema, is a historian whose special interest is the Italian Cinema of the 1930s and 1940s. He is in charge of the Cineteca at the Museo del Senio di Alfonsine (Ravenna). His published work includes: *La resistenza nel Ravennate* (Ravenna 1980), *Le foto dell'album dell'VIII Armata* (Bologna 1983), *La periferia dell'immagine* (Faenza 1985), *Le immagini dei fotografi di guerra inglesi nell'Aretino* (Arezzo 1987), *Rimini et ses alentours dans le cinéma. Les opérateurs de guerre britanniques filment la région de Rimini* (Florence 1988) and *Spettacolo e propaganda nel cinema italiano degli anni Trenta* (Ravenna 1989).

Kay Gladstone is Deputy to the Keeper of the Department of Information Retrieval.

Notes

1. AFPU sergeant cameramen and photographers operated in pairs and thereby ensured that British military operations were usually recorded simultaneously in still and cine form.
2. Luigi Carlo Farini (1812–1866), born in Russi, close to Ravenna, was an Italian patriot active in the struggle for independence.
3. Settimio Garavini was a partisan from Ravenna who was killed at the hands of the Germans, and whose name was adopted by the partisan unit operating in the pine woods of Classe, near Ravenna.
4. Wladimir Peniakoff, or 'Popski', who founded and commanded Popski's Private Army, a British raiding force which operated behind enemy lines in North Africa and Italy. Popski's activities in Romagna gained valuable information for the Eighth Army Command. Among other feats, he succeeded, with the help of a small number of local partisans, in saving the Basilica at Classe from destruction.
5. *Paisà* (1946) directed by Roberto Rossellini is a six-part dramatised journal depicting incidents in the Battle for Italy from 1943 to 1945.

Further Reading

Work of the Army Film and Photographic Unit

Gianfranco Casadio, *Immagini di Guerra in Emilia Romagna: I Servizi cinematographici del War Office*, Longo, Ravenna, 1987.

Peter Hopkinson, *Split Focus*, Rupert Hart Davis, London, 1969.

Ian Grant, *Cameramen at War*, Patrick Stephens, Cambridge, 1980.

General works in English on the Italian Campaign

C J C Molony, *The Mediterranean and Middle East* (History of the Second World War: United Kingdom military series), HMSO, London, 1973–1978.

W G F Jackson, *The Battle for Italy*, Batsford, London, 1967.

Dominick Graham and Shelford Bidwell, *Tug of War: the battle for Italy, 1943–1945*, Hodder and Stoughton, London, 1986.

Eric Linklater, *Campaign in Italy*, HMSO, London, 1951.

Books in Italian

A detailed bibliography prepared by Dott. Casadio relating to the war in Emilia Romagna is held by the Museum's Department of Printed Books, 91.9(45):01.

An appreciation of the shelter photographs taken by Bill Brandt in November 1940.

Joanne Buggins

Joanne Buggins is a research assistant in the Acquisitions and Cataloguing Section of the Department of Photographs.

Among its extensive and varied photographic collections the Imperial War Museum holds the original negatives of Bill Brandt's shelter photographs taken during the Blitz on London in November 1940. Brandt, who died in 1983, has long been regarded as one of the masters of British photography and this article examines the shelter pictures as a highlight of the Museum's photographic archive and places them in the context of his career as a whole.

Bill Brandt was born in Hamburg on 3 May 1904 into a wealthy middle-class family. His parents were both of Eastern European extraction, although his father, L W Brandt, became a British citizen. The main source of artistic influence in these early years, both for Bill Brandt and his brother Rolf, seems to have been their mother, Lili Merck, the daughter of a Hamburg family noted for its public service and interest in the arts.[1] At the age of sixteen Brandt contracted tuberculosis and was treated at a sanatorium in Switzerland for approximately six years. It was during his convalescence in Vienna that he decided to become a photographer. Rolf Brandt remembers that his brother was influenced by a mutual acquaintance, Dr Eugenie Schwarzwald, and how on one occasion 'she sat down with him and nominated suitable careers, checking them off her fingers one by one. For no known reason Bill Brandt stopped her at photography.'[2] Commencing his chosen career in a portrait studio in Vienna he found his early work disappointing and after receiving an introduction to the surrealist artist Man Ray in 1929 went to Paris to become his assistant. Brandt was always a modest and reticent man, highly reluctant to discuss his craft and influences. Evidence of his modesty is the fact that for many years he would only say that he was introduced to Man Ray by 'a family friend'. It has since emerged that this 'friend' was in fact the American poet Ezra Pound.[3]

At the time of Brandt's photographic 'apprenticeship' Paris was the centre of the *avant-garde*. He has said that 'these were exciting early days when the French poets and surrealists recognised the possibilities of photography' and that one could say that it was then 'that modern photography was born'.[4] Although it has been suggested that Man Ray was not the best of tutors,[5] Brandt could not have failed to be influenced by the surrealist artists (such as Brassai, Kertész and Cartier-Bresson) and the innovative art magazines (including *Bifur*, *Variétés* and *Minotaure*) that he came across during this period. He was also affected by the newly-discovered work of the documentary photographer Eugène Atget and the surrealist films – particularly *Un Chien Andalou* (1928), and *L'Age d'Or* (1930) – made by Louis Buñuel and Salvador Dali.

People sleep on the crowded platform of Elephant and Castle Underground Station on 11 November 1940.
D1568

On either side of a staircase at Elephant and Castle Underground Station men and women are bedded down for the night, 11 November 1940.
D1567

A group of men occupy their time playing a game of draughts at the Liverpool Street Underground Station, 12 November 1940.
D1581

A group of Orthodox Jews reading their bibles in an East End wine merchant's cellar on 5 November 1940.
D1508

A man and woman wrapped in a large floral quilt in a West End shop
basement shelter on 7 November 1940. D1521

Brandt settled in Britain in 1932 and gradually built up a reputation as a distinguished photo-journalist, drawing on the extreme social contrasts in these years as a source of great visual inspiration. Working as a freelance he photographed London and the industrial north and midlands. Of his pictures of London he said:

> I photographed everything that went on inside the large houses of wealthy families, the servants in the kitchen, formidable parlourmaids laying elaborate dinner-tables, and preparing baths for the family; cocktail-parties in the garden and guests talking and playing bridge in the drawing rooms: a working-class family's home, with several children asleep in one bed, and the mother knitting in the corner of the room.[6]

Examples of his early work can be found in his first two books *The English at Home* (1936) and *A Night in London* (1938), the latter commissioned by the publishers *Arts et Métiers Graphiques* as a companion to Brassaï's photographic book *Paris de Nuit*. Significantly this period saw the rise of the picture magazine and Brandt worked on numerous commissions for *Weekly Illustrated*, *Picture Post*, and *Lilliput*.

The shelter photographs were taken at a pivotal point in Brandt's career, between his initial social reportage in the nineteen thirties and his surreal, poetic post-war work. In September 1940 Brandt was commissioned by Hugh Francis, the Director of the Photograph Division at the Ministry of Information, to photograph life in London's underground shelters.[7] The London Blitz had begun on 7 September and continued for seventy-six consecutive nights save for 2 November when bad weather kept the raiders at bay. It wrought devastation on the East End, West End and suburbs showing the capital to be totally unprepared for the onslaught. Official thinking was opposed to the use of deep underground shelters such as the tube. It was feared that a 'shelter mentality' would develop and that:

> If big, safe shelters were established, the people would simply live in them and do no work. Worse, such concentrations of proletarians could be the breeding grounds for mass hysteria, even subversion.[8]

However, many Londoners, unable or unwilling to leave the capital and without adequate surface shelter provision, chose to ignore the official request. An Australian, Bert Snow, who joined the London Auxiliary Ambulance Service in the East End during the Second World War, commented that:

At first [sheltering in the underground stations] was a disorganised arrangement because the refugees were there in spite of official disapproval. They placed their bedding anywhere on the platform and it was not unusual to step over slumbering forms when using the underground at night. In a short time officials accepted the inevitable and special areas were marked on the platform for the nightly visitors.[9]

It is thought that at most only five per cent of Londoners sheltered in the underground with the highest estimate of the tube population for any one night being 177,000 on the night of 27 September 1940.[10] Contrary to official fears morale did not collapse during the Blitz and the shelterers behaved in an orderly fashion.

Brandt's photographs were taken after the Government had accepted that Londoners were using the deep underground shelters, but before plans to improve sanitation and render the areas more habitable had made much impact. Henry Moore who made drawings of the shelters in the early months observed that:

> Bunks were not provided . . . until several months after the bombing began, nor canteens and decent sanitary arrangements. But from my point of view, everything was then becoming too organised and commonplace. Up to perhaps the first two months of 1941 there was the drama and the strangeness, and then for the people themselves and for me it was all becoming routine.[11]

Brandt spent the nights of the entire week of 4–12 November visiting London shelters, and in this period of 'drama and strangeness', produced thirty-nine photographs. Perhaps his schedule was too rigorous, for in mid-November 1940 Brandt caught influenza and the project had to be abandoned. The shelter photographs were published in the leading arts magazine, *Horizon*, exhibited alongside Henry Moore's Shelter Drawings at the Museum of Modern Art in New York in 1941, and published (again with Moore's drawings) in the photographic magazine *Lilliput*. A set were also sent to President Roosevelt to illustrate the plight of Londoners during the Blitz.

The pictures show many aspects of life in the underground shelters such as the squalid, claustrophobic, uncomfortable conditions and the lack of privacy. One observer has recalled that the shelter floors were 'a sea of blankets, with all sorts of faces appearing above the surface in the most unlikely propinquity'.[12] Bill Brandt's photographs of the platform at Elephant and Castle Underground Station

A Sikh family sheltering in an alcove of Christ Church, Spitalfields on 5 or 6 November 1940.
D1516

At Liverpool Street Underground Station Londoners sleep in a tunnel, 12 November 1940.
D1576

A man sleeping in a stone sarcophagus in Christ Church, Spitalfields on
5 or 6 November 1940. D1511

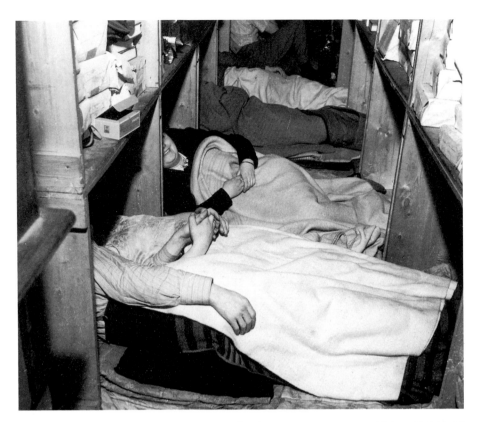

A row of people, their faces hidden by the wooden shelving, sleep in the basement of a book business in Bloomsbury on 7 November 1940.
D1523

Masses of people lie huddled together on either side of an unfinished tunnel in Liverpool Street Underground Station on 12 November 1940.
D1573

An old lady asleep in a makeshift bed, her silver handled umbrella safely stowed away behind her, at a Pimlico garage shelter on 4 November 1940.
D1503

crowded with sleeping people, and masses of Londoners lying on either side of an unfinished tunnel at Liverpool Street Station illustrate this well. One notes the ingenuity involved in the shelterers' attempts to make their lot bearable: such as the man who, avoiding all squeamish impulse, slept in an empty stone sarcophagus in Christ Church, Spitalfields; individuals resting between wooden shelving in the basement of a West End book business; and an old woman asleep on top of a row of barrels in an East End wine merchant's cellar. Brandt also had an eye for the oddities of life in the underground shelters such as an elderly lady asleep in a makeshift bed with her prize possession – a silver-handled umbrella looking curiously like a question-mark – safely stowed away behind her, and another showing a young couple, covered by a garish floral quilt in a shop basement shelter.

In a rare essay on his photography in the introduction to *The Camera in London*, a work which reproduced his photographs from the nineteen thirties and forties, Brandt spoke of the significance of 'atmosphere'. 'I only know it is a combination of elements, perhaps most simply and yet most inadequately described in technical terms of lighting and viewpoint, which reveals the subject as familiar and yet strange'.[13] In many ways therefore the shelter assignment was eminently suited to Brandt's preoccupations. All of the photographs have a rather surreal and jarring effect derived from capturing the incongruity of people living their private lives in the public shelters. Nor can one ignore the symbolism inherent in some of the pictures – for instance that of the Sikh family sheltering in an alcove in Christ Church, Spitalfields of whom it has been said that they 'combine the exotic flavour of the Magi and the humbleness of the Holy family'.[14]

For the shelter photographs, as for the majority of his assignments, Brandt used an Automatic Rolleiflex camera and his lighting equipment consisted of 'Kodak lampholders, some photoflood bulbs and enough flex to stretch the full length of Winchester Cathedral'.[15] His carefully composed photographs were the result of slow and deliberate work, although with characteristic modesty he claimed that his composition was often the result of good fortune rather than good judgement.[16]

Brandt created his atmospheric shelter photographs by careful lighting – a combination of flash bulbs and the artificial light in the shelters – and the use of very long exposures. In this manner he caught the play of light and

In an East End wine merchant's cellar an old woman sleeps in a bed constructed on top of a row of barrels, 5 November 1940. D1507

shadow on the long rows of sleeping bodies in the underground tube tunnels. The photographs display very distinct and intense contrasts, and this, although leading to a loss of detail, has the concomitant effect of increasing a picture's impact. Our attention is drawn to certain areas of the photograph: the rapt attention of a group of Orthodox Jews reading their Bibles in an East End shelter and the faces of sleeping Londoners oblivious to the camera.

Brandt's style was intensified by his work in the dark room. He often finished the composition of his pictures under the enlarger and cropped, retouched, lightened or darkened his prints dramatically. Indeed it is ironic that Brandt is regarded as a doyen of twentieth century photography because, contrary to the fashionable 'pure' photographers, he insisted on manipulating his work to whatever degree he thought fit in order to achieve a desired effect:

When young photographers come to show me their work, they often tell me proudly that they follow all the fashionable rules. They never use electric lamps or flash-light; they never crop a picture in the darkroom, but print from an untrimmed negative; they snap their model while walking about the room. I am not interested in rules or conventions. Photography is not a sport. If I think a picture will look better brilliantly lit, I use lights, or even flash. It is the result that counts, no matter how it was achieved . . . I do not understand why this is supposed to interfere with the truth.[17]

In later years Brandt's printing became even more dramatic with even starker black and white contrasts. Brandt commented towards the end of the Second World War that '. . . my style changed completely . . . the poetic trend of photography, which had already excited me in my early Paris days, began to fascinate me again. It seemed to me that there were wide fields still unexplored'.[18] In post-war years his work concentrated on portraits, landscapes and nudes. Brandt had begun taking portraits during the War, with a series called 'Young Poets of Democracy', and continued throughout the nineteen forties. He took to portraiture again in the late nineteen fifties and continued until a few years before his death. His portraits were generally of creative people in their own surroundings and it has been noted that 'his sitters seem fixed for all time, while the shadowed spaces they inhabit suggest ambivalences and uncertainties' – a comment which could also be applied to the shelterers of his Blitz photographs.[19] Between 1945 and 1950 Brandt concentrated on photographing British landscapes and a selection were published in *Literary Britain* in 1951. He often waited for the appropriate season, weather and the correct time of night or day in order to get a good picture. Many of his nude photographs were taken with a Kodak Wide Angle camera which had a fixed lens covering a 110 degree angle, creating a distorted image and very steep perspectives. Brandt claimed that he photographed what this camera saw: 'I interfered very little, and the lens produced anatomical images and shapes which my eyes had never observed'.[20] Some of the results can be seen in *Perspective of Nudes* published in 1961.

The shelter assignment came at a significant juncture in this internationally acclaimed photographer's career. It followed his photo-journalism of the nineteen thirties and was also a prelude to the more poetic portraits, landscapes and nudes taken in later years. Evocative and surreal, Bill Brandt's shelter pictures offer a rare glimpse of one aspect of life on the home front during the Second World War.

Notes

1. Haworth-Booth, M, 'Bill Brandt – Behind the Camera', *Aperture*, Number 99, Summer 1985, p 6.
2. Ibid, p 7.
3. Ibid, p 8.
4. Bill Brandt, *Album*, Album (Photographic) Ltd, Number 1, March 1970, p 47.
5. Haworth-Booth, 'Bill Brandt – Behind the Camera', *Aperture*, p 9.
6. Brandt, *Album*, op cit, p 47.
7. Craig, C, *The British Documentary Photograph as a Medium of Information and Propaganda during the Second World War*, M Phil CNAA thesis, 1982, p 139.
8. Tom Harrisson, *Living Through the Blitz*, Collins, 1976, p 35.
9. From the memoirs of H W Snow, p 38. Department of Documents, P394.
10. Harrisson, op cit, p 112.
11. Henry Moore in the introduction to *Henry Moore. A Shelter Sketchbook*, British Museum Publications Ltd, 1988, p 12.
12. Reverend J MacKay's observations on life in the Archway Central Hall Shelter, Archway Road, London, N19 during the Blitz. Department of Documents, 74/135/1.
13. Bill Brandt, *Camera in London*, Focal Press, London, 1948, p 11.
14. Mark Haworth-Booth, *Shadow of Light*, Gordon Fraser, London, 1977, p 19.
15. Brandt, *Camera in London*, op cit, p 89.
16. Interview for the BBC programme Master Photographers, *Bill Brandt*, 1983.
17. Brandt, *Album*, op cit, p 47. The original shelter prints are held by the Victoria and Albert Museum and the Museum of London.
18. Ibid.
19. Richard Ormond, *Bill Brandt: Portraits*, National Portrait Gallery Exhibition Catalogue, London, 1982, p 1.
20. Brandt, *Album*, op cit, p 47.

Further Reading

Book and catalogues of Brandt's photographs
The English at Home, (introduction by Raymond Mortimer), Batsford, London, 1936.
Camera in London, (commentary by Norah Wilson), Focal Press, London, 1948.
Shadow of Light, (introductory material by Cyril Connolly and Mark Haworth-Booth), Gordon Fraser, London, 1977.
Bill Brandt: Nudes, (introduction by Michael Hiley), Gordon Fraser, London, 1980.
Bill Brandt: Portraits, (introduction by Alan Ross), Gordon Fraser, London, 1982.
London in the Thirties, (introduction by Mark Haworth-Booth), Pantheon Books, New York, 1984.
Bill Brandt Photographs, (Arts Council of Great Britain Exhibition Catalogue, introduction by Aaron Scharf), London, 1970.
Bill Brandt: Early Photographs 1930–42 (Arts Council of Great Britain Exhibition Catalogue, introduction by Peter Turner), London, 1975.
Bill Brandt: A Retrospective Exhibition, (Royal Photographic Society Exhibition Catalogue, introduction by David Mellor), London, 1981.
Bill Brandt: Portraits, (National Portrait Gallery Exhibition Catalogue, introduction by Richard Ormond), London, 1982.

London during the Blitz
Angus Calder, *The People's War*, Jonathan Cape, 1969.
Tom Harrisson, *Living Through the Blitz*, Collins, 1976.
M Seaborne, *Shelters – Living Underground in the London Blitz*, Dirk Nishen Publishing, London, 1988.

Moving images? The Parliamentary Recruiting Committee's poster campaign, 1914–1916

Philip Dutton

Philip Dutton was a cataloguer in the Department of Information Retrieval from 1979 until 1989, when he left the Museum to take up a post with the Harding Housing Association.

'THE FAILURE OF RECRUITING
A SERIOUS SITUATION
THE NEED FOR DRASTIC REFORM'[1]

So ran a disturbing headline in *The Times* for 13 July 1914 reporting a series of parliamentary questions put to Prime Minister Asquith by, amongst others, Sir Samuel Scott, Sir Charles Hunter and the vigorous MP for South Birmingham, Leopold Amery. Except for a solitary dark reference to 'armed and organised warriors' in Ireland no hint was made of any impending war; rather press attention focused on the previous day's cricket at Lord's in which Eton had achieved 'a creditable and rather unexpected victory' over Harrow.[2] Nevertheless the questions posed to the Prime Minister reflected a deep concern felt by some at the military's failure to obtain the required levels of enlistment for both the Regular Army and the more recently established Territorial Force. *The Times* estimated the deficit to be between 25,000 and 40,000 over the past five years. The military manpower issue was not a new one for the Liberal government; indeed Mr Asquith's public interrogation may be seen as merely the consequence of the apparent failure of the Army's most recent attempts to improve the situation. In January 1914 the War Office initiated a short press campaign to hasten recruiting and repair 'wastage' (a purely technical term which was later to earn deservedly sinister overtones) of time-expired men. *The Times* chronicled this bold advertising campaign approvingly but not without displaying a slight degree of offended good taste:

> ... the campaign ... or the first move in it is apparently to extend over a week and to be carried on through such newspapers as are likely to fall into the hands of the class to which the appeal is particularly addressed.[3]

Commenting on the campaign Cyril Sheldon writing in *The Placard*, the specialist journal for professional bill poster producers and distributors, bemoaned the reliance on 'the cold colourless type announcement in the Press'.[4] Beneath the aggressive banner headline, 'Why not an Army Poster?'[5] Sheldon argued in favour of the full coloured poster bill of 'sufficient size' and 'with good commanding figure treatment' which would, with efficient distribution, make 'the Army posters popular and economical as a recruiting force'.[6] It is not without irony then that within eight months of *The Times*'s supercilious remarks on class readership that that most respectable of newspapers should have been among the first to carry the War Office's quarter-page typescript advertisement, later produced as a poster, voicing Kitchener's appeal for his 'First Hundred Thousand'. The Army's widely reported recruiting shortfall had found a remedy in the tragic context of British involvement in a general European War.

The response to the first state-sponsored cries for men was so overwhelming that the existing War Office machinery dealing with recruits became hopelessly swamped. The patent failure of existing procedures, adequate for the trickle of recruits in peacetime, led to the establishment of numerous voluntary civilian organisations to assist the Army in imposing order on the chaotic 'rush'; the early provision of food and shelter for the eager volunteers being of utmost importance. Later, as recruiting figures started to decline it became necessary to rekindle initial enthusiasms. One important semi-official organisation involved especially in the latter task was the Parliamentary Recruiting Committee (PRC), an all-party body formed at the end of August 1914. The PRC supervised, through its Publications Sub-Department, the most concerted leaflet and poster-based recruiting drive this country has ever seen. The PRC poster holdings of the Museum's Department of Art, although not complete, offer a sufficient number to allow a thematic study of the campaign's designs and messages. No attempt will be made to elevate these works into the category of high art but it is contended that the whole project represented an imaginative and energetic effort to mobilise manpower and one which used a surprisingly wide variety of images and arguments. Again, it may be argued that too much attention has been lavished on a select few of the posters and that for the most part the Committee's bills were well received by the public.[7] An essential aspect of the poster campaign was that it provided an extremely important and revealing index of contemporary social and moral attitudes, while at the same time chronicling the slow march away from the principles of voluntary enlistment to the grim prospect of compulsion, each step of which reflected the inbuilt weakness of the project; it could do no more than persuade.

It is customary for Kitchener, as reluctant Secretary of State for War, to receive sole credit for predicting the timescale of the war and, at the same time, for perceiving the need for a massive expansion of British military forces to meet the demands of a protracted continental commitment. Others too saw the problems; Haig, from the outset, believed in the reality of a war of years rather than months. Britain, he noted, 'must at once take in hand the creation of an Army. I mentioned 1 million as the number to aim at immediately.'[8]

On 7 August 1914, the day after Parliament had authorised an increase in the Army of half a million men, the first formal appeals for volunteers were made in local and national newspapers. The straightforward typescript message headed 'YOUR KING AND COUNTRY NEED YOU. A CALL TO ARMS', was entirely adequate to the task of rallying an already emotionally committed citizenry. On 25 August Kitchener delineated the proposed scale for the military forces in his maiden speech in the House of Lords (he had been a peer since 1898). Rising from the episcopal bench, the cause for some Lordly chortles, he drew the House's attention to the fact that the continental powers had 'almost their entire population in uniform' and announced his intention of creating a field army 'which in numbers not less than in quality will not be unworthy of the power and responsibilities of the British Empire'.[9] A new Army of 70 Divisions was to be formed, at the same time the current strength of existing Regular Army regiments and the Territorial Force would be maintained; all this would be attempted within the framework of the voluntary system of recruiting. Early enlistment figures suggested that these aims were not unrealistic. The single week between 30 August and 5 September witnessed a unique recruiting phenomenon. With rousing press accounts of the heroism and sufferings of the British Expeditionary Force's withdrawal from Mons the returns over the seven days were the highest for the whole of the war; 174,901 men were attested.[10] On 10 September, Asquith was able to report that up to the previous evening 'practically 439,000' men had been recruited into the Army since the declaration of war: 'We have been recruiting during the last 10 days every day substantially the same number of recruits as in past years has been recruited every year.'[11] The War Office admissions machinery, already creaking under the unprecedented demands of August 1914 came close to collapsing under the strain.

Kitchener was quick to appreciate these problems and appointed L S Amery, one of the July chorus of Asquith's critics, as Director of Civilian Recruiting for Southern Command. In an effort to induce local authorities to share the load currently borne by the War Office, Amery and Major-General H B Jeffreys (Sir Henry Rawlinson's Assistant Director of Recruiting) set off on 11 August to tour the towns and cities within their jurisdiction. The investigation revealed the need for 'a systematic scheme for enlisting public opinion and civilian drive behind recruiting over the whole country.'[12] Amery thus claimed, albeit retrospectively, a principal personal role in the creation of the Parliamentary Recruiting Committee.[13]

The actual origins of the Committee are to be found in the behind-the-scenes activities of Parliament. On Thursday 27 August 1914, the Conservative and Liberal Chief Whips, Lord Edmund Talbot and Percy Illingworth, together with the Conservative Party Chairman, Arthur Steel-Maitland and Major-General Sir Henry Rawlinson met in Illingworth's room in the House of Commons to discuss how 'the grave issues of the War should be fully comprehended by the people, and thereby to give a powerful impetus to recruiting'.[14] According to Jordan, Steel-Maitland suggested that a permanent bi-partisan committee should be set up to co-ordinate and oversee recruiting campaigns. Rawlinson, on behalf of Lord Kitchener, immediately gave his enthusiastic approval to the idea and assured the Committee that the War Office would welcome and facilitate their work.[15] A second meeting took place the following day at which, amongst other matters

> '. . . it was decided to recommend the formation of a PUBLICATIONS COMMITTEE, to include the Hon. Secretaries and one representative of each Party Publication Department, for the purpose of issuing literature supplementing that prepared by the War Office. It was agreed that the Honorary Secretaries should arrange as to any necessary printing, the cost thereof not to be borne out of the public funds.' [16]

On 31 August a large gathering in the Reception Room at 12 Downing Street formally established a Parliamentary Recruiting Committee under the joint presidency of Asquith, Bonar Law and Arthur Henderson. The full committee, comprising thirty-two members (including eleven Conservative, seven Liberal and four Labour MPs[17]) represented, according to its former Clerk, 'a remarkable and spontaneous display of British patriotism at a time of extreme peril to the nation'.[18] Other, less charitable, opinions have subsequently been formed, specifically David Sweet's observation that the PRC provided MPs 'with something useful to do which would divert their energies from attempts to question the government's policies or, worse still, to debate strategy'.[19]

The PRC's guiding principle was a commitment to use the local party constituency organisations to assist government and War Office in establishing order in the wake of the recent mass enlistments and, later, to stimulate recruitment as numbers began to fall off. The individual citizen was to be personally canvassed for war (rather than a general election) by house-to-house visits; by the comprehensive provision of meetings, speeches and rallies; by the more threatening and administratively complex 'Householder's Return' (an early attempt to estimate the potential number of recruits);[20] and indirectly by the production and distribution of millions of leaflets and posters. The January 1914 recommendation of *The Placard* calling for an Army poster was to be fulfilled beyond the wildest dreams of its proposer; as recruiting numbers started slowly to decline the poster bill was used increasingly in the urgent propaganda campaign to get the men 'in'.

The fruits of the Parliamentary Recruiting Committee's Publications Sub-Department's labours on display in the PRC HQ at 11 Downing Street. British Library, ADD 54192, 8251357. Reproduced by kind permission of the British Library

The Publications Sub-Department of the PRC

The Publications Sub-Department was set up by the PRC at its inaugural meeting on 31 August. Three days later the Sub-Department held its own first meeting[21] at 21 Abingdon Street at which it was agreed:

> . . . that attention should be drawn to the Union Jack posters for announcing meetings; that elaborate posters were not necessary; that no charge should be made for the Department's publications and that all reasonable demands should be met.[22]

It was the direction of R Humphrey Davies (then principal private secretary to the Parliamentary Secretary to the Treasury) as Clerk to the Committee and the unrivalled professional expertise of characters like Malcolm Fraser (later Sir) of Conservative Central Office and Charles Geake for the Liberals which particularly enhanced the overall effectiveness of the Department. HM Stationery Office undertook to oversee the printing of the posters and literature, and this appears to have been done with considerable speed and efficiency, made all the more remarkable by the apparently haphazard manner in which many of the posters seem to have been commissioned.[23] One method adopted was for a printer to make a suggestion for a bill which would then be considered by the Department and if approved would be drawn up and published. The printed output of the Publications Department was vast: print runs of 25,000 or 40,000 posters were not considered unusual. Overall, it was estimated that 13 million leaflets and over 1 million posters had been issued by early

January 1915, while at the end of March the figures were 20 million and 2 million respectively.[24]

Estimates of the total number of PRC poster designs differ widely; in July 1915 *The Placard* reported that more than ninety different designs had been employed.[25] Writing in 1920 Hardie and Sabin stated that the Committee had commissioned more than a hundred posters, of which two and a half million copies had been distributed throughout the British Isles.[26] An incredible and unsubstantiated statistic – 'by Autumn 1915, 54 million posters had been distributed' – is used to qualify a much later claim that 'about 130 designs'[27] had been issued and a recent work of scholarship submitted that the total was 'over 200 different poster designs'.[28] The IWM's incomplete holding (there are several small sequential breaks, the latest poster in the group is numbered 164 and dated February 1916) comprises 176 separate issues.[29]

Indisputably the first poster in the numbered series bears the code W.78 10–14 and displays the message used by Nelson at Trafalgar. There is no evidence to suggest that it was issued on the anniversary of the battle, 21 October, but it is clearly a product of that same month. Given the remarkable recruiting figures for August and September 1914 one is tempted to question the need for additional recruiting stimuli. The fact is that a significant diminishment in collective war enthusiasm occurred after the second week of September with an accompanying drop in recruiting returns. Various factors have been identified as responsible for this cooling process. The stories which had filtered through to the uncommitted, telling of disorganisation at the depots and temporary camps, certainly had some effect on slowing the rush.[30] It has also been claimed that improved war news, the end of the Allied retreat and the check administered to the Germans on the Marne served to dampen martial spirits. A third factor, 'official action', was the consequence of the War Office's efforts to come to terms with the initial rush. An increase in the minimum height stipulation was sanctioned.[31] Although only a temporary restriction it served to confuse and frustrate many willing citizens who, later, needed to be reconvinced of the importance of their coming forward. Thus the PRC's immediate role was to rekindle the enthusiasm of the first six weeks of the war. It was approached in two main ways: by direct appeals based on a continued public excitement over the war; and by a commitment to educating or informing the citizen of his obligation of duty to the state.[32] Ultimately, with the failure of persuasion in all its manifest forms, the poster campaign changed to one of direct instruction, in terms of the time-honoured government proclamation. The last posters in the series attempt to clarify the demands implicit in the schedules of the first Military Service Act.

'Posters are propaganda – the manipulation of public opinion through significant symbols'[33] – a thematic breakdown of the PRC's poster campaign's images and messages

Responsibility By far the largest number of posters issued by the PRC fall into the category of appeals for recruits based on exhortations to patriotic duty. The tone of this grouping is set by the first five in the series. Embellished with either the Union Jack or Royal Arms above their typographical messages they speak of 'DUTY', of the need to 'RALLY ROUND THE FLAG' and to hear and respond to the calls YOUR KING AND COUNTRY NEEDS YOU and 'MEN OF THE EMPIRE TO ARMS'. As the campaign gained pace the Committee employed a richer vocabulary of symbols. Portraits of British heroes, past and present, and personifications of the national spirit were brought to bear: the recently deceased Lord Roberts[34] (PRC 20), Nelson (PRC 101), St George (PRC 108) and John Bull (PRC 125) together with a multiplicity of bills using the Union Jack and tasteful arrangements of the Allied flags (eg PRC 71B, 'KEEP THESE FLAGS PROUDLY FLYING'). The image of King George V, a photographic portrait by W and D Downey, is used in a single poster (PRC 83, 'SURELY YOU WILL FIGHT') though it is Kitchener's level-eyed frown and pointing finger which have always been associated with the PRC's simple and direct appeal. But the poster based on Alfred Leete's *London Opinion* design held by the Department of Art bears neither the PRC's imprimatur nor an official series number (the only other PRC poster without a series number is the optimistic 1915 issue 'A HAPPY NEW YEAR TO OUR GALLANT SOLDIERS' though its PRC origins are acknowledged on the base margin) and it is possible that this particular poster ('BRITONS', IWM Art catalogue number PST/2734) was the product of a different recruiting campaign.[35] Kitchener's image was used in a summer 1915 appeal, 'LORD KITCHENER SAYS' (PRC 113) which also contains a barely veiled threat that 'compulsion' may not be far off. The effective image of the pointing Field Marshal imposed a powerful legacy on subsequent poster design: within the PRC's output derivatives of this irresistable format were enlisted in a variety of beckoning full-length forms. A British Tommy, pausing on his way to action, gestures in a friendly fashion for assistance, 'AN APPEAL TO YOU' (PRC 88); the innovative untitled PRC 129, making use of a large straight photograph, according to Harper a practice not found in Germany or France, has only the image of a vindictively-moustachioed Recruiting Sergeant wagging his finger furiously to attract the latecomer (September 1915).[36] In 'WHO'S ABSENT?' (PRC 125) John Bull impugns a noble appeal with low suggestions but nonetheless assumes a recognisably Kitchener-like inquisitorial stance. The theme of 'urgency' informs other general and individualised appeals: ' "HELP!", "JOIN NOW", "COME ON!" and most significantly "DON'T THINK . . . ACT!" indicate the . . . instinctive response required' [37] and reflect the bitter fortunes of the British Expeditionary Force although the elegant silhouette depictions of troops in action hardly convey the scale and ferocity of the engagements. A further sub-group within this general class of 'call to arms' used map-like representations of the homeland which emphasised the proximity of the fighting front across the Channel. The appeal to the Empire, first voiced in November 1914, is repeated in 'THE EMPIRE NEEDS MEN!' (PRC 58) which depicted lithe lion cubs, the fledgling Dominions, helping the old lion, Britain, to defy her foes.[38] But pure patriotism had its limits as a recruiting ploy:

> . . . We ran the gamut of emotions which make men risk lives and all the forces which defer them from doing so.[39]

Legitimacy It is hardly surprising that the German violation of Belgian neutrality in August should have been used prominently in appeals to draw men into the Army. Great play was made on the precise terms of the Treaty of London (1839), the derided 'scrap of paper', so much so that facsimiles of the document were produced clearly showing the signatures of the representatives of the guaranteeing powers – Bülow's for Germany is clearly displayed, 'THE SCRAP OF PAPER' (PRC 7 and PRC 15), 'A WEE "SCRAP O'PAPER" IS BRITAIN'S BOND' (PRC 17). This early group of poster images emphasises the morally binding obligations and responsibilities of great powers in respect of weaker and smaller ones: the war was represented as a crusade and appeals were made to the idealism of the people. Later posters in this category spoke of Britain's role in the defence of a more broadly defined 'freedom' and carefully introduced the theme of German war 'crimes'. 'HELP TO END THE WAR' (PRC 42) urges that the Germans be punished.

> . . . for the barbarous treatment of unoffending civilian populations by carrying the fight into the enemy's country.

'FIGHT FOR FREEDOM WITH THE STRENGTH OF FREE MEN' (PRC 48), urges men forward to battle 'for the freedom of Europe and to defend your mothers, wives and sisters from the horrors of war'. Asquith's Mansion House speech of 9 November 1914 was effectively summarised on 'WHY MORE MEN ARE NEEDED' (PRC 59). In it the Prime Minister's realistic appraisal of the likely length of the war, 'It is going to be a long drawn-out struggle', is followed by an uncompromising demand for the restoration of German-occupied Belgium and France together with the promise that Britain would fight 'Until the rights of the smaller nations are placed on an unassailable foundation' and 'Until the military domination of Prussia is finally destroyed'.

Hate Although published in January 1915 'GERMANY'S BATTLE CRY' (PRC 39) links the theme of a fight to defend freedom from tyranny with the notion of defending civilisation against a hateful and inhuman barbarism. The stakes at issue are precisely defined and the degradations for 'mothers, wives and sisters' consequent of failure made dismally obvious.

The recruiting appeals based on inflammatory anti-German propaganda may be summarised by the three posters 'REMEMBER BELGIUM' (PRC 16), 'REMEMBER SCARBOROUGH' (PRC 29) and 'REMEMBER THE LUSITANIA' (PRC 91). The first, using the image of a burning village and its fleeing inhabitants, endeavoured to stir hearts and minds to action by reference to little Belgium battered and despoiled by an aggressive and dishonest neighbour. The poster anticipates the Bryce Committee's report[40] on German contraventions of the rules of war. The second poster, one of a series bearing the same title and chronicling the aftermath of the German Navy's attack on Scarborough on 16 December 1914, details the cost in human terms – the deaths of innocent British women and children – of an attack on the homeland. The impossible had happened and feelings were encouraged to run high. PRC 29 refers to the Germans as 'barbarians' and PRC 41, bearing the splendid figure of Britannia in the habiliments of war, speaks of vengeance and urges men to the colours as a means of striking back. PRC 51 utilises the modernistic imagery of press photography to record the post-bombardment devastation in a Scarborough terrace and coldly displays the butcher's bill with the clearly rhetorical question 'MEN OF BRITAIN! WILL YOU STAND THIS?'. The sinking of the Cunard liner *Lusitania*, 7 May 1915, provided yet another opportunity to underline the theme of German criminality and inhumanity. No calm appraisal of the ambiguities posed by the vessel's dubious cargo was permissible in the press of events. PRC posters 91 and 92 record in closely worded detail the horrific event, the casualties and unarguable cause; they both indict

> the said submarine, the Emperor and Government of Germany . . . with the crime of wilful and wholesale murder before the civilised world

PRC 95 fulsomely reports the tale of a survivor and PRC 97 beginning with a powerful criticism of the sinking, boils up into a bitter denunciation of German actions and ends (for dramatic effect) with a patent catalogue of alleged crimes:

> Germans have wantonly sacked cities and Holy Places. Germans have murdered thousands of innocent civilians. Germans have flung vitriol and blazing petrol on the Allied troops. Germans have killed our fisherfolk and deserted the drowning. Germans have inflicted unspeakable torture by poison gases on our brave troops at Ypres. Germans have poisoned wells in South Africa. Germans have assassinated our wounded.

One of the most memorable images emerging from this campaign was Bernard Partridge's figure, much admired at the time, of a classically draped avenging 'Justice' rising from the sea near the stricken *Lusitania*, 'TAKE UP THE SWORD OF JUSTICE' (PRC 111). A variant of this work, PRC 123, displaying only the sword in its scabbard, appeared later and a reference to the weapon appeared in PRC 100 which also included stirring words from Kitchener and Asquith.

Comradeship and Adventure Pre-war recruiting posters had used the idea of 'fulfilment', both personal and sartorial, offered by the Army as a professional career; the archaic splendours of traditional uniforms were displayed on athletic physiques against a background evoking the delights to be had in Army sport and travel. The posters are reserved in tone and contrast starkly with a powerfully 'chummy' group of PRC poster images whose purpose was to tempt recruits in on the basis of the happy and healthy communal lifestyle offered by the Army and the adventures to be had on active service. As distortions go this category of appeal has not received its due weight of opprobrium. 'COME ALONG BOYS!' (PRC 22), at least sets the camaraderie within the context of impending military action: a cheerful pipe-smoking 'Tommy', clearly not a victim of trench foot or neurasthenia, invites men to join him in the fight and a quotation from General Sir Horace Smith-Dorrien gives factual evidence for outrageous British claims of unquenchable cheeriness in the face of the enemy. Later posters were content to settle for images of comradeship, happiness and contentment with no direct reference to the fighting at all. The *Evening Standard*, which endeavoured to ascertain the most popular recruiting poster of 1915 by balloting its readers, was highly approving of 'LINE UP BOYS' (PRC 54), and one of its Scots readers was moved to strong feeling in a letter to the paper praising it. Of the four smiling kilted soldiers striding purposefully to left he wrote '. . . their smooth and pink young faces alight with laughter and gay carelessness'[41] and claimed it as the 'best'. The theatricality of this image is repeated in 'JOIN THE BRAVE THRONG' (PRC 118), with its six grinning British infantrymen and 'HE'S HAPPY AND SATISFIED' (PRC 96). Others, more subtle perhaps, attempted to draw men in by communicating the unaffected ease with which civilians could be transformed into efficiently 'trained men' (conveniently ignoring the well established traditions of brutality and tedium that had hitherto characterised the 'other ranks' experience of Army life). 'STEP INTO YOUR PLACE' (PRC 104) used the picture of a column of civilians, representatives of a wide range of trades and professions, winding its way into the distance. Roughly at its midpoint the trail of civilians gradually metamorphoses into a column of khaki-clad marching soldiers. 'THERE'S STILL A PLACE IN THE LINE FOR YOU' (PRC 35 – a poster which attracted favourable attention in the April 1915 issue of *The Placard*, 'a noticeably strong design and ought to do good work for the Army') similarly implies that all that was required of a volunteer to qualify for uniform, arms and serious work as regards the Germans was that he should be 'fit'. Other images within this category included welcoming crowds holding back from imminent embarkation in order to wait for additional jolly volunteers: 'THERE'S ROOM FOR YOU' (PRC 122) has a crowded troop train, packed with cheerful soldiers, momentarily delayed as a beckoning soldier convinces the reader that his company is definitely required. Depictions of accoutrements and uniforms are again resorted to in more traditional appeals such as 'IF THE CAP FITS YOU' (PRC 53) and 'COME NOW' (PRC 130).

Understandably there are very few reproductions in PRC posters of actual fighting at the front: it would have been perverse to expect men to respond to calls which demonstrated the genuine horrors of the battlefield. Lack of battle experience on the part of the illustrator was a further inhibiting factor. 'Secondhand' attempts to portray the fighting were despised by veterans as nothing better than picturesque and distorting travesties. The effects of war are to be seen and read about in the second and third poster categories but there are (if one excludes the stylised silhouette battle scenes together with Lawson Wood's static kilted soldier in a Belgian village, in 'A WEE "SCRAP O'PAPER" IS BRITAIN'S BOND', PRC 17, and the marginal action of 'SINGLE MEN', PRC 120) only two direct representations of British troops in action in the PRC series and both are rendered in dramatic but clearly not disastrous circumstances. In 'AT THE FRONT!' (PRC 84), field gun teams come under shell fire just close enough to lend excitement; no casualties, men or beasts, are to be seen. In the other, 'FORWARD!' (PRC 133), which formed the last of the rousing rally-style posters of the PRC's campaign (October 1915, it was followed by typographical explanations of the Derby Scheme) has a cavalryman charg-

He did his duty. Will you do yours?
1914.
PRC poster no 20
Lithograph 76 × 51cms
IWM:PST:5100

'A Happy New Year to our Gallant
Soldiers!', 1915.
PRC poster, unnumbered
Lithograph 75.6 × 49.1cms
IWM:PST:6070

Designer: Alfred Leete
(1882–1933)
Britons . . . . 1914.
Photo-lithograph with type
74.9 × 50.5cms
IWM:PST:2734

An appeal to you, 1915.
PRC poster no 88
Lithograph 97.6 × 61.8cms
IWM:PST:5166

Who's absent? 1915.
PRC poster no 125
Lithograph 74.2 × 50cms
IWM:PST:5251

Designer: Arthur Wardle
The Empire needs men! 1915.
PRC poster no 58
Lithograph 74.9 × 50.2cms
IWM:PST:352

The Scrap of Paper, 1914.
PRC poster no 7
Type 76.3 × 50.6cms
IWM:PST:5083

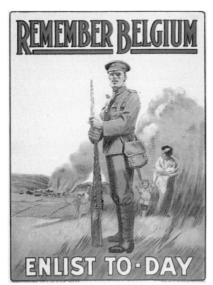

Remember Belgium, 1915.
PRC poster no 16
Lithograph 100.4 × 74cms
IWM:PST:5075

Men of Britain! 1915.
PRC poster no 51
Lithograph 125.1 × 76cms
IWM:PST:5119

Line up, boys! 1915.
PRC poster no 54
Lithograph 75 × 49.8cms
IWM:PST:5122

Artist unknown
Step into your place, 1915.
PRC poster no 104
Lithograph 50.5 × 75.8cms
IWM:PST:5904

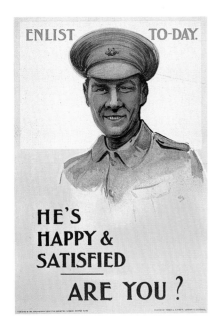

Designer: 'O.R.' (unidentified)
He's happy and satisfied. Are you? 1915.
PRC poster no 96
Lithograph 75 × 49.4cms
IWM:PST:321

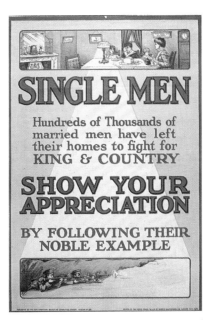

Single men, 1915.
PRC poster no 120
Lithograph 74.5 × 49.8cms
IWM:PST:5051

Designer: Lucy Kemp-Welch (1869–1958)
Forward! 1915.
PRC poster no 133
Lithograph 75.4 × 49cms

Designer: Baron Low
Everyone should do his bit.
PRC poster no 121
Lithograph 75 × 49.6cms
IWM:PST:5060

Designer: Lord Baden Powell
(1857–1941)
Are you in this? 1915.
PRC poster no 112
Lithograph 75.5 × 49.5cms
IWM:PST:2712

Designer: Savile Lumley
Daddy, what did YOU do in the Great War?
PRC poster no 79
Lithograph 74.6 × 49.2cms
IWM:PST:311

ing full tilt towards the reader (again within the dramatic setting of smoke and shellfire no casualties are apparent). It must be admitted that the output of other poster campaigns, especially those sponsored by the popular press, used a far more lurid imagery which did not shun the representation of death or wounds; a notable image accompanied the *Weekly Despatch's* publication of 22 November 1914, 'Will they never come?'.[42] Nonetheless it was perhaps inevitable that traditionally heroic images of the soldiers serving a noble cause should be presented to the public as a means of encouraging recruiting; poster art could not but reflect

> '... the pictorial representation of the soldier by such artists as R Caton Woodville, W B Woolen and Fortunino Matania, whose work appearing in popular illustrated periodicals and children's literature, invariably depicted gallantry, self-sacrifice and determination, while, death somehow contrived to be tasteful.'[43]

Interrogation and Intimidation The most contentious group of posters produced for the PRC were those which used arguments for recruiting based on social pressure and moral reproach. An early example (December 1914) of the former category used the theme of the eligible unenlisted civilian who was characterised as merely thoughtless in his neglect of duty to the state; this tardiness (perhaps reflecting the failure of the authorities adequately to make clear their needs) was roused by images conveying the self-sacrifice and generosity of those already in the fight: 'WHY ARE YOU STOPPING HERE WHEN YOUR PALS ARE OUT THERE?' (PRC 27) and 'THINK! ARE YOU CONTENT FOR HIM TO FIGHT FOR YOU?' (PRC 37). Later approaches were more refined and the sharper points more difficult to dodge: 'THINK IT OVER!' (PRC 43), includes within its condemnation of the unsporting reliance on the efforts of others, the question 'You're proud of your pals in the Army of course! But what will your pals think of you?'. The step from nudging persuasion to open confrontation with the fundamental moral question of duty left undone, (and all the associated implications of cowardice) was but a short and easy one. One of 'ENLIST TO-DAY' 's (PRC 68) disturbing questions asks '... WHO will remember us with pride and exaltation and thankfulness if we do our duty today?' and answers ominously 'Our children'. Other posters in this category resorted to dramatically urgent appeals, 'DON'T STAND LOOKING AT THIS ... GO AND HELP!' (PRC 73) and 'DON'T STAY IN THE CROWD AND STARE' (PRC 74). Some used the images of the soldiers at the front to voice the appeal: 'LADS, YOU'RE WANTED' (PRC 78) and 'BOYS! COME ALONG YOU'RE WANTED' (PRC 80). The use

of the affectionate terms 'Lads' and 'Boys' suggests that the men to whom these calls were addressed were regarded merely as rascally laggards rather than devious skrimshankers and that their immediate enlistment would result in a ready inclusion in the comradeship of the rank and file. Other more provocative poster arguments were used which were notable for the singular absence of any form of 'chumminess'. '3 QUESTIONS TO EMPLOYERS' (PRC 70) represented an indirect appeal to those who were employing men eligible for the Army which, if stark, was relatively fair. In contrast '5 QUESTIONS TO MEN WHO HAVE NOT ENLISTED' (PRC 57), published in January 1915, includes precisely the question posed later by Saville Lumley (see PRC 79) and which was to put a shadow over the whole poster campaign – 'What will your answer be when your children grow up and say, "Father why weren't you a soldier too?"' Later examples of this type of argument stopped little short of bullying and moral blackmail and their embittered tone perhaps reflected the disappointment of the recruiting organisations in the failure of their audience to respond. In 'WHAT WILL YOUR ANSWER BE?' (PRC 61), an insufferable Boy Scout poses the question to his clearly perplexed father, an agony in part relieved by the anonymity derived from the silhouette format:

> Father, – what did you do to help when Britain fought for freedom in 1915?

Probably the next best known British recruiting poster of the First World War, after Leete's 'Kitchener', is Saville Lumley's 'DADDY, WHAT DID YOU DO IN THE GREAT WAR?' (PRC 79). A vast amount has been written about this work, almost to the exclusion of the rest of the PRC series, but if its trite origins are to be believed the obloquy is undeserved; they are described in a letter[44] to the IWM from Mr Paul Gunn, of the printers Johnson, Riddle and Co Ltd. The incident may be summarised; his father, worried about the war and concerned whether he should volunteer, postulated a future scenario in which his children might embarrass him by asking what he had done to defend them. Apparently this distressing image was the source of much consolation to him; he immediately had Lumley sketch the imagined scene and volunteered himself a few days later. Subsequent reactions to the poster help register the degree of offence and opposition the work generated: both Arthur Marwick and Peter Simkins quote the reputed reaction of Robert Smillie, the Scottish miners' leader, to the invidious though innocently conceived question:

> I tried to stop the bloody thing[45]

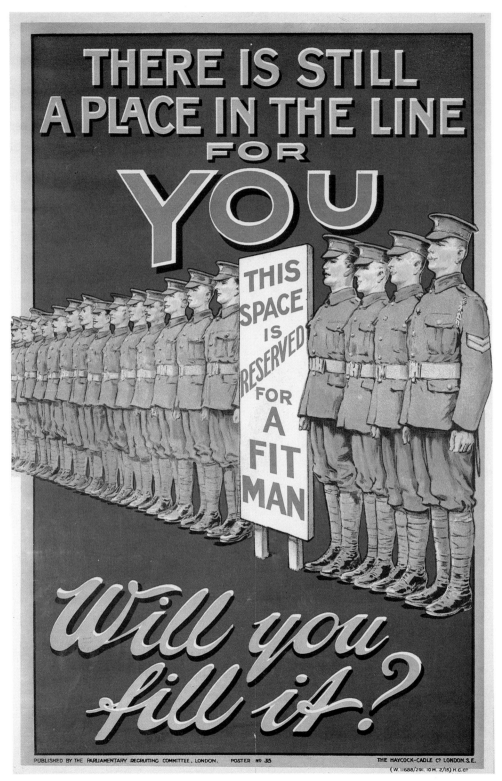

There is still a place in the line for you, 1915.
PRC poster no 35

Lithograph 76.6 × 50.3cms
IWM:PST:0316

and H G Wells's late 1915 estimation of the poster recruiting campaign – 'ridiculous placards and street corner insults' (quoted in *The Times Recruiting Supplement*, 3 November 1915) may well have been fostered by this and other similar tendentious messages. Certainly George Orwell's much later (1940) response to the poster was equally derisory:

> I have often laughed to think of that recruiting poster and all the men who must have been lured into the army . . . and afterwards despised by their children for not being conscientious objectors.[46]

As well as children, images of women were used to inspire or shame men into joining up. The pressures put on men to enlist by such appeals were quite obvious; less well remarked on were the disturbing claims placed on women to yield their sons, brothers or husbands up to the war. In addition to the emotional pain of unwilling separation genuine cases of economic hardship occurred within households following the departure of the principal wage earner into the forces. The failure of the War Office to provide obligatory separation allowances as early as September 1914 did not go unnoticed.[47] Nevertheless posters like, 'TO THE WOMEN OF BRITAIN' (PRC 55), unhesitatingly struck at the security of the home:

> To the Women of Britain. Some of your men-folk are holding back on your account. Won't you prove your love for your country by persuading them to go?

In more recent years the recruiting posters which used women to convey their messages have been criticised on the grounds of distortion and exploitation. They have been seen as attempts to portray females as a privileged caste, exempt from the horrors of the actual fighting, who were only too willing to offer up their 'men-folk' on the high altar of machine warfare. Certainly the appalling 'TO THE WOMEN OF BRITAIN' (PRC 69), 'WOMEN OF BRITAIN SAY – GO!' (PRC 75) and 'GO, IT'S YOUR DUTY LAD' (PRC 109) may be cited as wonderful examples of this particular aberration. The smiling unconcern of the elderly dame in the last, as she invites the young man to 'GO' is barely short of a parody. But the posters accord perfectly in spirit with the patriotic activities of such feminist organisations as Emmeline and Christabel Pankhurst's 'Women's Social and Political Union' and Mrs Henry Fawcett's 'National Union of Women's Suffrage Societies'. Both had abandoned their militant campaign for the vote in order to demonstrate their patriotism in time of crisis by supporting

calls for recruits.

Two posters, Lawson Wood's 'A CHIP OF THE OLD BLOCK' (PRC 18) and 'THE VETERAN'S FAREWELL' (after a painting by Frank Dadd – in monochrome and colour formats, PRC 24 and PRC 63), make sentimental use of the elderly. In the former a bewhiskered and bemedalled veteran shakes the hand of a young soldier as he bids farewell; the fateful leave train waits in the background. The old man's encouraging and patriotic commendations 'To maintain the honour and glory of the British Empire' though trite are perhaps more persuasive than the complacent remarks of the secure Chelsea Pensioner to the recently enlisted soldier in the second poster:

> Goodbye my lad, I only wish I were young enough to go with you.

which could hardly have convinced the determined laggard.

Other approaches

Homeland Despite Caroline Dakar's assertion, in her recently published study *The Countryside at War*, that throughout the conflict propagandists used images of rural England to inspire men to enlist, idealised bucolic scenes do not feature prominently in the PRC's poster campaign.[48] 'YOUR COUNTRY'S CALL' (PRC 87), is the only pictorial poster which attempts to exploit the unspoilt loveliness of the homeland, and idyllic vision of the British rural scene, as a recruiting ploy; the argument moves from 'the old country in danger' to the 'countryside endangered' by war's destructive power. But the poster presents a compromise landscape and features an ambiguous kilted soldier (who points to the beauties all around) designed to appeal to all the Home nations. The image is in marked contrast to Brangwyn's social realist lithographs (used in other propaganda campaigns) in which the more desolate and harsher industrial face of Britain is displayed to extol the workers' commitment to the war effort. Specific local appeals were also made by the PRC; posters in Welsh for the Principality[49] and the huge manpower potential of the capital was addressed by 'MEN OF LONDON!' (PRC 50).

Literary appeals Asquith's eloquent speeches (part of a great campaign of public speaking undertaken by leading politicians) featured in a number of posters and his exquisitely constructed sentences were applauded by Graves and Hodge who later claimed that Asquith was 'the last politician whose speeches could be printed as decent examples of English prose'.[50] But it is hard to believe that his words were easily intelligible to the masses, 'THE PRIME MINISTER, MAY

4th . . . 1915' (PRC 98), being a case in point. It reads:

> Let there not be a man or woman among us who, when the war is over, will not be able to say: 'I was not idle. I took such part as I could in the greatest task which, in all the storied annals of our country, has ever fallen to the lot of Great Britain to achieve.'

. . . and is typical of a small group of PRC posters which relied on the encouraging words of political and military leaders. Even the Bard himself was co-opted in the persuasive and inspirational task; 'STAND NOT UPON THE ORDER OF YOUR GOING' (PRC 52), uses a quotation from Macbeth which is 'carefully identified' and 'typifies the gentlemanly appeal to an educated class seen in many British posters'.[51]

Images of working class strength and solidarity (and appeals for effective manpower allocation) PRC posters 26, 28 and 36 effectively make use of the symbol of the clenched fist to summon working class support for the war effort either by encouraging workers to join the Army or to use their skills in essential war industries. PRC 26, produced in the shape of a right arm (the fist is clenched), exhorts the reader to 'LEND YOUR STRONG RIGHT ARM TO YOUR COUNTRY' and PRC 28 (December 1914) carries the reassuring message 'Britain's strong right arm and YOURS WILL CARRY US THROUGH'. The vital interdependence of soldiers and workers, the importance of which was only properly appreciated following the first wave of enlistments (which took with it thousands of skilled workers) in August 1914, was illustrated by three posters: 'WE'RE BOTH NEEDED TO SERVE THE GUNS!' (PRC 85C), in which, true to traditional images of socialist unity, a British infantryman and munition worker amicably shake hands as the text urges the reader to 'FILL UP THE RANKS' and 'PILE UP THE MUNITIONS'; Lieutenant-General Sir Robert Baden-Powell's 'ARE YOU IN THIS?' (PRC 112), is centred on a music hall-style 'tableau-vivant' composed of representatives from the Army, Royal Navy, Boy Scouts, Nursing Services, munition and industrial workers demonstrating their busy commitment to the war effort (at the same time displaying the unity of all classes in the common aim) while an, as yet, uninvolved civilian looks on; 'THE KEY TO THE SITUATION' (PRC 116) with the minimum of fuss resolves the issues to their barest essentials; victory requires 'Munitions, Men and Money'.

Allowances and explanations (separation allowances and the post-October 1915 exposition of the Derby Scheme) Informational posters detailing revised scales of separation allowances appeared from May 1915 onwards and attempted to make clear the recently altered (March 1915) arrangements.[52] After the pictorial poster 'FORWARD!' (PRC 133) rousing images disappear from the campaign; instead there were issued explanations of the scope, purpose and functioning of the Derby Scheme.[53] Asquith's oratorical skills were again brought into play and 'THE PRIME MINISTER'S ADVICE' (PRC 135), a characteristically literary and over-subtle poster, is notable in that it helped to seal the fate of the unhappy project. Asquith made a binding pledge to married men that all available single men would be eligible for military service before them. This pledge had to be 'redeemed' and once the attestation returns (statements of willingness to serve as and when required) had revealed a large pool of eligible single men who had no intention of enlisting voluntarily, compulsion became inevitable. The very last posters of the PRC campaign explain the detailed provisions and demands of the first Military Service Act which, passed by Parliament in January 1916, brought in conscription for single men aged between 18 and 42 on Thursday 2 March 1916.

An assessment of the effectiveness of the PRC's poster campaign is fraught with difficulties. Apart from generalised notions of the degree of 'attention' roused by particular images no methods operated for accurately determining how effective a poster had been. Again, the messages in the PRC series did not exist in isolation but formed part of a great national propaganda campaign which encompassed most known forms of advertising techniques. A straightforward correlation with known recruiting figures for a specified date or area in which a poster was issued may provide the basis for some tentative evaluations and certainly this has been attempted with regard to Leete's memorable image of Kitchener; analysis yielded a surprising conclusion:

Join the brave throng that goes marching along, 1915.
PRC poster no 118
Lithograph 60.1 × 186cms
IWM:PST:5036

Far left: Designer: Lawson Wood
(1878–1957)
Your King and Country need you,
1914.
PRC poster no 18
Lithograph 74.5 × 50.1cms
IWM:PST:5254

Left: *Your country's call*, 1915.
PRC poster no 87
Lithograph 75.7 × 50.2cms
IWM:PST:0302

In view of the fact that it became arguably the best known poster in history it is perhaps churlish to note that its widespread circulation in various forms did not halt the decline in recruiting.[54]

Earlier, Osborne, much interested in the loudly-voiced claims of the positive effects of military and naval setbacks on recruiting, attempted to quantify the results of the 'REMEMBER SCARBOROUGH' poster series. Acknowledging that any analysis of the late 1914 recruiting figures was significantly affected by the Christmas holiday he concludes that 'the claim of a new rush in the days following the raid is spurious.'[55] But this fact, little regarded at the time, did not destroy the faith maintained in poster appeals to 'passion' and the same writer, basing his findings on the undisputed decline in recruiting figures during 1915 argues convincingly that the release in January 1915 of 'official reports' on the Belgian atrocities, the use of poison gas by the Germans at Ypres in late April 1915 and the torpedoing of the *Lusitania* soon after 'all failed to stimulate recruiting.'[56]

At the time of their issue the PRC's pictorial posters received much criticism on the grounds of artistic merit – or rather lack of it. Even such a partisan journal as *The Placard* judged 'some of them good, not a few of them – well, less so'.[57] Widespread doubts were expressed as to the success of some of the images; they were deemed deficient in original conception, effective design and technique:

> ... the earliest days of the war saw available spaces everywhere covered with posters cheap in sentiment and conveying childish and vulgar appeals to a patriotism already stirred far beyond

the original conceptions of the artists who designed them or the authorities responsible for their distribution.[58]

Hardie and Sabin admit of 'very much better work' in 1915 but again remonstrated against the British poster artist's obsession with narrative and wordiness instead of concentrating on the virtues of directness and simplicity (exemplified by contemporary German poster art). An exhibition of British recruiting posters in Germany (opened 2 October 1915, in Berlin, in aid of the German Aeronautic Association) generated, from admittedly hostile critics, insights: 'The exhibition is a great material success not withstanding the general disappointment at the poor and inartistic designs.'[59] It would be fair to comment that the Publications Sub-Department had from the very outset expressed the opinion that 'elaborate posters were not necessary' (see footnote 25). It is also worth remembering that the PRC relied in many instances on civilian printing firms, whose in-house artists (humble to the point of failing to name themselves in their works) made decisions on designs and typography, inevitably resulted in a prosaic poster output. Civilian printers produced civilian-flavoured images in a deliberately unrefined popular style with obvious working class appeal. But this is not to say that the whole of British First World War poster design was inferior to the products of Germany; some British charities for example commissioned well-known artists like Louis Raemaekers and J P Beadle and were responsible for a far more sophisticated group of poster images. Again the London Underground, under the guidance of Frank Pick, commissioned first class poster art by some of the finest designers in the field. Nonetheless, up to mid-1915 the British press had been filled with confident assertions concerning the

Artist unknown
We're both needed to serve the Guns! 1915.
PRC poster no 85c
Lithograph 51.1 × 74.5cms IWM:PST:5112

quality and effectiveness of the poster recruiting campaign and claimed 'that the hoardings of England had never borne a better message conveyed in a better manner'.[60] In fact many of the hoardings had been underused and much unfavourable comment was expressed over the actual poster campaign strategy. *The Placard* in particular was very critical of the War Office's arrangements for billposting; these were for the most part left to the individual enterprise of the local recruiting officers. Some worked admirably, others less so; all lacked sufficient funds. Naturally the journal took the line that the War Office would have been better to entrust the matter to professional billposting contractors.[61] In addition to the inherent difficulties of recruiting as an advertising proposition and working in harmony with the stiff formalities of a distinguished government department other problems came to light. The size of the PRC's poster bills were much criticised by the professionals:

> There has been too great a readiness to run after small bills and to get them put up free. Like other beginners, the Government directors of billposting have probably been scared of the printing cost of many-sheeted posters – not realising that economy in display and effect makes large bills relatively cheap.[62]

The PRC's poster campaign's failure, despite the energy behind it and variety of the images and messages used, is chronicled in its own detailed expositions of the implications of the first Military Service Act. The new law made the Committee redundant but it continued to function up until July 1916. At one of its last meetings (now formally the Joint Recruiting Committee), 10 April 1916, the patriotic and

responsible nature of its membership was revealed in the sad task of forming a sub-committee:

> to consider the question of the reserves of posters raised in the memorandum by the Publications Department – and the most advantageous manner of disposing them with a view to benefitting some war charity . . .[63]

The PRC's poster scheme, which started out as a guardian of a cherished British ideal – the principle of voluntary enlistment – was unable to satisfy the war's unquenchable thirst for men and ended by announcing the system which was to replace it: compulsion. But the power of the poster as a medium for the dissemination of information was underlined by the War Office's decision to retain the use of the poster bill (and not the newspapers) to call up attested men and 'those deemed to have attested under the law of conscription'. The hard won lessons of experience were put to good use:

> It (the War Office) knows the universal advertising medium and employs posters: 40,000 were put up in the London area in a single night in February![64]

Notes

1. *The Times*, 13 July 1914, p 6.
2. Ibid, p 5.
3. Quoted by Maurice Rickards, *The Rise and Fall of the Poster*, David and Charles, 1971, p 25.
4. *The Placard*, October 1915, p 23 (includes a reprinted extract from the January 1914 issue).
5. Ibid, p 22.
6. Ibid, p 23.
7. An article in *The Times*, 21 March 1986, encapsulates popular attitudes to the poster recruiting campaign. Concentrating on Lumley's 'Daddy, what did YOU do in the Great War?', the exegesis emphasises their naivety and cruelty, postulating the existence of an underlying 'sick psychology'. It makes no attempt to suggest the range of persuasive messages used and place the arguments in their appropriate historical context which is labelled simply as 'a sad, mad era'. In contrast see Roy Douglas, *Voluntary Enlistment in the First World War and the Work of the Parliamentary Recruiting Committee*, Journal of Modern History, vol 42, 1970, p 568, which provides a far more coherent assessment.
8. Haig's *Diary* quoted by Peter Simkins, *Kitchener's Army*, Manchester University Press, 1988, p 47.

9. G H S Jordan, *The Politics of Conscription in Britain, 1905–1916*, 1974 PhD thesis, authorised facsimile distributed by UMI Dissertation Information Service, Ann Arbor, Michigan, 1987, p 63.
10. Simkins, op cit, p 65.
11. Great Britain Parliamentary Debates (Commons), 5th series, vol 66, September 10, 1914, columns 664–665. Quoted by Roy Douglas, op cit, p 569.
12. L S Amery, *My Political Life*, vol II, p 28. Quoted by Simkins, op cit, p 53.
13. Asquith has also been identified as the vital prime mover; specifically, his Parliamentary reply to J Norton-Griffiths, see *Great Britain Parliamentary Debates (Commons)*, 5th series, vol 66, 26 August 1914, column 28. Quoted by Roy Douglas, op cit, p 566.
14. *Minutes of the Preliminary Meeting of the Parliamentary Recruiting Committee*, 27 August 1914, p 1 (Add Mss 54192, Book I, British Library, Manuscripts Department).
15. Ibid, p 1. See also Jordan, op cit, p 71.
16. *Minutes of the Parliamentary Recruiting Committee*, 28 August 1914, pp 4–5 (Add Mss 54192, Book I, British Library, Manuscripts Department).
17. Simkins, op cit, p 61. The *Minutes of the Parliamentary Recruiting Committee*, 31 August 1914, p 1 (Add Mss 54192,

Book I, British Library, Manuscripts Department) provides a full list of those who were present: Percy Illingworth (in the Chair), the Duke of Devonshire, Lord Colebrooke, Lord Edmund Talbot, Sir Henry Rawlinson, Sir Jesse Herbert, Sir Robert Hudson, Major Gosset, A D Steel-Maitland, H Pike Pease, W Jenkins, Wedgwood Benn, William Jones, Geoffrey Howard, Henry Webb, James Parker, F W Goldstone, John Boraston and Clerk to the Committee R H Davies.

18. Letter, R H Davies to British Museum, dated 4 May 1971 contained in Add Mss 54192, British Library (Manuscripts Department).

19. David Sweet, *The Domestic Scene. Parliament and People*, chapter 2, p 15, of *Home Fires and Foreign Fields*, edited by Peter Liddle, Brasseys, 1985.

20. The idea for the 'Householder's Return' was supplied by Sir Jesse Herbert; its introduction was opposed by Arthur Steel-Maitland who regarded it as 'inquisitorial', see *Minutes of the General Purposes Committee*, 21 October 1914, p 5 (Add Mss 54192, British Library, Manuscripts Department).

21. Present were Illingworth in the Chair, Lord Edmund Talbot, Arthur Henderson, Sir Jesse Herbert, Boraston, Charles Geake, Malcolm Fraser, Pringle and R H Davies.

22. *Parliamentary Recruiting Committee, Publications Sub-Department Minutes*, 3 September 1914, p 1 (Add Mss 54192, British Library, Manuscripts Department).

23. Letter, R H Davies to British Museum, dated 4 May 1967 in Add Mss 54192 (British Library, Manuscripts Department).

24. Douglas, op cit, p 568. His figures come from *The Times*, issues for 6 January and 30 March 1915.

25. *The Placard*, July 1915, p 3.

26. Martin Hardie and Arthur K Sabin, *War Posters Issued by Belligerent and Neutral Countries 1914–1919*, A and C Black, London, 1920, p 8.

27. Barry Curtis, *Posters as Visual Propaganda in the Great War*, article published in *The Block*, (2), 1980, p 50.

28. Simkins, op cit, p 123.

29. One of the principal obstacles to computing the precise total published lies in the Publications Sub-Department's curiously erratic numbering system. Some quite different poster designs (and smaller show-cards) share the same PRC series number; others bear identical numbers with merely differentiating letter suffixes. Again, many posters bearing identical images or text were issued in a variety of sizes and formats, each issue being given a unique number within the system. These inconsistencies are further compounded by the fact that some posters carry a wealth of production detail – designer, publisher, print run, date of issue – and others carry no additional information at all (save the statement 'Published by the Parliamentary Recruiting Committee'), up to the point of ignoring the printer who produced and, in many instances, designed them.

30. The complaints were sufficient to stimulate questions in Parliament concerning the reported lack of facilities in some of the newly created temporary camps, see Simkins, op cit, pp 73–74 (*Parliamentary Debates, House of Commons*, 1914, LXVI, cols 607–15). Contemporary writers also remarked on conditions: 'They had in those early days, few leaders and less equipment . . . They were herded, fourteen, sixteen, and twenty together, in leaking tents with never a floorboard between their one blanket and the mud below . . . And when the sodden camps chosen for them stood two feet in greasy slime, when neither their single blankets nor their single suits could be dried, when fires would not burn and the sick parade marched double-company strong to the doctor's tent half a mile away – then they were vaccinated, willy nilly, and left to cure their swollen arms as best they might, jostling against each other in their crowded sties!' (Gilbert Frankau, *Peter Jackson; Cigar Merchant*, Hutchinson and Co, London, 1919, p 80).

31. The height requirement for recruits was raised from 5 feet 3 inches on 8 August to 5 feet 6 inches on 11 September (although the age limit for enlistment was increased from the original 19–30 to an upper limit of 35 years). See Ian F W Beckett, *The Nation in Arms*, p 8 of an article in *A Nation in Arms*, edited by I F W Beckett and K Simpson, Manchester University Press, 1985.

32. John Morton Osborne, *The Voluntary Recruiting Movement in Britain 1914–1916*, PhD thesis, authorised facsimile distributed by UMI Dissertation Information Service, Ann Arbor, 1983, p 156.

33. Paula Harper, *War, Revolution and Peace. Propaganda Posters from the Hoover Institution Archives 1914–45*, exhibition catalogue, 1971, pp 4–5.

34. Ancient hero of the Indian Mutiny and South African War; held in affectionate esteem ('Bobs') by the British public. Died of pneumonia in St Omer, 16 November 1914 whilst visiting the Indian Corps. The use of his image so early in the campaign is not without irony – he had been a vigorous president of the pro-conscriptionist National Service League.

35. 'Alfred Leete's famous Kitchener poster first appeared on the front cover of the magazine *London Opinion*, 5 September 1914. The following week, in response to a large number of requests for reproductions, the magazine offered post-card sized copies at ¼d per 100 (reported in *London Opinion*, 12 September 1914). The PRC also obtained permission to use the design with slightly amended text which included, at Kitchener's insistence, the words 'God Save the King'. But it was not until the end of September that the design began to be issued as a poster'. See Simkins, op cit, p 122 and *London Opinion*, 26 September 1914.

36. Harper, op cit, p 40.

37. Barry Curtis, op cit, p 51.

38. 'As originally designed this poster specifically acknowledged the services of Australia, Canada, India and New Zealand. No mention being made of South Africa. This . . . caused much indignation in the omitted colony, being described in "South Africa", the leading London weekly devoted to South African interests, as "unimperial" and even "offensive" in leading articles which set forth the services of the colony and wanted to know why it did not get its meed of thanks in the poster . . . The agitation resulted in the term "Oversea (sic) States" being substituted for the offending list.' *The Placard*, July 1915, p 2.

39. Eric Field (ex-Caxton Advertising Agency), *Advertising : the Forgotten Years* pp 28–29. Quoted by Cate Haste, *Keep the Home Fires Burning*, Allen Lane, London, 1977, p 52 and Simkins, op cit, p 123.

40. The Bryce Committee (chaired by British statesman and scholar Lord James Bryce, a member of the International Court at the Hague) was appointed in December 1914 to investigate charges that German soldiers, either directed or condoned by their officers, had been guilty of widespread atrocities in Belgium. The Committee reported its findings (not favourable to German actions) in May 1915. The conclusions based on the unverified depositions of Belgian civilians and British and Belgian soldiers though welcomed at the time as evidence of German 'frightfulness' have more recently come under closer scrutiny and criticism; see Trevor Wilson, *The Myriad Faces of War*, Polity Press, Cambridge, 1986, pp 182–191.

41. *The Placard*, July 1915, p 3.

42. PST/3294, (Department of Art poster collection) 'IT'S 4 TO 1', by John Hassall uses a similar image to 'Will they never come?'

43. Beckett, op cit, p 17.

44. The letter is quoted by J Darracott and B Loftus in *First World War Posters*, Imperial War Museum, London, 1972, p 6.

45. Arthur Marwick, *The Deluge*, Bodley Head, London, 1965, p 52; Simkins, op cit, p 123.

46. George Orwell, *My Country Right or Left*, in *Collected Essays*, volume 2, quoted by Barry Curtis, op cit, p 46.

47. Simkins, op cit, pp 106–107. Also Gilbert Frankau, op cit, p 80: 'Their wives and children starved because their separation allowances were not paid . . .'

48. Caroline Dakar, *The Countryside at War*, Constable, London, 1987, p 16.

49. Clive Hughes, *The Welsh Army Corps, 1914–15 : shortages of khaki and basic equipment promote a 'national' uniform*, in *IWM Review*, No 1, IWM, London, 1986, pp 91–100.

50. Robert Graves and Alan Hodge, *The Long Week-End*, Faber and Faber, London, 1940, p 46.

51. Harper, op cit, p 40.

52. See PRC posters 72, 89, 114 and 115.

53. Launched in October 1915 under Lord Derby (who became the country's first civilian Director of Recruiting) the scheme purported to make the voluntary system more effective by systematising enlistment on the basis of a National Register. It aimed to reconcile the needs of the Army with those of industry, calling men up by 'groups' (based on age) as they were required and making loud its claim to take single men first. The process of registration (or 'attestation') was not compulsory and when the returns revealed a large pool of single men who had failed to indicate their willingness to serve the voluntary system was certain to be replaced by conscription.

54. Simkins, op cit, p 122.

55. Osborne, op cit, p 159.

56. Ibid, p 160.

57. *The Placard*, July 1915, p 3.

58. Hardie and Sabin, op cit, p 2.

59. Ibid, pp 11–12.

60. Ibid, p 12.

61. *The Placard*, January 1915, p 28.

62. *The Placard*, October 1915, p 24.

63. *Joint Recruiting Committee Minutes*, 10 April 1916, p 56 (Add Mss 54192, Book II, British Library, Manuscripts Department). The Sub-Committee comprised Colonel Gosset, Geoffrey Howard, Pike Pearse and George Roberts.

64. *The Placard*, April 1916, p 2.

Des illusions ..
Désillusions .. :
an introduction
to parties,
personalities
and posters in
collaboration-
ist France,
1940–1944

Michael Moody

Michael Moody is a research
assistant and exhibitions organiser
in the Department of Art.

This article gives a brief outline of French collaborationism – the Vichy régime and its more politically
extremist associates – illustrated by posters of the period. All
of the examples reproduced are from the collection of the
Museum's Department of Art. Although material of this type
is becoming increasingly scarce, most of these items are fairly
recent additions to the collection, acquired within the last
decade.

For those unfamiliar with the complexities of this
particular period, the posters will provide only part of the
overall picture. Many present a purely localised political
viewpoint, albeit within a European context, which is not
immediately accessible to the British reader. Also, they do not
constitute masterpieces of graphic art. The artists responsible
remain either unknown as names or completely anonymous.
However, the posters present a rich variety of political her-
aldry and symbolism which supplies a key to their respective
meanings.

The major characteristic of collaborationist posters is the confusion of political imagery. Traditional emblems
of a Republican France and those recalling Napoleonic
grandeur were blatantly used in conjunction with an
authoritarian and often openly fascist iconography. Portraits
of Marshal Pétain, the embodiment of the conservative *État
Français* were circulated everywhere, his image appeared
frequently juxtaposed against the Republican *Tricolor*, a symbol of the nation's Revolutionary legacy. This conflicting
theme continued through the graphic vocabulary which
dominated the recruiting posters of the main collaborationist
parties. While politically these posters voice now discredited
ideologies, their visual content only reflects the confusions of
their epoch.

The fall of France was the culmination of a German Blitzkrieg campaign lasting only six weeks, the details
of which are well known. The reasons for the *débacle* were
rooted in the polarisation and fragmentation of French political life during the Third Republic. Through its failure to produce either strong leaders or stable government combined
with attendant financial scandals, corruption and rapid
ministerial changes, the Third Republic became an object of
popular contempt. After the Armistice of 1918, the *union sacrée*[1]

Enamel lapel badge showing the
symbol of L'État Francais, the
francisque gallique, double-
headed throwing-axe of the
ancient Gauls. The haft is
represented by a baton of a
Marshal of France.
Author's collection

N'oubliez pas Oran! Lithograph 1940 118.5 × 86.5cms
A painterly image of a drowning French sailor holding the *Tricolor* aloft:
anti-British poster issued after the Royal Navy's sinking of the French
Atlantic Squadron at Mers-el-Kebir (Algeria) 3 July 1940

Designer: Philippe H Noyer. *Révolution Nationale.* Lithograph 1940
39 × 30.8cms
Marshal Philippe Pétain, head of *L'État Francais*, whose 'National
Revolution' aimed to create a reborn France out of the humiliation of
defeat. IWM:PST:3341

Ils donnent leur sang. Donnez votre travail . . . . Lithograph 1943
156 × 118.8cms
A more strident call for French labour, compulsory by 1943, underlining
its crucial rôle in the defence of Hitler's Europe against Bolshevism.
IWM:ART:15778(2)

Le Feu Lithograph 1941 79 × 60cms
Collaborationist politics as
fantasy. Promising national
regeneration through action, *Le
Maître du Feu* appeals to the
French people in return for
support of his German-backed
party.
'People of France
I would save you from oppressive
lies

I would stop their criminal ways
I would save the Empire from
rogues who would sell it
I would save France from those
who do not know how to defend
her
(signed:) Fire Master
Everyone must join "Fire"
To delay, is Treason – to refuse, is
death'
IWM:PST:3335

En travaillant en Allemagne. Lithograph 1942 56.8 × 38cms
A subtle appeal to French artisans to volunteer for work in Germany in exchange for the repatriation of prisoners of war. The stylisation of the emblems of industry is suitably redolent of official Nazi sculpture, which based its aesthetic on the classical ideal and its technique on the nineteenth century academic tradition. IWM:PST:3321

RNP Rassemblement National Populaire Lithograph 1941
157.5 × 115.7cms
The choice of party logo – the horseshoe – was intended to symbolise the union of both agriculture and heavy industry. IWM:ART:15778(3)

Designer: Roger Folk *A temps héroiques jeunesse héroique . . . Combats avec les JNP* Lithograph 1942 118 × 77.6cms
The *Jeunesse Nationale Populaire* was the youth affiliate of the RNP under its *chef national* Roland Silly. The JNP's fight for a 'National and Socialist Revolution', also acknowledges the Republican spirit of 1792. IWM:PST:6023

Designer: 'Eric' *Milice Française contre le Communisme* Lithograph 1944
106.5 × 79.7cms
Recruiting poster showing the Milice logo, a white gamma motif – the zodiacal sign of Aries (the Ram) – symbolising strength and renewal. The Milice purported to represent the power and energy of a reborn France within the New European Order. IWM:ART:15778(5)

Designer: Michel Jacquot *Communisme Enemi de la France* Lithograph 1942 158 × 102.2cms
A PPF member in combat with the communist enemy, traditionally represented as a wolf of the Asiatic steppes. IWM:ART:15778(11)

Designer: Coulon *France Libère-toi, adhérez au PPF* Lithograph c.1941
120 × 80cms
France breaks free from the chains of a potential international
Communism. A curious mixture of Republican and Fascist symbolism.
IWM:ART:15778(7)

which had bound the nation together during the Great War, however slightly, dissolved, and both Left and Right wings emerged displaying more vivid ideological markings. Although the political heritage of the Left – the Great Revolution of 1789, the barricades of 1830 and 1848 – had faded with the passage of time, memories of the failed 1871 Paris Commune were still relatively fresh. Then the possibility of a government of the proletariat had almost appeared a reality.

As has been pointed out, it was on the achievements and mistakes of the Commune that Lenin based his own successful revolution in Russia in 1917 – an event which injected new life into the French Left.[2] As we shall see, it was the bogey of International Bolshevism that was to present a constant threat – real or imagined – to the men of the Right.

The flowering of the French Right prior to the outbreak of war in 1939 was essentially a rejection of the values of the stagnant society based on the old bourgeois values of 'stability, harmony and permanence' expressed by the weakness and vacillation of the Third Republic. Successive conservative governments had failed to meet the challenges of the 1920s and 1930s: a declining birthrate, a halting economy and the terrible disillusionment and exhaustion which followed the end of the Great War.

A combination of both middle-aged war veterans and a young, frustrated bourgeoisie impatient with the political ineptitude of its elders and only too aware of the Fascist reconstruction in Italy and the Nazi accession to power in 1933, considered more authoritarian alternatives to parliamentary democracy. The drift to the Right was characterised by the numerous *ligues* which rose to prominence during the 1930s prior to their dissolution before the outbreak of the Second World War. Charles Maurras's[3] *Action Française* spawned its own youth section the *Camelots du Roi* (The King's Hawkers) which perpetuated Maurras's monarchism, Catholicism and anti-semitism. The violently nationalistic and anti-Communist *Jeunesses Patriotes* were the successors to Paul Déroulède's *Ligue des Patriotes* originally formed to avenge the defeat of 1870. Colonel Casimir de la Roque's *Croix de Feu*, a war veterans' association, was committed to the purging of the Republic's corrupt institutions. The perfume magnate François Coty formed *Solidarité Française* in 1932 which sported the para-military dress of blue shirt and black beret, a uniform *de rigueur* for most collaborationist groups after 1940. Coty also founded a newspaper in support of his organisation, *L'Ami du Peuple*,[4] whose masthead bore the legend 'With Hitler against Bolshevism'. Although none of these bodies could be called openly Fascist, they provided the seed-bed from which more extreme elements were to grow under the German occupation. It was against this background – of political factionalism, public apathy, and the spectre of a million and a half dead in the First World War

Designer: O Anton *Coude à coude contre l'enemi commun!* Lithograph 1944 154.5 × 113.8cms
Recruiting posters for the French Division of the Waffen-SS, formed in August 1943. The initial intake amounted to some 800, rising to 1,688 by July 1944. In September of the same year, the volunteers were amalgamated with former LVF and Milice personnel to form the SS Division 'Charlemagne', of which many were to die in the ruins of Berlin. IWM:ART:15925

Left: Jacques Doriot, leader of the *Parti Populaire Français* (seated, in German uniform) at a press conference on his return from the Eastern Front (date unknown) MH 25260. Right: Joseph Darnand, head of the *Milice Française*. Behind him is a recruiting poster for its parent organisation the *Service d'ordre légionnaire* (SOL) whose personnel formed the nucleus of the *Milice*, established in January 1943. MH 25261 Reproduced by courtesy of the Comité d'histoire de la deuxième guerre mondiale.

– that a wavering Third Republic went to war against Germany, and lost.

France was the only defeated European country with which Nazi Germany signed an armistice. This was completed on 22 June 1940 at Compiègne, in the same railway carriage in which the French had presented their terms to the German delegates in 1918. It had been sought by the aged Marshal Philippe Pétain, 'Victor of Verdun', last premier of the Third Republic on 17 June (the date of his accession) in a radio broadcast to the nation. Pétain believed that France's defeat was primarily the work of the politicians. He was reluctant to admit, however, that 'the greatest army in Europe' had been thrown into a war for which it was totally unprepared: German tactical and technological superiority had rendered the trench mentality redundant. The German armistice terms dictated that France be divided into both occupied and unoccupied zones; the former comprising the entire Atlantic and Channel coasts including the richer northern and eastern *départements*, two-thirds of the country. A French government was to be responsible for the administration of both zones though in cooperation with the occupying power. All land forces were to be demobilized, and, with the exception of a token 'armistice army' of 100,000 men, retained within the unoccupied zone. The French fleet, its reputation unsullied by the recent *débacle*, was to remain intact, though demobilized, at Toulon. Two further agreements were to prove of increasing importance to France; the daily maintenance costs of the occupation army (400,000,000 francs) and the retention of some 2,000,000 French prisoners-of-war by the Germans until the expected British defeat.

All the traditional enmity and suspicion which had soured Anglo–French relations for centuries now resurfaced. Anti-British feeling was further exacerbated by the sinking of the French Atlantic Squadron by the Royal Navy at Mers-el-Kebir on 3 July in order to prevent its requisition by the Germans. The resulting casualties, over 1,600 dead and wounded, led to a virulent anti-British propaganda campaign, eagerly endorsed by pro-Nazi ideologues. The future arch-collaborationist, Pierre Constantini, leader of the quasi-Fascist *Ligue Française*, independently declared war on Great Britain.[5]

Pétain's armistice government settled on the spa town of Vichy, in the unoccupied zone, as its temporary capital pending the anticipated British defeat, after which it would return to Paris. There, on 10 July 1940, in an extraordinary session orchestrated by Pierre Laval, the Third Republic voted its own demise and full governmental powers to Pétain. In its suspension of the republican constitution, France passed, overnight, from democracy to autocracy – *L'État Français*. Laval, Pétain's appointed *chef de cabinet* quipped that the Marshal possessed 'more power than Louis XIV'.

The octogenarian Marshal's assumption of power was greeted with a patchy enthusiasm. Committed rightists felt that their hour had come but to the general public Pétain was still remembered for his heroic defence of Verdun in 1916 and his humane quelling of the army mutinies of the following year. A ready-made father-figure, willing to expiate the sins of the Third Republic, the Marshal became the focus of a cult – a fever which verged on religious hysteria, the song *Maréchal, nous voila!*[6] replacing the Republican *Marseillaise* as the unofficial anthem of Pétain's Vichy régime.[7]

Vichy's compliance with Hitler's New Order materialised in the *Révolution Nationale*, the keystone of Pétain's domestic policy, a policy which promoted arch-conservative, clerical and rural values, underscored by a strong sense of moral purpose. The ideals of self-sacrifice and obedience were furthered in Vichy's dropping of the now discredited Republican legend, *Liberté, Fraternité, Egalité* in favour of the portentous *Travail, Famille, Patrie*.

The slogan reflected the authoritarian Vichy's desire to retain some 'social' content. In 1941 a Labour Charter attempted to push the country in a corporative direction, to eliminate class conflict by banning trade unions and employers' organisations, and replacing them with professional bodies reminiscent of the medieval guilds, thus reconciling both managerial and shop-floor interests within the state context. In reality it simply allowed the business community to rationalize the economy without any actual restructuring of the existing social order. Other reforms included the introduction of old age pensions and the creation of several youth groups with an emphasis on physical training. There was also a decree against alcohol.[8]

Divorce was made more difficult and, in view of the declining birth-rate, larger families encouraged – a reflection of the strong clerical influence in Vichy's domestic policy. The more sinister aspects of this policy were made plain in the first anti-semitic laws of 1940, excluding Jews from all posts in government, teaching, business management and the media – legislation which culminated in mass round-ups and deportations.

Pétain's deputy, Pierre Laval, saw collaboration in more ambitious terms. Twice premier during the Third Republic, his two periods of office under Pétain were marked by intrigues with the Germans in a bid to gain more favourable post-armistice concessions, through manoeuvres which were fuelled by personal ambition and a fear of the possibility of a one-party 'Fascist' state as envisaged by the radical Right.[9] Laval's collaborationist policy was to integrate France into Hitler's New Order, reassuring the Nazis of a French desire not only to cooperate but to accept the defeat and thus ensure a favourable peace settlement. On 22 June 1942, the anniversary of Germany's invasion of the Soviet Union, Laval made his notorious radio broadcast in which he expressed his 'hope for a German victory', and at the same time, launched an appeal for French volunteer labour. Known as *La Relève*, this scheme came in response to Hitler's demands for foreign labour to work in German factories to replace those called up for military service. Hailing it as a patriotic duty Laval promised the repatriation of French prisoners-of-war in exchange. In practice the exchange balance was three volunteer workers for one liberated prisoner. The programme met with such scant response that forced labour, *Service du Travail Obligatoire*, was introduced later in the year. The result was that thousands of eligible Frenchmen either went underground or joined resistance cells.

The allied landings in French North Africa on 8 November 1942 spelt the end for *L'État Français*. Three days later the unoccupied zone was peacefully overrun by German troops. Now no more than a Nazi satellite, Vichy was drawn into a more committed collaborationist net, and the weak nature of Pétain's régime led to its bolstering by more extremist elements from Paris. Criticised for being too *attentiste* and insufficiently enthusiastic in its support for the Reich, Vichy had been continually attacked by the pro-Fascist Right. The true *homo fascista*[10] was, until the end of 1942, confined to Paris, in the occupied zone. The collaborationist world of the unofficial capital provided a stage which numerous potential leaders strove to dominate. From the beginning, all of the *Ultra* parties found themselves, unwittingly, in an impossible situation. Disavowed by Vichy, *Les Ultras* were only of use to their German masters in so far as they provided an extremist stick with which to threaten Pétain's régime. The possibility of a French totalitarian state, with its implications of a national renaissance was never a Nazi aim. To Hitler, collaboration with the French meant only their exploitation by the Germans.

National regeneration as embodied in a Fascist *parti unique* was, of course, exactly the aim of the various Paris-based organisations. Although most collaborationist parties issued virtually identical manifestos, their chiefs were divided by personality differences. Forced to play a waiting game, the *Ultra* factions competed for favour and backing from an occupation authority already split by inter-service rivalry. This complete lack of unity and compromise, which was abetted by both Vichy and the Germans, was a prime cause of their ultimate failure. Although the major parties attracted quite substantial followings, they remained essentially urban movements in a largely agrarian culture, for which, with its traditions deeply rooted in the ideals of 1789, a French form of National Socialism held little appeal. It was these same ideals of the Revolution that were constantly evoked in collaborationist outpourings. But it was an evocation of revolutionary style, not content, aimed not at changing the existing social order, merely redefining it in terms of a Spartan totalitarianism.

Bonaparte, an earlier architect of a new Europe, provided a further collaborationist reference point. Pierre Constantini, mentioned above, infused his *Ligue Française* with a Bonapartist ideology, as did *Le Feu*, a German-backed organisation formed and dissolved in 1941. '*Le Feu sauvera la France*,' proclaimed its leader, self-styled *Maître du Feu*, François-Henry Prométhée.[11] Common to all parties was an almost psychopathic hatred of Communism. Germany's invasion of the Soviet Union on 22 June 1941, gave the *Ultra* parties an opportunity for more active collaboration and greater participation in the New Order. It was the only occasion on which they would act in concert. The *Légion des volontaires français contre le Bolchévisme* (LVF) was run as a private organisation by an eight-man steering committee of prominent *Ultra* representatives formed just two weeks after invasion. Pétain approved the enterprise as did the Germans, though with some reserve.[12] Cardinal Baudrillart, Archbishop of Paris, known to keep a facsimile of the LVF banner on his desk, regarded the volunteers as 'the finest sons of France'.

With Germany now posing as a defender of European civilisation, successive propaganda campaigns stressed the unthinkable consequences of a Soviet victory. Even the anarchic writer Louis-Ferdinand Céline expressed his own horror of Bolshevism when he conjured up a vision of 'Asiatic commissars grazing their ponies in the Bois de Boulogne . . .' By 1943, many of the collaborationists, who had pinned their hopes on ultimate German victory, pushed less for the French Fascist *parti unique*. Their energies began to concentrate on the defence of a German Europe in which they realized that France would play a much more subordinate rôle.

Serious pretensions to power were left to the two major *Ultra* parties, Marcel Déat's *Rassemblement National Populaire* (RNP) and, more importantly, the *Parti Populaire Français* (PPF) led by Jacques Doriot. The RNP, founded in February 1941, was an ambiguous combination of both Republican and radical Right elements. The party's contradictory nature was very much a reflection of Déat himself. As a pre-war Socialist Deputy and pacifist, he had favoured appeasement prior to the outbreak of war, becoming an open advocate of Franco–German collaboration after 1940. Exclusion from the Vichy government led him to form the RNP in direct opposition. He attacked Vichy for its conservatism and royalism, clericalism and reliance on business interests, while setting forth his own programme for an authoritarian and corporatist state. Although party membership continued to rise through 1942, it was unable to prepare seriously for power. The ambitious Déat was finally given a government post at Vichy in March 1944 as Minister of Labour and National Solidarity.

Déat's most formidable rival, both politically and personally, was Jacques Doriot, leader of the *Parti Populaire Français*. Doriot founded the organisation in 1934, following his expulsion from the Communist party, as a result of doctrinal differences. With all the commitment of the converted, the 'le bon athlète Doriot'[13] made the PPF the major French Fascist party. After Hitler's invasion of the Soviet Union, Doriot became a member of the original steering committee of the *Légion des volontaires français contre le Bolchévisme*. With the exception of Pierre Clémenti, head of the *Parti Français National-Collectiviste* (PFNC),[14] he was the only *Ultra* leader to see action with the Legion as a volunteer on the Eastern Front. PPF fortunes reached an apex in November 1942 when at the 'Congress of Power', Doriot laid claim to absolute governmental authority though working within the framework of the New European Order. The campaign ran into direct opposition from Hitler who made it clear that he preferred a compliant Pétain and Laval in Vichy to a strident and power-hungry Doriot in Paris. As long as the Vichy government was willing to meet increasingly exorbitant German demands, Hitler regarded Doriot as superfluous, though a useful tool with which to threaten Vichy should the occasion arise. In September 1944, after the liberation of Paris, after Pétain's and Laval's joint refusal to exercise their authority further, Doriot found himself within sight of his goal. He was finally nominated by Hitler to lead a new 'national and revolutionary' French government. By then it was too late.

Doriot's PPF, the most politically astute and single-minded of all the *Ultra* parties, was indeed a source of alarm for Vichy. Laval responded to the threat by creating his own political and paramilitary élite, the *Milice Française*. Formed in January 1943, the *Milice* was a pro-fascist internal security force designed also to combat the growing Resistance movement, a task it accomplished with notorious efficiency. Although Laval was its titular head, the real leadership of the *Milice* rested with his nominee Joseph Darnand. A convinced patriot and devoted *Pétainiste*, Darnand was a decorated hero of both the Great War and the Battle of France in 1940. In opposition to Laval, who looked to the *Milice* as a support to his own political vulnerability, Darnand intended to use the force as an instrument with which to realise – if somewhat belatedly – Pétain's *Révolution Nationale*. To Darnand, this meant a total commitment to the New European idea and all it implied. As the Nazi war situation worsened, so its reliance on foreign manpower increased. The German decision to form a French unit of the Waffen-SS in the summer of 1943 brought Darnand's *Miliciens* under SS authority. Darnand himself entered the Waffen-SS as *Sturmbannführer* in August 1943, thus committing himself – and ultimately Vichy – to yet closer identification with Hitler's cause. Increased Resistance activity was repaid with bloody *Milice*

reprisals bringing France to the verge of civil war. The need to bolster Vichy was remedied by German pressure: on 30 December 1943 Darnand was named Secretary-General for the Maintenance of Order. But his extended powers only served to increase the violence of his organisation.

The Allied landings in Normandy signalled the beginning of the end for collaboration. From London de Gaulle called for general insurrection; from Vichy, Laval appealed for public calm, claiming that France was not in the war. A week before the liberation of Paris (25 August), Hitler ordered the forced removal of the Vichy Government to Belfort on the Franco–German border, despite protests from Pétain and Laval. From Belfort, the ministers were escorted to Germany, to Sigmaringen castle in Württemburg. Here they were joined by the *Ultras* and their followers, including 4000 of Darnand's *Miliciens* fleeing eastward from the advancing allies.

Pétain and Laval, now virtually German prisoners, refused to exercise their governmental powers. They were followed by several of their cabinet colleagues,[15] thus leaving the field open for further *Ultra* power struggles. *Les Ultras* felt that this imposed exile was merely temporary, pending the expected reversal of German fortunes after the deployment of new and devastating 'secret weapons'. In an atmosphere of total unreality the self-styled 'adolfins'[16] found a luke-warm unity in a *Délégation Gouvernmentale Française pour la Défence des Intérêts Nationaux* presided over by Comte Fernand de Brinon.[17] The *Délégation* included Déat, representing French workers still in the Reich, and Darnand, who aided the German induction of his *Miliciens* into the newly-formed Waffen-SS 'Charlemagne' Division. De Brinon's intrigues were in direct opposition to the wishes of both Pétain, now inactive, and Hitler, whose nominee was Doriot. The excluded Doriot, quartered with his PPF entourage at Meinau (Lake Constance), responded by forming his own *Comité de la Libération Française* in January 1945. Doriot's political acumen enabled him, at the last moment, to absorb de Brinon's *Délégation*; on 22 February, while on his way from PPF party offices at Lindau to Mengen where reconciliation with Déat was imminent, his car was strafed by a fighter plane killing him instantly.[18] Following the failure of the German Ardennes offensive[19] the death of Doriot proved to be the end of the collaboration. He was buried at Mengen.

With Doriot gone, the *Ultra* camp fragmented once more. By April, the approaching allied armies forced the Sigmaringen notables to move on for the last time. While their military colleagues in the 'Charlemagne' Division defended the *Führerbunker* in Berlin to the last, most of the *Ultras* were rounded up.[20]

The return of democracy to a liberated France was followed by an anti-collaborationist purge which lasted until 1949. Among the many prominent *Ultras* who faced the firing squad was Laval, Péta.n's head of government. To a vengeful French public, support for Vichy and support for Hitler meant one and the same thing. Pétain's own death sentence was commuted to life imprisonment. The Victor of Verdun ended his days in prison, on the Ile d'Yeu overlooking the Atlantic, until his death in 1951. His wish to be buried alongside his soldiers at Verdun was refused. For the remaining collaborationist subculture, his tomb on the Ile d'Yeu is now regarded as a shrine.

Whereas a radical Right remains active in French political life, this particular episode in its evolution is long over. Its participation in the four years of the German occupation was erased from the national memory.

'The voices of the collaborationists were added to those of Legitimists and Bonapartists in France's museum of lost causes.' [21]

Notes

The title of this article and its opening quote come from Jean Hérold-Paquis, *Des illusions . . . Désillusions! . . . Mémoires 15 août 1944–15 août 1945* Bourgoin, Paris, 1948. Hérold-Paquis, a prominent collaborationist and one of the 'stars of Radio-Paris', was notorious for his pro-German broadcasts. He concluded his daily broadcasts with the catchphrase 'England, like Carthage, will be destroyed'. His anglophobia acquired him the nickname 'The Great Destroyer of Carthage (*Le Grand Pourendeur de Carthage*) in the novel *D'un Chateau l'Autre* (Gallimard, Paris, 1957) by Louis-Ferdinand Céline.

1. See Michael Moody, '*Vive La Nation*', *IWM Review No 3*, Imperial War Museum, London, 1988, pp 34–43.

2. Alistair Horne, *To Lose a Battle, France 1940*, Macmillan, London, 1969.

3. Charles Maurras (1868–1952) was tried for collaboration in 1945 and sentenced to life imprisonment.

4. Paradoxically, *L'Ami du Peuple* was the title of the broadsheet edited by the revolutionary Jean-Paul Marat (1743–1793).

5. Constantini, a Corsican and right-wing activist of the 1930s imbued his *Ligue Française* (founded 1940) with suitably Bonapartist ideals. In 1945 he was declared mad by a Liberation court and institutionalised.

6. Montagnard, Courtioux-Montagnard 1941.

7. Special authorisation was required from the Nazi authorities for public performances of *La Marseillaise*.

8. Pétain, a man of austere habits, drank very sparingly. Under his régime, the famous Pernod factory was closed down and demolished. Fortified wines and aperitifs were limited to an alcoholic content of 16%. It had been claimed that the consumption of alcohol in France, which had doubled between 1918 and 1939, was a contributory factor in the decadence and eventual fall of the Third Republic.

9. As late as 1944, following the liberation, Laval proposed the reconvening of the National Assembly, in order to make a legal transfer of power to a de Gaulle administration, in which he envisaged playing a major rôle. Needless to say, Berlin dismissed the idea.

10. A term coined by the collaborationist and fascist writer Robert Brasillach, who, like many of his colleagues expressed an awe for the German military triumph of 1940 – the manifestation of a new virility. He would attempt to compete in intellectual terms. Brasillach (1909–1945), journalist and novelist was initially a disciple of Charles Maurras and a contributor to *Action Française*, becoming editor of the notorious Right-wing weekly *Je suis partout*, in Paris 1933–1939, 1941–1944. He was executed for collaboration in 1945. A petition for clemency signed by sixty fellow writers, including François Mauriac and Colette, was presented to de Gaulle but dismissed. Among those who refused to sign were Sartre and Simone de Beauvoir.

11. Aptly named; François – of the French, Henry – ruler of the house, Promethée – Prometheus, the Titan who according to the Greek myths, stole the secret of fire from the gods. Promethée's real name was Maurice Delaunay, former deputy for Caen. He was assisted by a *Maîtresse du Feu*, an aristocratic lady whose identity is now sadly lost to us. The party published a weekly broadsheet, *La Tempête*, 'the organ of regeneration through fire'.

12. Hitler was mistrustful of the scheme and stipulated a maximum intake of 15,000. However, the Legion's full strength only ever reached 5,800.

13. The compliment paid to Doriot by the Fascist novelist and intellectual Pierre Drieu la Rochelle. As quoted in Alistair Hamilton *The Appeal of Fascism*, Macmillan, New York, 1971, p 219.

14. One of the smallest *Ultra* parties, the PFNC was established in 1934.

15. *Paul Marion*, Secretary-General for Information. After the liberation condemned to ten years hard labour. *Jean Bichelonne*, Secretary-General for Industry. He died in mysterious circumstances at the SS hospital at Hohenlychen (East Prussia) undergoing an operation on a broken leg. *Abel Bonnard*, 'La Gestapette', Secretary-General for Education. Expelled from the *Académie Française*. He was sentenced to death *in absentia* after flight to Spain in 1945.

16. The Spanish collaborators who had supported Napoleon's brother Joseph, on the Spanish throne in 1808, fled to France after the popular Spanish uprising supported by Wellington's army had forced the French troops out of Spain. These Spanish collaborators were called 'josefins'; thus the French collaborators in Sigmaringen became the 'adolfins'.

17. De Brinon, a successful journalist and president of the *Comité France–Allemagne* published the first interview with Hitler to be published in France (1933). In 1940, Laval appointed him delegate general of the French government in the occupied zone, with the title of *Ambassadeur de France*. Tried for collaboration, he was executed in 1947.

18. The circumstances of Doriot's death still remain a mystery. Doriot was well acquainted with aircraft identification; his secretary, who survived the attack, claimed that the PPF leader had confidently asserted that the plane overhead was German. However, there are no reports of Allied aircraft operating in that area at that time.

19. *Ultra* fantasies of re-entering Paris in triumph following the defeat of the Allied forces were reinforced by the promise of the possible German victory in the Ardennes. At the castle, theatrical events, poetry readings, dances and an original musical composition 'The Retaking of the Ardennes' celebrated the event. For a very humorous first-hand account, see Louis-Ferdinand Céline, *D'un Château l'Autre*, Edition Gallimard, Paris, 1957, pp 249–261.

20. The most notable exception was Marcel Déat. Condemned to death *in absentia*, he successfully evaded arrest until 1955 when he died in Turin, a Christian convert.

21. Bertram M Gordon, *Collaborationism in France during the Second World War*, Cornell University Press, Ithaca and London 1980, p 312.

Further Reading

Robert Aron, *The Vichy Régime*, trans. Humphrey Hare, Beacon, Boston, 1969.

Sven Aurén, *The Tricolour Flies Again*, trans. Evelyn Ramsden, Hammond, Hammond and Co Ltd, London, 1946.

Louis-Ferdinand Céline, *D'un Chateau l'Autre*, Editions Gallimard, Paris, 1957.

Milton Dank, *The French Against the French, Collaboration and Resistance* Cassell, London, 1975.

G and W Fortune, *Hitler Divided France*, Macmillan, London, 1943.

Bertram M Gordon, *Collaborationism in France during the Second World War*, Cornell University Press, Ithaca and London, 1980.

Alastair Hamilton, *The Appeal of Fascism*, Macmillan, New York, 1971.

Jean Hérold-Paquis, *Des illusions . . . Désillusions! . . . Mémoires 15 Août 1944–15 Août 1945*, Bourgoin, Paris, 1948.

Pascal Jardin, *Vichy Boyhood: An Inside View of the Pétain Régime*, trans. Jean Steward, Faber and Faber, London, 1975.

David Littlejohn, *The Patriotic Traitors: A History of Collaboration in German Occupied Europe 1940–1945*, Heineman, London, 1972.

Robert O Paxton, *Vichy France: Old Guard and New Order 1940–1944*, Knopf, New York, 1972.

David Pryce-Jones, *Paris in the Third Reich, A History of the German Occupation, 1940–1944*, Collins, London, 1981.

Jules Roy, *The Trial of Marshal Pétain*, trans. Robert Baldick, Faber and Faber, London, 1968.

A gift for Christmas: the story of Princess Mary's Gift Fund, 1914

Diana Condell

Christmas 1914 saw the usual crop of seasonal treats, many with a patriotic theme. Gamages' '1914 Christmas Fair and War Tableaux' invited parents, looking for a way to entertain their offspring, to – 'Bring the Boys and Girls to see the English and Allies beat the German Army' with 'Looping and Bomb-Dropping Aero planes' and 'Cannon fired by real gunpowder'.[1] If this were not excitement enough, then a visit to Peter Robinson's 'Wonderful Bazaar' could, for the fortunate child, culminate in high adventure involving a visit to 'Father Neptune by submarine'.[2] For theatrical entertainment there was, as the saying goes, something for everyone. Thomas Hardy's 'The Dynasts' was playing at the Kingsway, 'David Copperfield' at His Majesty's, 'Peg O' My Heart' at the Comedy, 'Alice in Wonderland' at the Savoy and rousingly patriotic in its theme, 'The Flag Lieutenant' at the Haymarket.[3]

The famous London emporia such as Harrods, Fortnum & Mason, Jacksons, Robinson and Cleaver, Mappin and Webb, the Army & Navy, and Debenham and Freebody, to name but a few, offered a staggering array of foodstuffs, clothes and trinkets, much of it aimed at the shopper seeking something to give the officer on active service. Fortnum, whose hampers were already legendary, offered their 'Choice Matured York Ham', 'Raised Game Pie', and Stilton cheeses at one guinea each ('Christmas Hampers from one to five guineas').[4] Debenham and Freebody, with what *The Sphere* described as 'excellent discretion', issued a special catalogue of Christmas presents' of a practical character suitable for officers serving in his Majesty's Forces at the Front'.[5] A random selection of advertisements, culled from the pages of newspapers and magazines of the time, shows the variety of goodies on offer. Silver propelling pencils at 14/-, Tinder lighters 6/6d in silver or 3/- in electro-plate. Pocket lighters ('A PRACTICAL PRESENT FOR ACTIVE SERVICE') at 6/6d in silver or 33/6d in 9ct gold; silver tobacco tins ('equally useful as a "Meat Lozenge Box"') 25/- and a selection of photo-frames (silver of course!) ranging in price from 10/6d to 25/-. Other suggestions included 'Xmas Handkerchiefs', and every conceivable variety of what were then, and indeed still are, rather quaintly referred to as 'smokers' requisites'. These included pipes, matchbox covers, tobacco ('You'll march at ease as long as Three Nuns tobacco burns in your pipe'), cigarettes (3d for ten) and matches, which Messrs Bryant and May offered in bulk at one pound for enough to supply a whole battalion.[6]

Amid the welter of commercially generated advertisements for Christmas gifts and treats, could be found others which, in their appeal for money to provide comforts

Diana Condell is a research assistant in the Department of Exhibits and Firearms.

and bring seasonal cheer to the men serving in the forces, perhaps more closely reflected the desire on the part of many ordinary people to mark this first Christmas of the war, as one of particular importance. The habit of charitable giving, nurtured in the traditions of Victorian philanthropy, was to find ample expression during the First World War in the thousands of appeal funds which were set up to aid every conceivable cause.[7] But perhaps the most memorable of these was the Christmas Gift Fund launched on 14 October 1914, by Princess Mary.[8]

Her Royal Highness The Princess Victoria Alexandra Alice Mary, third child and only daughter of Their Majesties King George V and Queen Mary, was born at York Cottage, Sandringham on 25 April 1897.[9] She was thus just over seventeen years of age when war broke out, and as the *Sunday Times* was later to point out, the Fund to which she lent her name, was the 'first great national cause' with which she became associated.[10] It was originally the Princess's wish to pay for a personal gift to each soldier and sailor out of her private allowance. For whatever reason, this was found to be impracticable, and it was therefore proposed that she lend her name to a public fund which would raise the necessary monies to provide the gift.[11] From the beginning, the young Princess took a real and very personal interest in the work of the Fund. Accompanied by her mother's Lady in Waiting, Lady Katharine Coke, she was present at the Fund's inaugural meeting held at the Ritz Hotel on 14 October.[12] The following day, Buckingham Palace released a letter, signed by the Princess, in which she explained her purpose in launching the Fund. With its youthful charm and obvious sincerity, the appeal must have been very hard to resist:

'For many weeks we have all been greatly concerned for the welfare of the sailors and soldiers who are so gallantly fighting our battles by sea and land. Our first consideration has been to meet their more pressing needs, and I have delayed making known a wish that has long been in my heart for fear of encroaching on other funds, the claims of which have been more urgent. I want you now to help me to send a Christmas present from the whole nation to every sailor afloat and every soldier at the front. On Christmas-eve when like the shepherds of old, they keep their watch, doubtless their thoughts will turn to home and to the loved ones left behind, and perhaps, too, they will recall the days when as children themselves they were wont to hang out their stockings wondering what the morrow had in store. I am sure that we should all be the happier to feel that we had helped to send our little token of love and

HRH The Princess Mary, 1914. A copy of this photograph, of which some 836,470 were printed, was included with each gift distributed under Class A. Copyright reserved. Reproduced by gracious permission of Her Majesty The Queen.

Dies for the Embossed Brass Box and Proof Box. These, together with a complete set of the gifts sent out by the Fund, were presented to the Imperial War Museum in 1920. Following the winding up of the Fund the Secretary, Rowland Berkeley, handed over the records to the Museum where they now form part of the Women's Work Collection administered by the Department of Printed Books. MH 30526 sympathy on Christmas morning, something that would be useful and of permanent value, and the making of which may be the means of providing employment in trades adversely affected by the war. Could there be anything more likely to hearten them in their struggle than a present received straight from home on Christmas day?

Please will you help me?' [13]

A General Committee, including the Prime Minister, the First Lord of the Admiralty, the Secretary of State for War and the High Commissioners for the various Dominions, as well as notable industrialists and bankers together with senior serving and retired officers from the Royal Navy and Army, was appointed to set up and administer the Fund. It was obviously impracticable for busy men such as these to take a direct hand in the day to day running of the Fund, so a much smaller Executive Committee was established to give effect to the Princess's wishes.[14] It was upon this Committee chaired by the Duke of Devonshire, with Rowland Berkeley as Honorary Secretary, and Lord Revelstoke as Treasurer that virtually all the work of the Fund devolved.[15] What is perfectly clear, is that none of the members of the Committee, least of all Rowland Berkeley upon whom much of the burden fell, could have foreseen that the work of the Fund, which turned out to be a major undertaking, would occupy them on and off for the best part of the next six years.

Viewed from the distance of more than seventy years, the Princess's gift, of an embossed brass box, a pipe, a tinder lighter, tobacco, cigarettes and a Christmas card, does seem a rather eccentric choice. However, as has been noted, these sorts of gifts were very much in vogue. That being said, it was one thing to decide on the form the gift would take; it was quite another to find sufficient quantities to provide individual presents for an, as yet unknown, but very substantial, number of recipients. The Committee's first priority therefore was to reach a decision on who would, and who would not qualify for the gift, bearing in mind Princess Mary's desire that 'every sailor afloat and every soldier at the front' should have the present. The criteria eventually agreed upon were that all sailors serving under the command of Admiral Sir John Jellicoe, and all soldiers under the command of Field Marshal Sir John French, should receive the gift.

The Committee's Admiralty representative, Captain Cecil Foley Lambert RN, thought that about 145,000 men would qualify, including Royal Marines. General Sidney Seldon Long CB, Director of Supplies and Transport at the War Office, co-opted on to the Committee to represent the Quartermaster General, Major General Sir John Cowans,

explained that, including all officers and men and the 'Indian Contingent', the figure for the Army was in the region of 350,000.[16] This gave the Committee a figure of nearly half a million to work on. They estimated that in the region of £55,000–£60,000, would need to be raised to cover the cost of 500,000 presents. With just over two months to go before Christmas, the Committee decided to take a gamble. Confident that the generosity of the British Public would prove equal to the task of providing the funds, the Committee went ahead and placed an order for the embossed brass boxes.[17]

The box, designed by Messrs Adshead and Ramsay, formed the principal feature of the gift. It seems that before the war the manufacture of brass boxes had only been carried out to a very limited extent in the United Kingdom, and as a result the Committee encountered considerable reluctance on the part of manufacturers to undertake the work. After some pressure had been applied four firms did agree to co-operate, and contracts were duly let for 498,000 boxes at a cost of $6\frac{1}{4}$d per box.[18] In fact the problems with the boxes stemmed, not unexpectedly, from difficulties in the supply of raw materials. The manufacturers had undertaken to obtain the brass strip as well as supply the finished boxes. However as soon as it became clear that the firms were experiencing real difficulty in this area, a difficulty that at one point seriously threatened the breakdown of the whole scheme, the Committee decided to undertake the supply to the box makers direct.

A manager of brass supply was engaged, contracts let and a warehouse opened in Birmingham as a collection and distribution point. As things turned out, the Committee's efforts were not noticeably more successful than those of the manufacturing firms, and in the end all the original contracts were abandoned due to the failure of the metal suppliers to fulfil their obligations. While there was enough brass obtained in Britain for the initial despatch of gifts, with the later expansion of the scheme the Committee had to look elsewhere, and eventually placed a contract for the shortfall in the United States. This was an ill-fated move, however, for the bulk of the brass strip supplied under this arrangement went down with the Cunard liner the RMS *Lusitania* when she was torpedoed off the Old Head of Kinsale in May of the following year.[19] The problems over the supply of raw materials, particularly the brass, would continue to 'engage the unremitting attention', of the Committee throughout the scheme.[20]

Although the Committee encountered many difficulties, most of which they overcame, raising the necessary monies was fortunately not one of them. On 18 October, four days after the official launch of the Fund, the *Sunday Times*, reporting the 'Splendid Response' to the initial request for help, published a list of some of the well known names who had already donated money.

The Embossed Brass Box finished in lacquered bright brass, was designed by Messrs Adshead and Ramsay and manufactured for the Fund by four different firms, Barringer Wallis & Manners Ltd, Hudson, Scott & Sons Ltd, O.T. Banks Ltd and Barclay & Fry Ltd. The final total of boxes produced was 2,620,019. Bearing the portrait effigy of the Princess, and the legend 'IMPERIUM BRITANNICUM', the design incorporated the names of Britain's allies, France, Belgium, Japan, Russia, Serbia and Montenegro, with their flags. At the top can be seen a representation of a bayonet and scabbard, and at the bottom the twin bows of two dreadnoughts. MH 30529

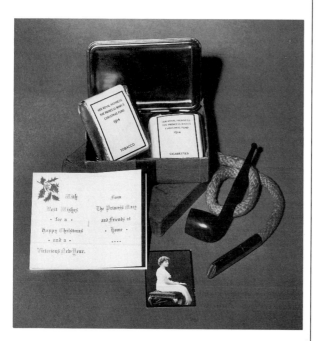

The smokers' gift distributed under Class A consisted of the embossed brass box, one ounce of pipe tobacco, twenty cigarettes, a pipe, the tinder lighter, Christmas card and photograph. The tinder lighter included here formed part of the gift received on Christmas Day 1914 by Corporal Joseph Allen of the Army Service Corps. MH 30527

Amongst these were The King and Queen, the Prince of Wales, the Princess herself, and in order of generosity, Lord and Lady Rothermere (£1,000), Sir William H Lever Bt (£500), the splendidly named Sir Sigismund Neumann Bt (£262 10s 0d), Harrods Ltd (£262 10s 0d), Mr H Mallaby-Deeley MP (£262 10s 0d), The Duke of Devonshire (£250), Lord Ashton (£250), Lord Portman (£200), Lord Revelstoke (£100), and Lord Rothschild, Mr Leopold de Rothschild, and Mr Alfred de Rothschild, (£100 each).[21] When the Committee met for the second time on 20 October, Berkeley was able to report that contributions to the Fund already stood at just over £12,000.[22] Seven days later this figure had risen to nearly £31,000.[23] The total monies eventually subscribed to the Fund amounted to £162,591 12s 5d, and while there were some substantial single donations, most of this sum came from thousands of small gifts sent by ordinary people from all parts of the United Kingdom. Much of the credit for the success of the fund raising effort must go to Hedley Le Bas.[24] Firmly grasping the nettle, and ably abetted by Rowland Berkeley, he launched what could only be described as a 'Blitzkrieg' of a campaign, the results of which would undoubtedly stand comparison with any achieved by the 'professional' fundraisers of the nineteen eighties.

By 27 October, Le Bas was able to report that over 39,200 appeals had gone out by post. Apart from those sent to private individuals he also sent out 7,000 specifically directed at 'those who kept more [than] five servants', 1,500 to social clubs, 1,500 to golf clubs, 1,600 to schools, and 2,600 to Masonic Lodges.[25] While the Committee was happy to sanction collecting boxes being placed in premises, such as shops, hotels theatres and the like, it came down very firmly against street collections, which its members deemed 'very undesirable'.[26] Le Bas also despatched 12,000 appeals to various commercial organisations making a point of ensuring that most of these were directed at firms who were, as the Committee put it, 'benefitting by contracts for war supplies'.[27] He also targeted certain specific areas of the country, sending out 18,000 appeals to addresses in Kent and Hampshire, counties in which there were large concentrations of troops, either in training or in transit. This proved a veritable goldmine for the Fund, and with the Committee's agreement, he sent out a further 500,000 to other counties in two stages, the first batch on 7 November and the second seven days later. Of the final sum collected over £135,713 6s 5d came from general donations, £6,822 11s 4d from municipal collections, organised by Mayors and Mayoresses, £4,399 10s 5d, from Church collections, £6,252 2s 2d from the schools, £1,333 0s 0d from employees of commercial undertakings, £1,748 10s 1d from card collections, £4,017 19s 3d from flag days and collection boxes, and £2,269 4s 11d from the proceeds of concerts and entertainments. A special charity matinee, held at

Drury Lane on 28 November, alone netted over £1,500.[28] The Committee, always at pains to keep the administrative expenses of the Fund to the minimum, tried to get the Post Office to agree to free postage for the appeals. The Duke of Devonshire undertook to approach the Postmaster General on the matter, but a few days later he was obliged to report failure. The Postmaster General decreed that free postage 'was a concession that could not properly be allowed'.[29]

It is worth remarking, in passing, that, with one or two exceptions, the Fund received remarkably few gifts in kind from the commercial and business undertakings with which it had to deal. The management of the Ritz Hotel, and later that of the Piccadilly Hotel, provided free accomodation for the Committee meetings, and Messrs De la Rue & Co, who designed and printed the Christmas Cards and the photograph, generously did so at cost, but donations of gifts in kind apart, the Committee had to pay the going rate for virtually everything else.[30] Although this may seem to represent a rather less than wholehearted response, distinctly lacking Christmas spirit, it should be borne in mind that in the period immediately following the outbreak of war, there was high unemployment in what were popularly regarded as 'non-essential' industries.[31] Indeed the members of the Committee were acutely conscious of the need to justify their efforts beyond simply relying on the obvious goodwill which the Fund had engendered. As the Duke of Devonshire was at pains to point out in a letter, dated 25 November, sent to the Editor of *The Morning Post* and subsequently re-printed in *The Observer*, the Fund's administrators were well aware of the problem:

> It is difficult to give an exact estimate of the number of persons employed in connection with the present, but it is safe to say that the number runs into thousands. In subscribing to her Royal Highness's fund the public have the satisfaction of knowing that they are not only contributing to the present itself but are affording much-needed relief in industries which are suffering in the war.[32]

There was a tremendous amount of press and public interest in the Fund, and the organising Committee received much unsolicited advice on how to conduct their affairs, as well as requests from other Christmas gift appeals to be allowed to join in. One of these came from the *Daily News*, which had launched a fund to send 'Plum Puddings' to the troops. Discussion on this proposal got as far as the Committee, but was rejected.[33] Evidently the notion of the popular press muscling in on what was, after all, a Royal appeal, was thought somewhat unseemly. However in other areas popular opinion did persuade the Committee to change its mind.

Quite early on, Rowland Berkeley reported that he had received strong representations that an alternative gift should be made available for non-smokers. When this matter was first raised, the Committee seems to have taken the view that since non-smokers constituted only a very small minority of the total, and an unknown one at that, they would have to have what was on offer, and be done with it. But after some discussion the Committee agreed that non-smokers should be regarded as a special group and alternative provision made for them. The principal difficulty was determining the proportion of non-smokers to smokers, but they eventually settled on the figure of 2 non-smokers' gifts for every 56 smokers'.[34] The Committee decreed that the non-smokers should receive the brass box, a packet of acid tablets, a khaki writing case containing pencil, paper and envelopes and, of course the Christmas card and photograph of the Princess.[35]

Non-smokers were not the only minority group whose tastes the Committee were now obliged to consider. Although it had originally been intended that everyone, irrespective of rank, race or religion should receive precisely the same gift, it was soon borne in on the Committee that if the dietary rules of various religious groups were to be respected, changes would have to be made in the gifts intended for Indian Troops. To this end, they sought help from five 'old India hands' who, after due deliberation, came up with a solution.[36] The Gurkhas were to receive the same gift as the British troops; Sikhs the box filled with sugar candy, a tin box of spices and the Christmas card, and all other Indian troops, the box with a packet of cigarettes and sugar candy, a tin box of spices and the card. Authorised 'Camp Followers', who for the purposes of this exercise were all grouped under the title of Bhistis, were to receive a tin box of spices and the card.[37]

Yet another group to engage the Committee's attention were the members of the various military nursing services.[38] Smoking was not then considered a socially acceptable habit in which well brought-up women indulged. Although the war would to some extent alter this state of affairs, in 1914 there was never any question of the nurses receiving the smokers' gift, or for that matter the non-smokers'. For nurses at the front in France, of whom there were estimated to be about 400 who qualified (the eventual number was 1,390) the Committee settled on the box, a packet of chocolate and the card.[39] In the midst of sorting out the various problems concerning the non-smokers, Indians and nurses, the Committee, on 17 November, approved the letting of the remaining contracts for the initial order for tinder lighters, cigarettes, tobacco and Christmas cards for the first 500,000 gifts.

The non-smokers' gift comprised the box, a packet of acid tablets (not shown), a khaki writing case with paper, envelopes and a pencil, the Christmas card and photograph. The gift given under Classes B and C consisted of the box, a bullet pencil and a New Year Card. The card bore the date 1915 and the message, 'With Best Wishes for a Victorious New Year from the Princess Mary and Friends at Home'. The box and bullet pencil illustrated here were received by Lieutenant D A B Williams, 6th Battalion The Rifle Brigade. MH 30528

Asprey & Co Ltd were to supply half a million tinder lighters at 5½d each, De La Rue & Co 350,000 Christmas Cards at 25/- per thousand, Harrods Ltd, together with seven other firms, 483,875 pipes at a total cost of £12,340 11s 5d, while four firms of tobacco and cigarette manufacturers between them eventually supplied 44,840 lbs of tobacco and 13,050,000 cigarettes at a total cost of £10,722 17s 5d.[40] Unfortunately, as things turned out, Asprey were unable to fulfil the terms of their agreement.[41] While the Committee made every effort to find another supplier, shortage of time eventually forced them to abandon that part of the scheme. Although they were able to obtain some tinder lighters, under the terms of the original agreement, the number proved insufficient. This placed the Committee in something of a quandary, since it meant that even if the troops in the trenches on Christmas Day had first call on these limited supplies, there were still not enough to go round. The Committee solved the problem by hurriedly buying in an assortment of substitute gifts: bullet pencil cases, tobacco pouches, shaving brushes, combs, pencil cases with packets of postcards, knives, scissors, cigarette cases and purses.[42] Those sailors under Jellicoe's command, who should also have received the lighter as part of their gift, were given instead, a handsome bullet pencil in a silver cartridge case which bore Princess Mary's monogram, an 'M' surmounted by a coronet.[43]

When, towards the end of November, the Committee sat down and did its sums, it became clear that there was a surplus of £37,000 accruing to the Fund's accounts.[44] This happy state of affairs now made it possible for the whole scheme to be extended, so that every man 'wearing the King's uniform on Christmas Day, 1914', would eventually receive a gift from the Princess's Fund.[45] The very large increase in the numbers of those now eligible, estimated to be in excess of 2,620,019, meant that there was no possible way in which the Committee could arrange for the manufacture, supply and entire distribution on Christmas Day itself. Accordingly

74

it was decided to divide the potential recipients into three classes designated as (Class A) the Navy, including minesweepers and dockyard officials, and Troops at the front in France, (Class B) all British Colonial and Indian troops serving outside the British Isles (but exclusive of those provided for in Class A), and (Class C) all troops in the British Isles.

Under Class A, those who were to have the gift on Christmas Day, the Committee also included the wounded in hospitals and men on furlough, prisoners and men interned (for whom the gift was reserved), members of the French Mission with the Expeditionary Force, nurses at the front in France, and, in a touching gesture, the widows or parents of those who had been killed.[46]

At the meeting held on 8 December, Berkeley was able to report that 220,000 gifts for the Army and 150,000 for the Navy would be ready for delivery on Saturday 12 December.[47] It was, by any standards, a remarkable achievement, and one of which the Committee could be justly proud. By arrangement with the War Office the Fund had been given the use of the Army Depot at Deptford in South-East London where the bulk of the goods had been delivered and where the packing was carried out using Army personnel. The Fund did however defray the costs of packing materials paying the War Office 6d each for 10,000 packing cases. It had been at General Long's suggestion that the Fund had sought the War Office's agreement to the use of their Depot.[48] Long, the Director of Supplies and Transport (no doubt the reason he was co-opted onto the Committee in the first place!), could obviously see the sense in having the main distribution point at a railhead, and since the Army was to undertake the task, it made even more sense for them to organize the packing and shipping.

In the two weeks prior to Christmas Day over 450,000 parcels, and two and a half million letters were despatched from Britain to the troops serving in France.[49] Add to this, not only the Princess's gift, but also the card sent from the King and Queen to each man and woman serving with the forces, and it is just possible to imagine the strain imposed on an already overloaded supply system. Indeed, for those charged with overseeing the distribution of the Fund's gift, the days leading up to Christmas became something of a nightmare. Major G D Jeffreys, Second in Command of the 2nd Battalion, Grenadier Guards, found the whole business rather too much of a good thing, confiding to his diary that:

> Everything seems hung up just now for all the Christmas parcels, which are becoming a positive nuisance. I am told that the rations of the army are to be held up for twenty-four hours to enable Princess Mary's presents to come up, and I have had reams of orders as to their distribution . . .

> It was the longest order I have had since I have been out, . . .[50]

The Major was not the only one to remark upon the delays caused by the tons of Christmas post. Major General Wilfred Smith, writing to Colonel Sir Henry Streatfield complained, albeit mildly, that:

> The Field Glasses have not arrived yet. I expect many things are hung up by the quantity of Christmas presents. The men have had the Plum Puddings to-day, [Boxing Day] and Princess Mary's present and many other good things, for all of which the men are very grateful. It has been rather a labour serving them all out![51]

But, all these problems aside, the gift in all its 'not inconsiderable splendour' was pleasurably received by senior officer and junior soldier alike. Lieutenant-General Sir Henry Rawlinson, commander of IV Corps, was delighted with his gift and, on Boxing Day wrote in appreciative terms to the King's Assistant Private Secretary, Colonel Clive Wigram:

> I received last night a charming little packet containing pipe tobacco & cigarettes which I am told is sent me by Princess Mary – It is just what I want, for my old pipe is rapidly coming to an end, and tobacco is not too plentiful – The least I can do to shew my gratitude is to return to H.R.H. one of my Xmas Cards – Will you give it to her for me and say how much we all value her kind gift of tobacco & cigarettes –.[52]

It wasn't only the Generals who felt impelled to write and say 'thank you', as a report in the *Manchester Guardian* of 11 February 1915 shows:

> Among the packages sent to soldiers at the front at Christmas-time containing Princess Mary's gift-boxes was one which was specially packed by the Queen in person, and which contained a card indicating the fact. The recipient of this particular package at once wrote thanking the Queen, but thinking his letter might have gone astray he forwarded a second letter addressed to her Majesty's private secretary, who received it yesterday. In his letter, Private John Duffy, of the Leinster Regiment wrote; "I was a very lucky man to have received it. It reached me in the trenches on Christmas evening." '[53]

Christmas Day 1914 is perhaps now chiefly recalled for the unofficial truce which took place at various points along the front line. During the course of the day officers and men from both sides climbed out of their trenches and crossed in to 'no-man's-land'. In exchanging Christmas greetings many also took the opportunity to exchange Christmas gifts and souvenirs.[54] At this distance in time it can only be a matter of conjecture how widespread the exchange of gifts was, and it is impossible even to hazard a guess as to the number of Princess Mary's gifts which found their way into German hands. However at least one participant, the writer Henry Williamson, at that time a private soldier in the London Rifle Brigade, records the instance of a German soldier who, having come into possession of one of the photographs of Princess Mary included with the gift, was heard wandering around, muttering ' "Ah, schöne, schöne Prinzessin." ' ("Oh beautiful, beautiful Princess").[55]

One indication that the Princess's gift was regarded as something special is that, although plenty of the tobacco and cigarettes were consumed, and the pipes smoked, a great many men carefully repacked their presents and sent them home to their wives and families.[56] For one young soldier at least, the receipt of the Princess's gift marked more than simply Christmas Day; in a very personal sense it also marked his passage into adulthood. Rifleman Leslie Walkinton of the Queen's Westminster Rifles was especially gratified to have the present because, as he put it, his 'family at home thought I was too young to smoke and it made me feel rather older and bigger'.[57]

On 5 January 1915, with delivery of the Class A gifts successfully accomplished, the Committee re-assembled at Devonshire House. Although the members of the Committee were obviously gratified by the success of the Fund's work to date, they were not content to rest on their laurels. If anything the task which now faced them, the supply and distribution of gifts for those in Classes B and C, was the more daunting simply because of the numbers involved. The figures which Berkeley had obtained from the War Office give an indication of the size of the problem. There were 1,337,889 troops designated as New Army, Territorial Army and Dominion at home in the UK. A further 100,000 men, of whom 37,000 were British, were under the control of the War Office in various parts of the world; 112,000 assorted personnel came under the control of the India Office, including some British troops, Territorials and members of the various Indian Volunteer Corps plus a further 155,000 Indian troops and 5,000 members of the Indian Marine. In addition to these there were also 38,000 Canadians, 15,258 New Zealanders and 40,000 South Africans making a grand total of 1,803,147. The Committee, no doubt mindful of the problems they had previously encountered, clearly felt unequal to the task of tackling the dietary and religious differences of so large a number of individuals. They announced that the gift would be given without reference to race or rank, and settled on the brass box, a New Year's card and a pencil. That matter having been resolved the Committee decided that, further regular meetings being unnecessary, they would reassemble only if there were special matters requiring their attention.[58]

Three weeks later, on 26 January, just such an occasion arose when Princess Mary paid a visit to the members of the Committee at Devonshire House, the London home of its Chairman. The purpose of the visit seems to have been to thank the Committee for all their hard work, but in the event, it was also the occasion for the Committee to make their own unique presentation to the Princess of a rather special version of the gift box, not in brass, but in silver-gilt. Inscribed on the inside of the lid were the names of the members of the Executive Committee. At the same occasion Berkeley was able to give the final figures for the distribution which had taken place on Christmas Day. 355,716 gifts had gone to the British Expeditionary Force, 66,168 to the men at home either on furlough or on sick leave, 4,600 to the French Mission to the BEF and 1,390 to the members of the various army nursing services, all of which added up to a grand total of 426,724 gifts.[59]

Although the administrative work of the Committee was now virtually over, since distribution was a matter left to the various service authorities, Rowland Berkeley remained as Honorary Secretary of the Fund until November 1919, after which it was wound up. The sum remaining, after all the Fund's liabilities were discharged, was later transferred to Queen Mary's Maternity Home, a Home founded by the Queen and intended for the benefit of the wives and infants of sailors, soldiers and members of the newly formed Royal Air Force.[60]

In 1920 Princess Mary presented specimens of the gifts to the Imperial War Museum, together with the dies of the embossed lid and a proof box. In the intervening seventy years or so, these have been joined by a large collection of embossed brass boxes, some with the contents intact. It was Princess Mary's expressed wish that each recipient of her gift should have something of permanent value by which to remember that first Christmas of the Great War. That so many of the boxes have survived the vicissitudes of over seventy five years and a second world war is ample evidence that her wish was more than fulfilled. Along with the trio of First World War medals, and the Next-of-Kin Memorial Plaque, the Princess Mary's Gift Fund Box has proved one of the most enduring mementos of the years 1914–1918.[61]

Postscript: the 'Lusitania Connection'

In March 1915, in pursuit of the increasingly elusive supplies of brass strip needed to make the boxes, the Committee decided to purchase 200 tons from the Phosphor Bronze Co Ltd of America. The price was set at £101 os od per ton and, subject to shipping space, delivery was to be completed within six weeks. On 16 March the Admiralty, through its Transport Department, informed the Committee that shipping space was available from New York, for the forty-five tons that were ready, and that the remainder would be delivered to the docks for shipment by 15 May.

In due course the Committee was notified that the first shipment was to leave New York on 9 April aboard the SS *Portsmouth*. However three days before the expected sailing the Committee learned that the American contractors had declined to put the brass in the *Portsmouth* since they had discovered that part of her cargo consisted of Sulphuric Acid. The consequence of this delay meant that the brass strip was still in New York, some 3000 miles from where it should have been. Berkeley got in touch with the Admiralty at once, and eventually, on 21 April received a further letter from the Transport Department which indicated that the brass had left New York aboard the SS *Drum of Airlie*. Three days later Berkeley received another communication which informed him that the brass was in fact still in New York.[62]

For no very apparent reason, it had been off-loaded from the *Drum of Airlie* and placed on board the Cunard liner the RMS *Lusitania* which sailed from New York, bound for Liverpool, on 1 May. Six days later, on 7 May, shortly after 2.10pm, the liner was struck amidships by a torpedo from the German submarine the U.20, and sank with the loss of 1,201 men, women and children.[63]

In the propaganda campaign subsequently conducted on both sides, much was made of rumours circulating at the time, that the *Lusitania*, in addition to her passengers, had been carrying armaments and munitions. The question of the *Lusitania*'s cargo has long been a controversial one. The British emphatically denied German claims that munitions of war were on board. However recent evidence, including the much-publicised dive on the wreck, does seem to confirm that she was carrying some ammunition. She was certainly carrying what could have been construed as the raw materials of war in the shape of forty-five tons of brass strip, shipped on orders of the Admiralty, and therefore not unnaturally suspect. The fact that its ultimate intended use was wholly innocent is irrelevant. After all, there is no reason to suppose that it would have occurred to the German authorities that in May 1915 the British were still busily engaged in the manufacture of hundreds of thousands of belated Christmas presents![64]

Acknowledgement

Extracts from letters held in the Royal Archive Windsor are reproduced by gracious permission of Her Majesty The Queen.

Notes

1. *Sunday Times*, 29 November 1914.
2. *The Sphere*, 5 December 1914.
3. Ibid, 12 December 1914.
4. *Sunday Times*, 29 November 1914. This issue carried two full pages advertising gift suggestions for Christmas.
5. *The Sphere*, op cit, 12 December 1914.
6. *Illustrated London News*, 12 December 1914.
7. The enormous number of such funds preclude any detailed listing of them here. For the interested reader, a fairly comprehensive survey can be found in the Catalogue of the Imperial War Museum Women's Work Collection which is administered by the Department of Printed Books. However a small sample will serve as an introduction. 'Miss Gladys Storey's Fund For Bovril'; the 'National Egg Collection Fund for the Wounded'; 'The Silver Thimble Fund'; the 'Ivory Cross'; the 'Blue Cross', and 'Lady Roberts' Field Glass Fund'.
8. Minutes of The Executive Committee of The Princess Mary's Gift Fund. (Hereinafter referred to as PMGF MINS.), 14 Oct, 1914. Department of Printed Books, W[omen's] W[ork] Coll[ection], BO 2 1/7.
9. To date no official biography of HRH The Princess Mary has appeared. However some impressions, all of which make one regret the omission, may be gained from James Pope-Hennessy, *Queen Mary*, George Allen & Unwin, London, 1959; Lord Harewood, *The Tongs and The Bones*, Weidenfeld and Nicolson, London, 1981; and Harold Nicolson, *King George V His Life & Reign*, Constable, London, 1952. See also the obituary which appeared in *The Times* on 29 March 1965. In 1914 the harsh light of publicity did not shine anything like as fiercely on the Royal Family as it does now, and the heir to the throne apart, the younger children of King George V and Queen Mary, grew up far removed from the intrusive gaze of the popular press. The young Princess was thus, in 1914, relatively unknown to the broad mass of the British public, although as the King's only daughter, she came to occupy a special place in their affections. Her first

official public engagement was in 1917, at an entertainment in aid of the Mesopotamia Comforts Fund, and was the beginning of a lifetime of quiet and unobtrusive service to the Country. The Princess took an active part in promoting the Girl Guide movement, of which she later became President, the VADs and the Land Army. She did canteen work at a munitions factory, and spent time as a VAD. During the Second World War she was Chief Controller of the Auxiliary Territorial Service and in 1950 became Controller Commandant of the Women's Royal Army Corps. In the same year she also assumed the appointment of Air Chief Commandant of Princess Mary's Royal Air Force Nursing Service. The Princess married, in 1922, Viscount Lascelles, later the 6th Earl of Harewood, by whom she had two sons, and who died in 1947. On 1 January 1932 the Princess was created Princess Royal, a title traditionally borne by the eldest daughter of the sovereign, and the one by which she is perhaps best remembered. HRH The Princess Mary, Princess Royal, Countess of Harewood CI, GCVO, GBE, RRC, TD, CD died at Harewood in Yorkshire on 28 March 1965.

10. *Sunday Times*, op cit, 29 November 1914.

11. *The Times* obituary, op cit.

12. PMGF MINS, op cit, 14 October 1914.

13. Typescript copy of a letter dated 15 October 1914. Held in IWM Department of Exhibits & Firearms' Ephemera Collection.

14. PMGF MINS, op cit, 14 October 1914. Final Report of The Princess Mary's Gift Fund, 1920 p.l. Copy in IWM W.W.COLL.BO 2 1/7.

15. Victor Christian William Cavendish KG GCMG TD PC, 9th Duke of Devonshire (1868–1938). Financial Secretary to the Treasury, 1903–5; a Civil Lord of the Admiralty 1915; Governor General and Commander in Chief Dominion of Canada 1916–1921; Secretary of State for the Colonies 1922–24; Chairman of Executive Council of the British Empire Exhibition 1924 & 1925. The Duke was a most conscientious chairman, missing only one meeting of the Committee until he left for Canada. John Baring, GCVO, PC, 2nd Baron Revelstoke (1863–1929). A Director of the Bank of England and partner in the family banking firm of Baring Brothers. Member of the Council of HRH The Prince of Wales, 1907 and Receiver-General of The Duchy of Cornwall. Rowland Comyns Berkeley (1845–?) was the son and son-in-law of

clergymen, unfortunately it has not proved possible to find any further information about him. For a full list of both the General Committee and the Executive Committee see Final Report, op cit, pl.

16. PMGF MINS 15 October 1914.

17. Ibid, 15 October 1914.

18. Final Report, op cit, p 4.

19. Ibid, p 4–5.

20. Ibid, p 5.

21. *Sunday Times*, 18 October 1914.

22. PMGF MINS, op cit, 20 October 1914.

23. Ibid, 27 October 1914.

24. Final Report, op cit, p 9. Hedley Francis Le Bas (1868–1926) Joint Honorary Secretary Prince of Wales National Relief Fund, Organiser of Lord Kitchener National Memorial Fund. During the First World War Le Bas, Director of the Caxton Press, was chief adviser to the Government in connection with publicity. He was knighted in 1916.

25. PMGF MINS, op cit, 27 October 1914.

26. Ibid, 20 October 1914.

27. Ibid, 3 November 1914.

28. Ibid, 22 December 1914. Final Report, op cit, p 9.

29. Ibid, 27 October & 3 November 1914.

30. Ibid, 3 November 1914. Final Report, op cit, p 9.

31. Arthur Marwick, *The Deluge*, Macmillan, London, 1973, p 34–35.

32. *The Morning Post*, 25 November 1914. *Observer*, 26 November 1914.

33. PMGF MINS, op cit, 15 October 1914.

34. Ibid, 24 November 1914.

35. Final Report, op cit, p 2.

36. The 'Indian Committee' comprised General Sir Alfred Gaslee, Colonel C S Wheeler, Colonel Ridgeway, Lieutenant Colonel O C Bradford and Brevet Colonel N A K Burn.

37. PMGF MINS, op cit, 27 October, 3 November, 10 November, 24 November, 1914. Final Report, op cit, p 3–7. Camp Followers were an important feature of life in the Indian Army and in those British Army Regiments stationed in India. They tended to be known by the name of the job they did, thus the water carrier was a 'Bhisti'.

38. The military nursing services comprised Queen Alexandra's Imperial Military Nursing Service (QAIMNS), its Reserve (QAIMNS(R)) and the two Territorial Nursing Services, the Territorial Force Nursing Service (TFNS) and its Reserve (TFNS(R)).

39. PMGF MINS, op cit, 24 November 1914.

40. Ibid, 3 November, 17 November

1914. Final Report, op cit, p 6.

41. Ibid, 1 December, 8 December 1914.

42. Ibid, 22 December 1914.

43. Final Report, op cit, p 7.

44. PMGF MINS, op cit, 24 November 1914.

45. Ibid, 24 November 1914. Final Report, op cit, p 2.

46. Final Report, op cit, p 2.

47. PMGF MINS, op cit, 8 December 1914.

48. Ibid, 3 November 1914.

49. Figures quoted in Malcolm Brown & Shirley Seaton, *Christmas Truce: The Western Front December 1914*, Leo Cooper/Secker & Warburg, London, 1984, p 43.

50. Diary of Major G D Jeffreys, 18 December 1914, quoted in Brown & Seaton, op cit, p 44.

51. Major General Wilfred Smith to Colonel Sir Henry Streatfield, 26 December 1914. RA.GEO.V.Q 832/92. Colonel Sir Henry Streatfield BT was an Extra Equerry to HM The King.

52. Lieutenant General Sir Henry Rawlinson to Colonel Clive Wigram 26 December 1914. RA.GEO.V.Q 2522/2/12. This letter is annotated 'Seen by The King'. Colonel Clive Wigram was knighted in 1926 and became Private Secretary to the King on the death of Lord Stamfordham in 1931.

53. *Manchester Guardian* 11 February 1915.

54. Brown & Seaton, op cit, p 126.

55. The Department of Exhibits & Firearms holds a considerable number of these boxes, several with their original contents intact. In any one year there may be anything up to fifty written enquiries and numerous telephone calls from members of the public seeking information about the origin of the box.

56. Leslie Walkinton quoted in Brown & Seaton, op cit, p 126.

57. PMGF MINS, 5 January 1915. Final Report, op cit, p 3.

58. Ibid, 26 January 1915.

59. Ibid, 26 January 1915.

60. Final Report, op cit, p 12.

61. Ibid, p 13. The three service medals (known as 'Pip, Squeak and Wilfred'), were the 1914 Star (or 1914–15 Star), British War Medal 1914–1920 and the Victory Medal 1914–1919. For the Next of Kin Memorial Plaque see Philip Dutton, 'The Dead Man's Penny: a history of the Next of Kin memorial plaque' in *Imperial War Museum Review No 3*, Imperial War Museum, London, 1988, p 60–68.

62. PMGF MINS, 16 March 1915 with Addendum.

63. Philip Dutton, 'GESCHAFT UBER ALLES': notes on some

medallions inspired by the sinking of the Lusitania' in *Imperial War Museum Review No 1*, Imperial War Museum, London, 1986, p 30. See also Colin Simpson, *Lusitania*, Penguin, London, 1974.

64. Simpson, op cit, p 32.

Further Reading

Malcolm Brown & Shirley Seaton, *Christmas Truce The Western Front December 1914*, Leo Cooper/Secker & Warburg, London, 1984.
Paul Fussell, *The Great War & Modern Memory*, OUP, 1975.
Arthur Marwick, *The Deluge*, Macmillan, London, 1973.

The German Biber Submarine

John Bullen

On 29 December 1944, the officer of the watch on HMS *Ready*, an Algerine-class minesweeper,[1] reported that one of the danbuoys marking the lap the *Ready* was sweeping 30 miles east of the North Foreland appeared to have drifted badly out of position. The Commanding Officer of HMS *Ready* and the Senior Officer of the 18th Minesweeping Flotilla, Commodore A V Walker DSC RN received this news with surprise since it was a calm day, and a quick look through his binoculars convinced him that the 'danbuoy' was the periscope and conning-tower of a German midget submarine.

The vessel was not under way and Walker hoisted a signal instructing the remaining ships of the flotilla to disregard HMS *Ready*'s motions. *Ready*'s sweeps were cut and the minesweeper steamed at full speed towards the submarine watching it carefully. HMS *Ready*'s motorboat was lowered and a party investigated the vessel. The pilot, seen through the glass light of the conning tower, was dead. The midget submarine, a Biber (Beaver) one-man submarine, was in immaculate condition and beautifully cellulosed.

The Admiralty was anxious to acquire one of these craft. More than one Biber had already been captured, but they had in all cases been subsequently lost by capsizing when in tow. Walker gave serious thought to hoisting the Biber on the motorboat's davits, since it was twenty-nine feet long and the length of the motorboat was twenty-five feet, but decided that it was too heavy. Also, the Biber still had a Type G7e 21-inch torpedo slung underneath it, which could have broken away and fired as the Biber was lifted out of the water.

Walker ordered the *Ready* to tow the Biber astern at five knots, the maximum speed recommended by the Admiralty. The other ships of the 18th Minesweeping Flotilla maintained an asdic sweep around HMS *Ready* as she made her slow journey back to the North Foreland. Walker was refused permission to take the Biber 90 (90 denoted the pro-

HMS *Ready*'s motorboat approaching Biber 90, now displayed in the Imperial War Museum, after the midget submarine was spotted drifting off the North Foreland on 29 December 1944. A28248

Dr John Bullen is a research assistant in the Department of Exhibits and Firearms.

duction number) to Sheerness and a large ocean-going tug rendezvous-ed with his flotilla off the North Foreland. Fog had closed in and the weather was deteriorating by the time the second tow commenced. The difficulties of entering Dover Harbour led to the tow being broken and Biber 90 was lost. It was recovered, badly battered, from the bottom of the harbour, ten days later.[2]

The subsequent post-mortem on the pilot showed he had died of carbon monoxide poisoning after inhaling the fumes from the Biber's petrol engine. In the weeks that followed the Biber 90 was modified by the Royal Navy for experimental purposes which included the installation of trimming tanks inside the two main ballast tanks, the addition of extension pipes to the port and starboard fuel tank hull filling valves to enable the craft to be refuelled whilst still in the water, and the fitting of an extension to the engine exhaust pipe.[3]

These modifications were carried out at Chatham Dockyard and Biber 90 was used in extensive trials carried out by British midget submarine officers and various methods of detection were used. The information gained was passed to the anti-submarine forces.

Biber 90 was transferred by the Admiralty from Capt (S/M) Fifth Submarine Flotilla, HMS 'Gosport' to the Imperial War Museum on 3 April 1946, and the Biber's periscope, binnacle, schnorkel and associated mount were transferred from the Flag Officer Submarines, Fort Blockhouse, Gosport on 9 September 1947.[4] Since that date Biber 90 has been one of the more unusual and interesting exhibits on display in the Imperial War Museum.

The genesis of Biber 90 and the large resources that Imperial and Nazi Germany were to commit to undersea warfare lay in the completion of U-1, the first German submarine, in 1906. During 1898 and 1899 the French Navy had built several successful submarines, which led the German Torpedo Inspectorate to suggest the completion of an experimental submarine for defensive operations. Admiral von Tirpitz, Secretary of State of the Imperial Naval Office considered the submarine of little value, but his attitude changed when the Imperial Russian Navy ordered three submarines, *Karp*, *Karas*, and *Kambala* from Germaniaweft (GW) Kiel, during 1904. In response, a German submarine, the U-1, similar in design to the Russian boats, was ordered from GW on 3 December 1904.[5]

At the outbreak of the First World War, in August 1914, Germany possessed 45 U-boats either in service or being commissioned. On 5 September U21 torpedoed HMS *Pathfinder*, a light cruiser, off St Abb's Head and on 22 September the obsolete U9 sank three old 10,000 ton armoured cruisers HMS *Aboukir*, HMS *Cressy*, and HMS *Hogue* thirty miles south-west of Ijmuiden. Nearly 1,500 British seamen were lost.

Biber 90 being secured by HMS *Ready*'s motorboat. The Biber's pilot had died of carbon monoxide poisoning caused by fumes from the petrol engine. The Biber carried a standard armament of two Type G7e 21-inch torpedoes mounted in semi-recessed positions on either side of the hull. This is the type of torpedo which is fitted to the Imperial War Museum's Biber 90. Alternatively, two mines could be carried. A28249

Biber 90 after being salvaged from the bottom of Dover harbour where it had lain for ten days. Its appearance reflects the battering it received. Note the smallness of the conning tower. Forward of the open hatch are, successively, the extension piece for the air intake, the periscope, and the projector binnacle. A28253

Rear view of Biber 90 after salvage, showing aft armoured glass port, exhaust valve, exhaust tank, and exhaust pipe. A28254

The submarine was a proven weapon of war.[6] The Imperial German Navy was to wage a relentless *guerre de course* against Great Britain's merchant shipping. In April 1917 nearly 900,000 tons of merchant shipping and cargoes – two-thirds of them British – were lost to submarine attack. By the time of the Armistice Britain had lost 11,135,000 tons of shipping.[7]

The Treaty of Versailles, ratified in June 1919, formalised the Armistice of 11 November 1918 and limited the size and composition of the German armed forces. Weimar Germany, in particular, was not allowed to possess U-boats. The U-Boat Inspectorate and the U-Boat Office were dissolved, and the existing U-boat fleet was either destroyed or handed over to the Allies. Yet both the dockyards and the new Naval Directorate wanted U-boat construction and development to be maintained. During the 1920s this development continued by subterfuge. Secret funds of the Reichsmarine's B5 (*Seetransportabteilung im Allgemeinen Marineamt 'B'* or Sea Transport Department) were used to support Dutch shipyards at Rotterdam which built German-designed submarines for Turkey, and work began in 1927. Other submarines, built to German designs, were constructed in Finland. Such clandestine activity enabled the Reichsmarine to stay abreast of the latest submarine technology.[8]

On January 30 1933 Adolf Hitler became Chancellor of Germany. He appointed General Werner von Blomberg as Minister for Defence and, in an address on 2 February, assured the senior Admirals and Generals that Germany would re-arm. 1935 was to be the crucial year for German naval re-armament. On 1 February construction work began at Kiel on the first U-boat flotilla and in June 1935 Raeder selected Kapitän zur See (Captain) Karl Dönitz to be in command of operational boats. The Anglo–German Naval Agreement of June 1935 limited the German Navy's (Kriegsmarine's) size in relation to that of the Royal Navy. Yet this formal Agreement legitimised Nazi Germany's construction of modern warships and abrogated the relevant terms of the Versailles Treaty. During 1935, also, work began on the first Type VII U-boat, the submarine which was to be the mainstay of the U-boat Force and to determine German naval strategy more than any other vessel.[9]

Nazi Germany was to attempt to challenge British naval dominance. The 'Z Plan' emerged in January 1939 and advocated the building of a large surface fleet by 1947 composed of 10 battleships, 3 pocket battleships, 12 battlecruisers, 8 aircraft carriers, 5 heavy cruisers, 60 light and scout cruisers, 148 destroyers and torpedo boats and 247 U-boats.[10] This projection envisaged the submarine as a major component of Germany's seapower. The plan was forestalled by Hitler's invasion of Poland and the subsequent outbreak of war between Germany and Britain on 3 September 1939.

The Kriegsmarine was unready for war against the world's greatest seapower. Once more, however, the German U-boats came close to defeating Britain during the Atlantic Campaign which began in September 1939 and did not end until May 1945, when the Third Reich capitulated. It was the longest campaign of the Second World War and the most crucial for Britain. The Third Reich's victorious campaigns during April–June 1940 enabled the Kriegsmarine to operate its U-boats from German, French and, later, Norwegian ports, and their depredations posed the most formidable threat to British merchant shipping and to Britain's ultimate survival.

Yet by the autumn of 1943 Nazi Germany's geo-strategic position was deteriorating after successive defeats in Russia, North Africa, and in the Atlantic. The invasion of Western Europe seemed imminent. The Kriegsmarine's small and depleted surface fleet could not hope to match Anglo–American naval power, and the U-boats were on the defensive after heavy losses in May 1943. Admiral Dönitz, now Commander-in-Chief of the Kriegsmarine, turned to midget submarines and other less conventional weapons as a means of defending the western sea frontiers of the Reich. Already the exploits of the Royal Italian Navy's 'chariots'[11] against the Royal Navy, and the latter's use of X-craft[12] against the *Tirpitz*, had shown what could be accomplished by these weapons. Dönitz conceived the *Kleinkampfmittel-Verband* (small battle-weapon unit, KdK, or K-Force) which was to be composed of midget submarines, explosive motor boats, frogmen and human torpedoes.

In December 1943 Vice-Admiral Hellmuth Heye, who throughout 1943 had urged the Naval High Command to form 'special attack' units, was appointed as the head of K-Force. Heye was a great admirer of Lord Nelson and, like the Royal Navy's foremost fighting admiral, accepting that high morale was vital in combat operations, aimed to establish K-Force as a Nelsonian 'band of brothers'. The operations that K-Force personnel would be called upon to mount were to prove extremely hazardous. Heye decided that K-Force personnel would not be overly subject to formal discipline and expected his men, in the tradition of the British and the Italians, both to work and play hard. He furthered this non-conformity by discarding all badges of rank.

The Kriegsmarine initiated development of midget submarines later than most of the other major navies. The premier advocates of 'special attack' submersibles, the Lübeck industrialist Heinrich Dräger and Kapitänleutnant (Lieutenant Commander) Hans Bartels, were ignored as the Third Reich continued to expand. The outstanding success of the Kriegsmarine's U-boats, moreover, precluded the development of midget submarines. By late 1943 Bartels's time had come.

Vice-Admiral Hellmuth Heye, who throughout 1943 urged the German Naval High Command to form 'special attack' units, shown presenting an award. HU2246

Korvettenkapitän (Commander) Hans Bartels who was chiefly responsible for the design of the Biber submarine. Bartels was a redoubtable individual and is wearing the Knight's Cross awarded for exploits in Norway. He personally tested the first Biber prototype, 'Adam', and led the first operational Biber group, K-Flotilla 261. HU2245

Heye and Bartels faced immense problems. Heye later stated:

The formation from scratch of a new force and the establishment of entirely new weapons in the fifth year of a war presented extraordinary difficulties. As speed was essential there was no question of lengthy tests and trials. At my suggestion the Commander-in-Chief gave me considerable powers which enabled me to short-circuit tedious bureaucratic procedure and to have direct contact with all departments of the Naval Staff and – especially important – with industrial concerns. Unless I had made full use of these powers, the formation and equipment of the K-Force would hardly have been feasible in the short-time available.[13]

On 22 November 1943 a British Welman midget submarine was captured during an attack on Bergen. The

Welman was a one-man submersible with a surface displacement of 4,600 lb. A 2.5hp electric motor gave it a maximum submerged speed of 3 knots with an endurance of up to 20 hours at 1.7 knots. Welmans were used on several occasions to attack Laksevaag floating dock which was used to service U-boats based at Bergen.[14]

This little craft was to influence the promoted Korvettenkapitän (Commander) Bartels who was to be chiefly responsible for the design of the Biber, the smallest U-boat to be deployed by the Kriegsmarine. Bartels's first negotiations about Biber began on 4 February with Flenderwerke Lübeck. On 15 March 1944 the first Biber prototype called both the 'Bunte boat' after Director Bunte of Flenderwerke, Lübeck, and also 'Adam', was ready for trials. Bartels ran trials in the 'Adam' boat, which had a different bow and conning tower from the production Biber models, on the River Trave. The prototype was inspected and approved by Admiral Dönitz and was taken into service on 29 March. Doubts were expressed about the use of a petrol engine by the Head of 'K' Office but Bunte and representatives of the Marinegruppenkommando Nord/Flottenkommando in Kiel approved. Petrol engines could be supplied in quantity and were almost noiseless, since a suitable diesel propulsion unit was not available.

The success of the trials led to twenty four Bibers being ordered from Flenderwerke to be delivered by 31 May 1944. Further contracts were placed with Klockner-Humboldt-Deutz and other firms. Production began in May and three Bibers were manufactured: six were made in June; nineteen in July; fifty in August; one hundred and seventeen in September; seventy three in October; and fifty six in November. Total production was three hundred and twenty four Bibers.[15]

The Biber was a one-man submarine which displaced 6.5 tons with its torpedo armament. It was 29.5ft long, 5.25ft in the beam, and of 4.5ft draught. Surface propulsion was provided by a 32hp Opel-Blitz Otto automobile engine which gave a range of 100 nautical miles at a maximum speed of 6.5 knots. Three torpedo battery troughs Type 13T210 and a 13hp electric torpedo motor gave the Biber a submerged range of 8.6 nautical miles at 5.3 knots plus 8 nautical miles at 2.5 knots.

The hull was made of 3mm sheet steel and gave a permissible diving depth of over 60ft although Bibers were dived to more than 100ft. There were no compensating or trimming tanks and before a voyage solid ballast was stowed. The Biber was reasonably manoeuvrable on the surface but could not maintain a consistent depth when it dived. Its main flaw was the Opel-Blitz Otto petrol engine and the carbon-monoxide it released. The operator sat in a potentially lethal atmosphere if he ran this engine for more than 45 minutes with the hatch shut. Pilots were therefore provided with breathing apparatus and 20-hours' supply of oxygen, but many, including the pilot of the Museum's Biber 90, succumbed to carbon monoxide poisoning.[16]

The Biber was built in three sections bolted together. The pressure hull was reinforced by ribs and four bulkheads. The bow compartment contained only the forward diving tank. Between the first and second bulkheads was the main compartment – the control room – in which sat the single operator, his head projecting into the 28-inch conning tower. The operator sat within easy reach of all the control valves and levers which were simple and uncomplicated (see accompanying photograph). This compartment also contained the batteries and petrol tank. The small hatch in the tower was the only means of access and exit. The pilot was issued with a special combat ration of chocolate which contained caffeine, kola nut extract and other stimulants. Navigation was accomplished mainly by eyesight aided by a wrist compass. Periscope observation was provided only in a forward direction. Since the Biber could not be maintained at periscope depth because of her lack of compensating and trimming tanks, attacks could only be carried out on the surface. The engine compartment, behind the pilot, was sealed off from the rest of the boat to avoid petrol leaks and petrol vapour. The rearmost compartment held the after diving tank.[17]

Biber carried a standard armament of two Type G7e 21-inch torpedoes mounted in semi-recessed positions on either side of the hull. Each torpedo was 23ft 7ins long, weighed 3,534lbs, was electrically powered, carried a 661lb warhead and had a range of 5470 yards at 30 knots. The torpedoes were clamped to the rail by a band which ran from a fitting on the keel to a swinging eyebolt above the rail. (This is still in position on the empty starboard rail of Biber 90.) The release sequence was uncomplicated. The fitting above the rail is a pneumatic cylinder to which air was admitted in order to fire. The piston in the cylinder travelled towards the rear, thus releasing a clamping eyebolt, and simultaneously forcing back a trip lever which can be seen in a slot towards the rear top side of the G7e torpedo on Biber 90. The torpedo then ran forward under its own power along the rail, suspended by two lugs within the rail until it cleared the bows of the submarine. The run to clear Biber was about 16 feet.[18]

One Royal Navy observer considered the Biber to be comparable to the British Welman, if of superior design on certain points. He also accepted that the Biber's use of torpedoes, rather than attaching heavy charges to the target, had certain advantages, especially against merchant shipping.[19] This is not to suggest that Biber was a 'wonder-weapon'. It was, in effect, an improvised defensive weapon

Internal view of Biber 90 taken from the stern showing the main compartment – the control room – in which sat the single operator. The rear section containing the petrol engine has been removed. The boxlike structure is one of the 26-cell batteries. The upper rod on the right controls the hydroplane and the lower is the reversing gear rod. A27777

The controls and instrument panel of the Biber 90. The austerity of the instrument fit is apparent. All the controls were within easy reach of the pilot who looked out through armoured glass ports. Especially prominent in this interior shot of the Museum's Biber 90 is the control wheel. On its lower left is the rudder indicator dial, and on its lower right is the hydroplane indicator. The five indicators above are, from left to right, for engine oil pressure, oxygen pressure, voltage, low pressure air gauge 0–50, and high pressure gauge 0–300. MH29893

for use against Allied invasion shipping, and was designed for mass production and a short life, utilising as far as was possible parts already being manufactured for other purposes.

The rapid production of Bibers led to the speedy formation of the first Biber flotilla, K-Flotilla 261, which was led by the redoubtable Bartels.[20] On the role of K-Force Vice-Admiral Heye later wrote:

We ourselves possessed no practical experience in this form of warfare. We knew broadly that the

Italians and the British possessed several different forms of small battle weapons, but we knew nothing of the Japanese operations with midget submarines. . . .

Our first intention was to design and build midget submarines on the English pattern, for penetrating into enemy harbours and other special operations.[21]

On 6 June 1944 overwhelming Allied air and naval supremacy ensured the successful landings of the Anglo-American armies in Normandy. The Kriegsmarine, including K-Force, had not been able to challenge effectively Anglo-American naval power. The Bibers' first operational deployment was on the night of 29–30 August 1944 by K-Flotilla 261, when an attack was planned on the invasion fleet from Le Havre. After 20 August 1944, however, the German front in Normandy no longer existed, since powerful Allied armoured formations had broken out of the bridgehead. Le Havre was evacuated and K-Flotilla 261 was re-directed to Fécamp, arriving with 20 Bibers after an epic five-day journey from Belgium in the teeth of marauding Allied bombers and fighter-bombers. Eighteen serviceable Bibers sailed from Fécamp on the night of 29 August. The weather was unfavourable with wind and a sea force four.

Two Bibers located an Allied convoy and claimed a Liberty ship and a large landing craft as sunk. All eighteen Bibers returned, one of the exhausted pilots, suffering from carbon-monoxide poisoning, not returning until 10am the next morning. Post-war records do not confirm the sinkings. On 31 August Fécamp was abandoned. The K-Force personnel were among the last Germans to leave, most of the Bibers were blown up, and those few which were placed on trucks were later destroyed in a night action with an advancing American armoured column.

The Bibers' operational debut was hardly auspicious in spite of the vessels surmounting the adverse weather conditions and returning safely. Indeed, Bibers were to achieve little against Allied warships or merchant shipping. The limitations of their design and the dangers besetting their operators – who were, of necessity, resolute men – presented formidable obstacles.

Each new Biber flotilla was sent overland to Rotterdam which became the base for attacks on Allied shipping in the lower Scheldt. The German radio interception station on Schouwen island reported the movements of convoys, but weather conditions often precluded Biber sorties, which had to be abandoned if wind and sea conditions exceeded four on the Beaufort scale. It was preferable, moreover, to send out the Bibers on an afternoon ebb tide which enabled them to cover the forty miles or more to the Western Scheldt more quickly, and arrive at the area of operations at dusk, which covered the Bibers' attacks, especially if there was no moon.

Bartels sent out his Bibers on intermittent operations throughout December 1944–February 1945. Altogether there were 110 Biber sorties from Rotterdam. When starting the missions, the Biber pilots kept the hatch open to breathe fresh air as long as possible until the open sea was reached at the Hook of Holland and between the islands of Goeree and Voorne. Casualties, especially from Allied fighter-bombers, were high, and no losses to the torpedoes of Bibers are recorded, although it is believed some Allied vessels were sunk by mines.[22]

The poor design and rapid wartime development of the Biber compromised its success and K-Force's more ambitious operations. One planned action – Operation 'Caesar' – involved an attack by Bibers on Allied escort vessels of the Russian convoys, anchored in Kola Inlet, Murmansk, on the Barents Sea. K-Flotilla 265 began training with Bibers at Harstadt, Norway in November 1944. Three Type VII-C U-boats, U-295, U-716, and U-318 were equipped to carry two Bibers each on their decks.

Murmansk was protected. Destroyers equipped with radar and asdic (sonar) patrolled between the island of Kildin and the mainland at Sjet Navolok. Net-and-boom defences had been placed on either side of Salny island. K-Flotilla 265's training intensified as it practised manoeuvres with the Type VIIs, dived under net obstacles, and made dummy attacks on German warships in Harstadt.

The Type VIIs were to carry the Bibers to within forty miles of the target area, release the deck clamps, and submerge beneath the midgets. The Bibers had twelve hours to penetrate into Murmansk and to attack at 3am on the 8 January by the light of a half-moon. It was anticipated that the Soviet battleship Archangelsk – formerly the Royal Navy's HMS Royal Sovereign[23] – and other warships would provide numerous targets.

Following the attack the Bibers were to lie on the shallow bottom and send acoustic signals to be received by the waiting U-boats. After the pilots were picked up the Bibers were to be destroyed by self-destructive charges. Alternatively, the Biber operators were to be rescued a day later from the Fischer peninsula, or make for Pers fjord, destroy the Bibers, and cross into Sweden. The operators were given maps and rehearsed the rescue procedures.

The three Type VIIs left Harstadt on 5 January 1945, passed Tromso, and lay on the bottom of Lyngen fjord. The journey was resumed at noon on 6 January. However, the vibrations of the U-boats, surface running on diesels, started leaks in the Bibers' fuel pipes and despite efforts to repair the faults, the mission had to be abandoned.[24]

A Biber submarine in 1945 camouflaged with branches and leaves around the periscope. This Biber was used in the attack on Nijmegen Bridge on the night of 12–13 January 1945. The attack was unsuccessful. HU56107

An abandoned Biber midget submarine with attached torpedo on a transport trailer after an attack by Allied aircraft being examined by a Royal Navy officer in battledress. The first operational Biber unit, K-Flotilla 261, took five days to travel by road from Belgium to Le Havre because of marauding Allied bombers and fighter bombers. A28250

A Biber being lowered into water. The small size of the midget submarine is apparent. HU2247

Another major Biber mission which proved unsuccessful was the planned attack on the Nijmegen road bridge over the river Waal, captured by the United States 82nd Airborne Division in September 1944. K-Force frogmen had already damaged the rail bridge in a daring raid. The British defences of the road bridge were strengthened, specifically by rigging four net-and-boom barriers across the Waal system upstream from the bridge.

On the night of 12–13 January 1945 the Germans, from their lines a few miles above Nijmegen, floated 240 mines downstream in four waves of 60 mines, to destroy the net-and-boom barriers. Twenty Bibers, their periscopes camouflaged to resemble drifting foliage, were to launch torpedoes at the bridge and sortied behind the mines. Allied troops held both sides of the Waal above the bridge and raked the river with artillery and machine-gun fire. The mines exploded and the following Bibers fired their torpedoes. Four more Bibers followed each towing a large tree trunk beneath which was a 6,600lb explosive charge supported by flotation chambers. The trunks were released. The change of light under the bridge was supposed to trigger photo-electric cells built into the upper sides of the trunks and fire the explosive charges, but Allied artillery fire destroyed the logs.

Heavy operational losses were aggravated by two serious accidents which led to the phasing out of Biber in favour of the two-man diesel-powered Type XXVII midget U-boat Seehund (Seal). Bibers operating from Rotterdam were towed by harbour tugs to the Hellevoetsluis lock on the Haringvliet, at the head of the Waal-Maas estuary. At the Hellevoetsluis lock the Bibers were serviced and early in January 1945 a mechanic inadvertently fired a G7e torpedo. The resulting explosion destroyed nearly thirty Bibers. A similar accident occurred on 6 March. Bartels had ordered thirty-five Bibers to be serviced for an operation and the pilots stood by for several days waiting for the weather to clear. On the evening of 6 March the pilots manned the Bibers, when suddenly a huge explosion and an eight foot tidal wave wrecked twenty of the midgets and killed thirty-two men. Again, a G7e torpedo had been inadvertently fired exploding a Biber carrying two mines and setting off a chain reaction. After the disaster, Bartels was relieved of his command and only a few Bibers were used for minelaying operations.[25]

The failure of the Biber and, in spite of the courage displayed, of K-Force reflects the failure of the Kriegsmarine's and, ultimately, Nazi Germany's ability to wage war successfully at sea. The organisation of K-Force came at a time when the Third Reich, through its flawed strategy, was being assailed on three fronts – in Italy, in Russia, and from the air – by a combination of the most powerful nations on earth. K-Force and the remaining ships of the Kriegsmarine failed to stop the invasion of Normandy in June

A Biber in the Hellevoetsluis lock on the Haringvliet at the head of the Waal-Maas estuary in the harsh winter of 1945. Bibers operating against Allied shipping in the Scheldt area were towed here by tug from Rotterdam. HU56108

1944 and the opening of a fourth front.

The Third Reich's strategic dilemma was part of a continuing historical process. Alfred Thayer Mahan, perhaps the greatest of naval historians,[26] wrote:

> This power (ie seapower) feels and is moved by many interests: it has a great history in the past, it is making a great and yet more wonderful history in the present.[27]

Two of the 'many interests' that move seapower are that only rarely in history does a great land power commensurately project its strength at sea; or, faced with a dominant naval protagonist, quickly create a powerful naval capability and defeat its opponent. In recent history no Great Power has been able to maintain both powerful armies and navies for an extended period of time without overreaching itself. In the post-war era even the two super-powers, the United States and the Soviet Union, are finding their economies strained in supporting large naval and military establishments.

Nazi Germany's flawed naval strategy followed this historical pattern. The abandonment of Plan Z and the defeat of the U-boats ended the Third Reich's attempts to expand at sea: and other strategic demands in the middle of the Second World War meant that Nazi Germany could not build a powerful navy to challenge Anglo-American maritime supremacy.

The creation of K-Force was a desperate and unsuccessful attempt to challenge the Anglo-American invasion fleet. Biber 90 is one of the Museum's more interesting items, but the failure of the Biber programme and others of Nazi Germany's midget submarine projects reflects the failure of the Third Reich's naval strategy.

Notes

1. HMS *Ready* was built by Harland and Wolff, and launched in 1943. She displaced 1,225 tons and was powered by 2-shaft geared turbines giving 2,000shp. and a top speed of 16.5 knots. Her dimensions were 225ft × 35ft. Her armament was 1 × 4in/45 QF Mk V HA, 8 × 20mm Oerlikons and 92 depth charges when used as an escort. Her crew was 85 men.
R Chesneau (Ed), *Conway's All the World's Fighting Ships*, Conway Maritime Press, 1980, p 65.
2. Memoirs of Captain A V Walker DSC RN, Department of Documents, 78/50/1, pp 160–163.
3. Report from David Hill to J R Bullen on Biber German Midget Submarines, May 1987, enclosed with letter dated 7 July 1987, Department of Exhibits and Firearms.
4. Admiralty to Imperial War Museum, 3 April 1946, Flag Officer Submarines to Imperial War Museum 9 September 1947, Department of Exhibits and Firearms, H390/46.
5. E Rössler, *The U-boat: The evolution and technical history of German submarines*, Arms and Armour Press, London, 1981, p 17.
6. J S Corbett, *History of the Great War: Naval Operations Vol 1*, Longmans, Green & Company, 1920, p 163 and pp 172–177.
7. D van der Vat, *The Atlantic Campaign: The Great Struggle at Sea 1939–1945*, Hodder and Stoughton, 1988, p 40.
8. Rossler, op cit, pp 88–95.
9. Ibid, p 100–101.
10. C Bekker, *Hitler's Naval War*, Purnell Books, 1974, p 372.
11. Among other exploits the Royal Italian Navy's 'chariots' sank the battleships HMS *Valiant* and HMS *Queen Elizabeth* in Alexandria Harbour, on the night of 18–19 December 1941. R O'Neill, *Suicide Weapons: Axis and Allied Special Attack Weapons of World War II: their development and their missions*, Salamander Books, London, 1981, pp 218–219.
12. The X-craft crippled the German battleship *Tirpitz* on 22 September 1943. Each one weighed 30 tons (submerged and without explosive charges) was 51.25ft long, had a crew of 4 men, and carried two 4,400lb side charges, which were released and became timed mines. O'Neill, op cit, p 58 and pp 60–63.
13. C Bekker, *K-Men: the story of the German Frogmen and Midget Submarines*, W Kimber, 1955, pp 18–19.
14. O'Neill, op cit, pp 64–65.
15. R Compton-Hall, *Submarine Warfare: Monsters and Midgets*, Blandford Press, 1985, p 143. Rossler, op cit, p 290. Bekker, 'K-Men', op cit, p 119.
16. Rossler, op cit, p 290. Bekker 'K-Men', op cit, p 119.
17. Bekker, 'K-Men', op cit, pp 119–121.
18. Letter from G Rayner (employed by Vickers Limited) to P Simkins, 24 March 1975, Department of Exhibits and Firearms.
19. D Hill to J R Bullen, op cit. Report on inspection of captured German Midget Submarine in Portsmouth Dockyard on 25 September 1944. W O Shelford (Commander RN) Department of Exhibits and Firearms.
20. Hans Bartels had an extraordinary career in Norway during 1940, capturing a destroyer and an entire torpedo-boat flotilla. He built his own minesweeper, followed by eleven more and invited Grand Admiral Raeder to pay for them. When Raeder refused, Bartels moved a minesweeper to Berlin and moored it in the canal outside Naval Headquarters where Raeder inspected it. Raeder took a dim view of Bartels's independence and had him promoted to First Officer in the destroyer Z34, in order that he might re-learn some naval discipline. J P Mallmann Showell, *The German Navy in World War Two*, Arms and Armour Press, 1979, p 27.
21. C Bekker, 'K-Men', op cit, p 19.
22. O'Neill, op cit, p 68. C Bekker, 'K-Men', op cit, p 116 and pp 122–123.
23. HMS *Royal Sovereign* was transferred to the Soviet Navy on 30 May 1944 and renamed *Archangelsk*. She was returned on 9 February 1949 and sold for breaking up.
24. Letter from Kapitän Ernst Plöger (former Commander of Biber Flotilla 265 in Norway 1944–1945) to John R Bullen 29 October 1988) to Department of Exhibits and Firearms.
25. For these operations see Bekker, 'K-Men', 113–114. O'Neill, op cit, pp 68–70.
26. Alfred Thayer Mahan 1840–1914. The most influential naval writer between 1889, and the publication of *The Influence of Sea Power Upon History*, until his death in 1914. His works, including *The Influence of Sea Power upon the French Revolution and Empire* (2 Vols), were studied by the world's leading navies and statesmen.
27. A T Mahan, *The Influence of Sea Power on the French Revolution and Empire*, Sampson Low Marston & Co, 14 Ed. Vol II, p 373.

The trench raid at Chérisy, 15 September 1917

Stephen Badsey

Dr Stephen Badsey was a cataloguer in the Department of Information Retrieval from 1980 to 1984. He is currently a freelance television researcher and historian.

The Imperial War Museum's Department of Photographs holds a remarkable series of three prints, believed to be the only aerial photographs ever taken of a British trench raid in progress on the Western Front. They were taken just north and west of the village of Chérisy (itself about ten miles south-east of Arras), timed at 4pm GMT on Saturday 15 September 1917, and show an improbably straight German trench, known to the British as Narrow Trench, as the raiders' objective. The raiders themselves, photographed from about 800 feet, show as small white dots with black shadows.

The Chérisy raid had its origins five months previously in the Battle of Arras, in which a British attack produced the salient at the village of Monchy-le-Preux. Needing to straighten out their line, the British then made a slow, grinding advance to the south of Monchy, in what became known as the Second Battle of the Scarpe. Chérisy village and its trenches had been intended as the German second line, and Narrow Trench had none of the curves and bays which protected properly made fire-trenches. The force of the British drive took their front line to within 250 metres of Narrow Trench, although due to a slight curve in the ridge neither side could see the other, except at special observation posts. Any trench built further out into no man's land would have been silhouetted on top of the ridge itself. For a time there was stalemate. But the German decision to hold Narrow Trench was an obvious mistake, for which they would eventu-

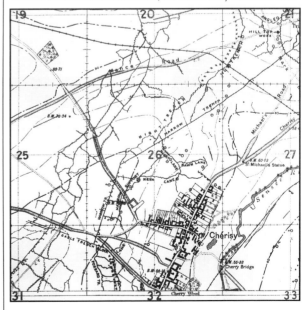

Section of trench map, 1:10,000 51B SW2 Vis-en-Artois, showing the village of Chérisy and Narrow Trench.

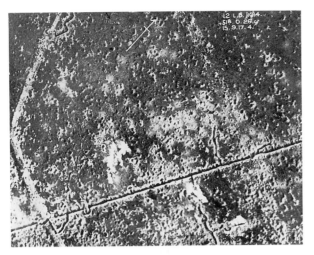

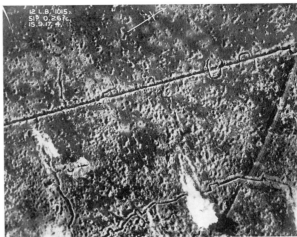

The first of the photographs taken by Captain Stevenson and Lieutenant Webster at the moment of the Chérisy Raid, flying over Narrow Trench. The numbers in the top right-hand corner indicate that this is photograph 1014 taken by 12 Light Bomber Squadron at grid reference 51B.026.c. on 15.9.1917 at 4pm. Shells from the British barrage are still bursting in no man's land. The fork in the road leading from Chérisy towards the British lines is on the left, with a sap jutting out across it. The men of C Company, 9th Durhams, can be seen as small white dots just above the North arrow at the top of the picture. A single German soldier (arrowed) of 6th Company, 2/76th Reserve Infantry can be seen in Narrow Trench towards the right of the picture. Q 58653

The second photograph of the sequence, number 1015, taken a few seconds later. The aircraft is flying north-eastwards and losing height. The German spotted in Narrow Trench is marked as gone from his position, which is now centre-left of the picture. Shells from the barrage are falling on Narrow Support and the communication saps. In the top right hand corner the small dots that are men from C Company and B Company have nearly reached Narrow Trench. The men are moving singly or in pairs, and any formation has broken down. Q 58654

ally have to pay.

The Chérisy raid was made by the British 50th Division, part of VI Corps, which was in turn part of the British Third Army. The pre-war Northumbrian Division of the Territorial Army, 50th Division had been fighting on the Western Front since April 1915. The divisional commander was Major-General Sir Percival S Wilkinson KCMG, CB, a typical 'dug out' officer who had joined the Northumberland Fusiliers in 1883 at the age of eighteen, but had spent most of his career in West Africa commanding native troops. In 1914 he was already a major-general, but had been passed over and was commanding a brigade of Indian infantry. The war revitalised Wilkinson's career, and exactly a year after its start he took command of 50th Division in France. In June 1916 he received as his GSO1, or chief staff officer, Lieutenant-Colonel Henry Karslake, a thirty seven-year-old career gunner who had won the DSO in South Africa in 1902. The First World War had halted his studies at the Staff College and he had gone to France as a captain with his battery. Thereafter a steady rise had culminated in his posting as the chief staff officer of a fighting division.

One battalion commander in Wilkinson's division was already something of a legend. In 1917, Lieutenant-Colonel Roland Boys Bradford, commanding 9th Battalion Durham Light Infantry, was just twenty-five years old. He had joined a Territorial battalion of the Durhams in 1910

and transferred to the Regular Army two years later. At the start of the war he went to France with his battalion, and in October 1916, already commanding 9th Durhams, he won the Victoria Cross on the Somme. He was one of four brothers from Milbanke, Darlington, only one of whom survived the war. His battalion, recruited from Gateshead, would together with 8th Durhams, recruited from Durham City, make the Chérisy raid. Both battalions belonged to 151st Brigade, known before September 1915 as the Durham Brigade, and commanded by acting Brigadier-General Neville J G Cameron. Forty-three years old, he was a true Cameron of the Cameron Highlanders, and his lifelong ambition was to command its 1st Battalion, in which he had started his career. He had already been twice wounded in action since 1914, and had each time returned to the Front.

The men who would defend Narrow Trench against the Durhams came mainly from the city of Hamburg. In the German Army the three battalions of a regiment served together as a brigade-sized unit, and 76th Reserve (2nd Hanseatic) Infantry Regiment was one of three regiments forming 17th Reserve Division. The regiment had suffered a bad summer, holding trenches only knee- or waist-deep against the British positions before Arras. On 14 August a surprise British bombardment had obliterated a 250 metre stretch of trench, and most of one company with it. On the last day of the month the regiment was finally taken out of line, only to be shifted

The third photograph of the sequence, number 1016. Stevenson and Webster's records indicate that they took at least twelve photographs over Chérisy, but only these are believed to have survived. The aircraft continues on its north-easterly course, and the picture now shows Neva Lane running from Narrow Trench at the top down to Narrow Support at the bottom. The British barrage is falling on Neva Lane, sealing off the left flank of the raid. At the top of the picture a few raiders can be seen on the left arriving at Narrow Trench, and in the centre, at the junction with Neva Lane, they can be seen (arrowed) inside the trench itself. Q 58655

southward to the badly sited position at Chérisy with Narrow Trench as its front line.[1]

The Northumbrian Division had come back into line opposite Chérisy on 15 June. Only two brigades held the divisional front of 3,000 yards, with the third brigade in reserve. The four battalions of each brigade moved between front line, support line, brigade reserve and rest, seldom spending more than four days at each. During August 9th Durhams spent altogether twelve days holding the front line, for the loss of three men dead and eleven wounded, in what they judged to be a quiet sector. On 1 September, having watched 76th Reserve Infantry come into line opposite them, they moved into brigade reserve. With a new, unidentified, enemy unit in the area it was only a matter of time before a raid was planned.

For the British the Chérisy raid would depend on five men. Bradford was one, and Lieutenant-Colonel J H Martin, commanding 8th Durhams, another. Brigadier-General Cameron would be responsible for co-ordinating the two battalions. Lieutenant-Colonel Karslake and his staff would draw up the plan, subject to Wilkinson's approval. The fifth man was actually on leave, so routine was raiding on the Western Front. He was Brigadier-General Herbert de T Phillips, the Commander Heavy Artillery (CHA) of VI Corps. His staff would supply the artillery support without which the raid would fail.

On 3 September 50th Division's own Commander Royal Artillery (CRA) issued new wire-cutting orders to his medium mortar crews. Each brigade had a light battery of six 3-inch Stokes mortars, with a battery of 9.45-inch heavy mortars and three batteries of 2-inch medium mortars (which threw an iron rod of that diameter to which was attached a sphere of high explosive) under divisional command. The mortars were to 'cut' German wire by simply blasting it away. Four days later the divisional artillery, six batteries of 18-pounder field guns and two of 4.5-inch howitzers, joined in the fire-plan by shelling Chérisy and the surrounding area. It was not a heavy bombardment, which might have warned the Germans of a raid, but the light, intermittent shellfire typical of the Western Front in a 'quiet' sector. The scale of such light shelling may be judged by the fact that, day and night for the next week, apparently by coincidence, 1,950 shells fell on the German positions near Chérisy.[2]

On 5 September Bradford's 9th Durhams were relieved from brigade reserve and marched back to their rest area south of Arras. On the following morning the officers were briefed on Karslake's written orders for the raid. These listed four objectives:

(a) To obtain an identification.
(b) To kill as many Germans as possible.
(c) To destroy all dugouts.
(d) To bring back or destroy machine-guns and trench mortars.

The raid would be in three phases, the third of which was still being finalised. The first phase would involve A, B and C Companies of 9th Durhams, the second only C Company of 8th Durhams, and the third would depend on Special Brigade Royal Engineers, the Army's experts on chemical warfare.[3] Borrowing an ordinary farm plough, 9th Durhams dug a replica of the German trenches and spent the afternoon practising over it. On the following day 151st Brigade came back into divisional reserve, and the divisional artillery fire programme began.

On the following morning Lieutenant-Colonel Martin reviewed his C Company, under Captain Bennett M Williams. A thirty-three-year-old qualified barrister, Williams had joined the Army as a volunteer in 1915. Like most fighting formations, C Company was notably under strength, and Martin detached ten men from each of his other companies to bring it up to five officers and 110 other ranks. C Company then had its first attempt at the replica trenches. Meanwhile the divisional Commander Royal Engineers (CRE), Lieutenant-Colonel Harold E F Rathbone, visited each of his three field companies. Early next day, 7th Field

Company was ordered to prepare a detachment for the raid. Second-Lieutenant William H Rebbeck, twenty five-years old, five feet six inches tall, nine stones in weight and with his commission barely six months old, was given four corporals and eight sappers, and after experimenting with gun cotton and Stokes mortar bomb charges on the abandoned dugouts of the Hindenburg Line produced seventeen explosive devices for the raid. Aerial photographs showed only eight dugouts in Narrow Support, immediately behind Narrow Trench. But the most recent reconnaissance also showed a machine gun nest built in a small sap projecting forward from Narrow Trench, just at the point where A Company of 9th Durhams were planning to attack.[4]

For the next two days the raiders continued to train. On Monday the divisional artillery switched to targeting Narrow Trench alone, leaving the mortars to continue wire cutting. On Tuesday 11 September the final preliminaries of the raid were set in motion. The heavy artillery of VI Corps joined in shelling Narrow Trench and Night Trench further north. Brigadier-General Phillips's staff arranged for supporting fire during the raid from two neighbouring divisions, and contacted 12 Squadron, the Corps reconnaissance squadron, for spotter aircraft. A day later Phillips returned from leave and approved the plan. Lieutenant-Colonel Rathbone made another routine visit to his Engineer companies, checking out some special equipment for the raid, and Second-Lieutenant Rebbeck left with his men to start training with 9th Durhams.

That afternoon 9th Durhams carried out a full dress rehearsal of the raid in its practice trenches, watched by senior officers including the commander of Third Army, General Sir Julian Byng. Later that day, Brigadier-General Cameron issued the final instructions for the raid, sensibly ordering that 9th Durhams would receive eight extra stretcher bearers from each of his other battalions. On the following morning Karslake released the date and times for the raid, the third phase of which remained only an option.

There was already some concern from VI Corps gunners about the poor weather and bad visibility, typical of the late summer of 1917. On 12 September the weather broke altogether, and it was cold and damp. C Company of 8th Durhams had their final trial over the practice trenches while 9th Durhams rested, taking a form of solace in an extra evening church parade (8th Durhams preferred a film show). Next day the brigade returned to the trenches, and by 11.45am 8th Durhams were back in the front lines opposite Chérisy, with 9th Durhams in the brigade reserve camp behind them. That night, 8th Durhams sent out two-hour patrols into no man's land at 10pm and 2am. One patrol heard noises from the German trenches opposite – it sounded as if they might, after all, be building new defences in front of Narrow Trench.

By summer 1917 the German Army had already adopted the tactic of defence in depth, concentrating their main strength in the Support trench and leaving the front line only lightly held. On 13 September 1st Battalion 76th Reserve Infantry, the regimental reserve in the village of Lecluse, some distance from Chérisy (which after a summer of bombardment was little more than rubble and brickdust) paraded for a visit by the Mayor and Secretary of the Hamburg Senate. That night the battalions rotated. 3/76th Reserve Infantry came out of the front line into reserve, 1/76th moved from Lecluse to Chérisy itself, and 2/76th deployed its four companies in the dugouts of Narrow Support, each company sending one platoon forward to hold Narrow Trench. The front line itself had no dugouts, only shelter holes (called 'funk holes' by the British) and German doctrine held that in an enemy attack these could be abandoned without a direct order. This change-over was the noise heard by 8th Durhams, and by the following morning most of 76th Reserve Infantry were in their dugouts, asleep.[5]

Friday was very cold, and rain fell on and off throughout the day. That day, the next night, and on into the following morning the gunners and fire planners of 50th Division and VI Corps fought a slow, persistent, subtle war with the front line platoons of 2/76th Reserve Infantry, to prevent the gaps in the wire being repaired and the damaged machine guns and mortars being replaced. The point of the game was that the Germans must lose without ever being allowed to guess that they were playing. In the afternoon C Company of 8th Durhams retired inconspicuously from its front line trenches and let the three companies of 9th Durhams crowd in to take its place. Bradford and his men slept in the front lines that night. To keep to routine, 8th Durhams sent out night patrols, and with them went a patrol of 9th Durhams which cut a series of gaps in the British wire, clearing the way for the attack the next day.

Saturday 15 September dawned to cold, mist, drizzle and the intermittent sound of shells bursting. A light wind from the south-west drifted smoke across the German trenches. By 10am the rain had stopped and the weather was clear. At midday a staff officer arrived from division with a vital piece of equipment – a watch. He was bearing the correctly synchronised time, which was passed on down to the battalions in the trenches. The extra stretcher-bearers arrived, and 9th Durhams prepared their raiding equipment, a lighter version of their normal fighting order, without gas masks, haversacks, water bottles or entrenching tools. Each man fixed his bayonet to his rifle, discarded the scabbard, and collected two Mills bombs. In the specialist bombing section of each platoon the appointed grenade thrower carried five Mills bombs and the other members ten each. Each man of the rifle-bomber sections collected six rifle grenades. The grenade, with the bayonet, was the principal infantry weapon of trench warfare. One man in each section was given an MSK bomb (a type of smoke grenade) and sergeants and platoon commanders were given wire cutters. Except for the lead platoon in each company, the Lewis gun sections were leaving their machine guns behind as too cumbersome, and taking only their rifles.

Meanwhile, six batteries of 6-inch howitzers and one of 60-pounder field guns were preparing to fire. Once the raid started they would attempt to cordon off the area from German reinforcements with a three-sided box of shellfire for which the French word *barrage* was already common usage. The divisional artillery would provide the fourth side of the box, moving ahead of the raiders as they attacked. Other guns and trench mortars finalised their roles in the raid, as did the Engineers of 7th Field Company, strung out to the north and south of where William Rebbeck sat with his explosives and detonators. With no more that he could do, Lieutenant-Colonel Rathbone went down into the trenches to join Cameron watching the raid.

Each of the five British Armies on the Western Front had its own Royal Flying Corps brigade, III Brigade in the case of Third Army. Part of this was 12 (Air) Wing, of which 12 Squadron formed the chief reconnaissance squadron. In September 1917 the squadron was still adjusting to its new Royal Aircraft Factory RE8 aircraft, with a top speed of just under 100mph and the ability to fly safely at half that speed. Six of these aircraft were to fly as spotters for the guns during the raid, and the remainder to fly 'contact patrols', shooting at anything German in the air or on the ground. Aircraft 3767 was flown by Captain Donald F Stevenson, who had volunteered for flying from the Northamptonshire Yeomanry in November 1915. His observer was Lieutenant John Webster, who had been commissioned in April 1917. Both men already held the Military Cross. The aircraft, in addition to its forward firing Vickers and observer's Lewis machine guns, carried two 20-pound bombs beneath the wings, and an aerial reconnaissance camera mounted on its fuselage next to the observer's cockpit. At 3.20pm Stevenson and Webster took off from their airfield at Wagonlieu, west of Arras, and forty minutes later they were airborne over Narrow Trench when the raid began.[6]

Since spring 1916 each brigade of a British division had been allocated its own company of Vickers medium machine guns, and in July 1917 a fourth divisional company was added. Normally, at least half these guns would be kept as replacements for 'wasteage'. For this special event, Karslake had concentrated every gun in the division, plus more borrowed from neighbouring divisions, opposite the raiders' target. At 4pm precisely, a total of seventy Vickers machine guns, firing on high trajectory to clear their own front line, opened fire at 250 rounds a minute, their maximum sustained rate of fire. Twenty two light mortars each began to fire off one round every four seconds, their own maximum rate; two heavy mortars and eighteen mediums joined in with three rounds a minute. Cameron, watching from the trenches, would later describe this bombardment as 'perfect'. At the same time forty eight field guns and seventeen howitzers started their own fire crashing down on Narrow Trench, 'intense' fire of one round per gun per minute onto the target, while the heavy guns of VI Corps started to build their barrage: five minutes of intense fire with sixty and hundred-pound shells, mixed with smoke from 4.5-inch howitzers and Special Brigade's 4-inch smoke mortars. Even 12 Squadron joined in: flying at 800 feet, far too low for safety, Stevenson and Webster dropped their two bombs into the barrage and fired off 500 rounds in an all-too-successful attempt to attract hostile fire. Stevenson noticed that the barrage fell precisely, with no stray shells, a clearly defined and edged box of smoke and exploding metal. After two minutes the field guns lifted their fire from Narrow Trench and the line of explosions began to creep forward at a barely perceptible 100 yards a minute. At that moment, Bradford's men left their trenches and, unable to see the enemy, launched themselves into the unknown. As they did so Stevenson, flying above C Company on the right, throttled back and Webster switched on his camera. The resulting photographs show the running men as odd white flecks, throwing black shadows to the north.

As rehearsed, the plan called for the three companies to attack in half-platoon waves. Each platoon formed two widely-spaced lines, each with its commander in the centre and NCOs on the flanks. In the lead platoons the Lewis gunner stood with the commander. After the first half-platoon wave had covered fifteen yards the second, with the company second in command, left the trenches. Then, after a further ten yards, the first wave of the second platoons started, with the fourth wave a further ten yards behind them, together with the company commanders and Rebbeck's demolition men. The third platoon of each company remained in the trenches. There was no overall commander, and Bradford himself remained with the third platoons. The men advanced as best they could, sliding around the shellholes and dodging German fire. Unlike some commanders, Cameron permitted them to open fire on the approach, sacrificing maximum speed across no man's land. 'It improves our morale', he argued, 'lowers that of the enemy, and causes a certain number of casualties'.

As the men of A Company left their trenches they came at once under fire from the new German machine gun position, and scattered as they did so. The raiders had been well rehearsed for this moment. Quickly and professionally the bombers of the leading platoon worked towards the gunner, throwing grenades to blind his fire, making a few yards in a crawl. It was never established how he died, but Cameron believed that he was shot by an unnamed company officer. The men brought his machine gun back with them. Three minutes after they had left their own trenches, the Durhams were all inside Narrow Trench, having lost – as far as anyone could remember – just one casualty.

Seconds before the three companies left their trenches, at two points each half a mile to the north and south of their lines flames were seen to billow, and figures to move. Other British troops appeared above their parapets, while a barrage fell in support in front of them. Also visible to the south was the unmistakable lozenge shape of a Mark IV tank. German fire poured onto these targets. It was meant to do so: the flames came from burning straw, the figures were dummies, and the tank had been built from wood and canvas by 7th Field Company, who managed to haul it on pulleys a short distance into no man's land before it stuck.[7] The deception plan to confuse the Germans about the extent and nature of the raid had begun. As the field guns lifted their barrage the 4.5-inch howitzers switched targets and joined the 4-inch mortars firing smoke in an effort to hide the SOS flares now rising over the German trenches, a signal to their own artillery that an attack was in progress. Should this fail, there were strung out at regular intervals along the British line a number of officers, each armed with a Very pistol and 150 coloured flares. Their job was to copy any flare pattern seen over the German trenches in the hope of duplicating the SOS signal and so attracting German fire away to the flanks of the raid.

Meanwhile, two special parties, each of an officer, a Lewis gun team, two rifle bombers and two snipers, were moving to set up blocks in the trenches to cover the flanks of the raiders. Second-Lieutenant Hall, commanding one of these flanking parties, was killed during the raid. But for a few precious minutes there was no SOS barrage, and in that time the Durhams took their first objective – Narrow Trench from the Chérisy Road to its first dog-leg. For a while at least the Germans believed that they were facing a full scale assault, and 3/76th Reserve Infantry was moved up from Lecluse in case the British broke through. The first German SOS fire began to fall about four minutes after the attack started, and few of the gunners knew their exact targets. No more than twelve batteries out of twenty six joined in a bombardment described by VI Corps as 'weak and ragged', by Stevenson, flying above it, as 'thin and scattered', and even by 8th Durhams on whose trenches it was falling as 'doing considerable material but little personal damage'. There was one tragedy: a trench mortar battery on loan from 62nd (2nd West Yorkshire) Division, firing in a support trench, took a direct hit on its bomb dump, killing eight men. 'Few traces' wrote

Roland Boys Bradford. A civilian portrait taken in 1914, just before his departure for war, at the age of twenty two. Despite his military appearance, this photograph hardly hints at Bradford's remarkable abilities. His elder brother, Lieutenant-Commander George Bradford, was to be killed winning the family's second Victoria Cross on the Royal Navy's Zeebrugge Raid on 23rd April 1918.
Q 79774

the divisional CRA 'of piece or detachment could be found afterwards'. The luck of Stevenson and Webster had also run out. As they turned over the battlefield a bullet severed one of the RE8's elevator cables, which wrapped itself around the aircraft's tail. As best he could, Stevenson pointed his machine towards home and began to lose height.

As the raiders collected themselves in Narrow Trench, the second stage of the operation began. At 4.05pm the machine guns slowed their fire to one belt of 250 rounds every two minutes. Half the mortars ceased fire, the rest slowed to one round a minute for mediums and ten rounds a minute for lights. The heavy artillery switched to their own version of slow fire with one round per battery per minute onto each target, including Thermit shells fired under the supervision of Special Brigade into the smokescreen. At 4.07pm the 18-pounders, having rolled their barrage out beyond Narrow Support, ceased fire. All the time, no-one could see what was happening on the far side of no man's land. Then, at 4.18pm, two minutes before the machine guns were due to cease fire, came the first flag signal from the German trenches that the raiders were safe.

The main force of the raid had fallen on 6th Company of 2/76th Reserve Infantry, whose men in Narrow Trench had quite properly fallen back when the attack came. The Durhams raced after them, using two of Rebbeck's charges to blast away wire blocks dropped across the communication saps. Of the eight dugouts marked on the British maps only three were found to exist, while two more were uncovered of which there was no previous record. In the confusion no-one was afterwards sure if they had twelve or eleven shafts leading to the surface. Most of 6th Company had been asleep underground when the bombardment started, and its violence coupled with the speed of the Durham's advance had trapped them below the surface. While battle raged around them the infantry of two opposing armies could not fight. The MSK smoke grenades circumvented this problem. Thrown into the dugouts, they drove some men to the surface where they were taken prisoner. The other alternative open to the raiders was recorded in 7th Field Company diary: 'three of the dugouts destroyed were undoubtedly occupied by the enemy, who in two instances tried to effect their escape, but were driven down by the demolition party and escort, the charges then being placed'. This was in keeping with the raid's stated aim of killing Germans.

To the north of the Narrow Trench dog-leg other Germans, mainly from 5th Company, left their dugouts in an attempt to counter-attack into the raiders' flank. They emerged straight into the British barrage, including the Thermit shells of Special Brigade. When the smoke cleared a British pilot estimated fifty bodies lying in the open. The Durhams never knew that it had happened. Another German party tried to bomb its way up from the south but was driven off by the blocking party. Three men of 1/76th Reserve Infantry, coming from Chérisy, managed to get through the barrage but achieved little other than to be taken prisoner. At 4.30pm the British machine guns again opened fire. Taking their wounded, their dead, their trophies and their prisoners, 9th Durhams began to retire back across no man's land. After five minutes the rate of fire slowed; five more minutes and the German SOS bombardment had died away. At 4.50pm all British guns, machine guns and mortars ceased fire, as the raiders walked straight back through the trenches towards brigade reserve camp. The third platoons remained holding the line until 6.45pm when C Company of 8th Durhams relieved them. For Bradford's men the raid was over.

The pilot who had spotted the German dead around Narrow Trench was Captain Stevenson, once more airborne with Webster. Despite his lack of control Stevenson had landed safely at Wagonlieu at 4.25pm and handed over his photographs. At 4.45pm both men took off in another RE8 to resume patrol, having a near miss with three Albatros scouts. Fifteen minutes later Webster spotted a German two-seater firing signal flares in an attempt to contact the men in Narrow Support below. The RE8 attacked and the German dived away to 200 feet, falling out of control. Convinced he had a kill, Stevenson pulled up and levelled out at 1,000 feet. Then, the luck of the two men ran out again: anti-aircraft shells punctured the aircraft's fuel tank. Had there been a spark, Stevenson and Webster would have faced the First World War airmen's dilemma of jumping to death or burning to death. In the event Stevenson landed the RE8, leaking fuel, in a field about a mile north-east of Wancourt. The two fliers had been shot down twice in ninety minutes.

That evening, 9th Durhams tallied their losses: one officer and five men killed, two officers and ten men seriously wounded, three officers and eight men walking wounded who would stay with the battalion. But the roll call failed to account for two other men. Their names are not known, and their story can only be guessed from the record. The battalion listed them as missing to division, and pragmatically added them to its own list of dead. A further mystery was the fate of three German prisoners. 9th Durhams believed that they had brought back twenty five Germans, but only twenty two reached Third Army prisoner of war cages. In the confusion, anything might have happened to the missing three men: they may have been hospitalised, or escaped, or been shot, or simply have never existed. Such was the power held by his captor over a prisoner of war in his first few hours.

The raiders later guessed that they had killed seventy Germans, a figure which gained the authority of repetition higher up the command chain. The exact German losses are not known, but for all practical purposes 6th Company had ceased to exist. The men of 76th Reserve Infantry worked for three hours in the wreckage of the trenches, carrying away the wounded, burying the dead, and searching for those who had been buried alive. Watching them overhead, flying at a safe 2,000 feet, was another of 12 Squadron's RE8s. Then at 7.40pm another barrage crashed down on the remains of Narrow Trench. The British were raiding again.

This was the main contribution of C Company 8th Durhams to the Chérisy raid, and it had only one stated aim, 'to kill Germans'. The target was the northern sector of the previous raid, and the time had been picked so that the raiders could retire in darkness. The scale was smaller, but the plan nearly identical to that of the previous raid:

Zero
7.40pm   Infantry leaves trenches
           Artillery 4.5s open medium barrage
           18 pounder barrage opens

	MGs open at 1 belt per minute
	TMs medium open at gunfire [3 rounds/min]
	lights open at 15 per minute
	Heavy artillery opens slow fire
7.41pm	Dummies exposed
7.42pm	18-pounder barrage lifts and creeps at 100 per min
7.44pm	Infantry enter final objective
7.45pm	MGs slow to one belt per 2mins
	TMs cease fire
7.47pm	18-pounder barrage halts
8.05pm	Infantry commence withdrawal
	TMs open at previous rate
8.10pm	Dummies cease
8.15pm	Infantry withdrawal complete
	All covering fire ceases.

Karslake and his planners were, however, optimistic to think that they could bluff the Germans twice in one day. As soon as C Company reached the British wire the SOS barrage began to fall, 'very intense' on the British second line where again the mortar crews took casualties. Flying overhead in the fading light the British RE8 took notes of the German flare patterns, hoping to break their code. Meanwhile C Company reached Narrow Trench, defended by just five Germans, one of whom lived to be taken prisoner. Leaving one platoon to hold the trench, Captain Williams led his men down the communications saps and into Neva Lane (known to the Germans as *Recken Graben* or Heroes Trench). The Durhams claimed that they found no resistance, and followed Neva Lane to the outskirts of Chérisy itself. The German version was that 5th Company, attacking from the flank, drove the raiders out immediately. In the confusion of trench warfare both impressions may have appeared true. C Company certainly found no difficulty in withdrawing.

One of Captain Williams's men was killed in this second raid and eleven seriously wounded. Three German prisoners had been taken, but only one survived the return journey across no man's land. Two machine guns were brought back, one of which soon vanished. C Company listed twelve Germans 'definitely dead' and estimated a further ten bodies, including the occupants of a funk hole, 'five Germans who refused to come out', as Cameron wrote, 'they were left dead'. Also left behind were forty copies of a pamphlet describing the delights of being a prisoner of war in Britain. But C Company did bring back the two men missing from the previous raid. They had been wounded and had managed to hide, probably in shell holes. They were too badly injured to return to 9th Durhams, which continued to list them as dead, and were passed rapidly back to a base hospital.

Unluckily, 8th Durhams' own battalion doctor, Captain M J McNiff RAMC, was also wounded in the head by shrapnel and had to be hospitalised.[8]

The night, in trench warfare, was for reconstruction and routine. Karslake and his planners had other ideas. There is, and of course there was meant to be, something frightening about the relentless brutality to which they subjected the men in the Chérisy trenches. At 4.04am on the morning of Sunday 16 September, J Company of Special Brigade fired off its Livens projectors. These were simple tubes of metal sunk into the earth with an explosive charge at the bottom, which when detonated by an electrical contact threw into the air a sixty five pound bomb, thirty pounds of which was liquefied phosgene gas.[9] Firing in salvoes, the Livens projectors delivered 552 gas bombs onto the German trenches, only twenty of the projectors failing to fire. The British sat for ten minutes waiting for the German stretcher bearers to arrive, then for a further ten minutes every machine gun, mortar, gun and howitzer in 50th Division fired into the gas cloud. When this bombardment stopped, the Chérisy raid was over.

That evening, 8th Durhams sent out their usual patrols into no man's land. They found, on approaching Narrow Trench, that it was empty, 76th Reserve Infantry was making no attempt to hold it. This, in trench warfare, represented the ultimate low point of morale. Already, at 9.45pm on the previous day, British General Headquarters had issued a statement on the raid to the press. 'This afternoon, Durham troops successfully raided the enemy trenches west of Chérisy and captured 22 prisoners. Our casualties were slight'. At 10.35am next day a second statement announced that 'Following on their successful raid yesterday afternoon west of Chérisy our troops raided the enemy's trenches in this neighbourhood a second time last night and penetrated the German position as far as the western outskirts of Chérisy.' No mention was ever made of the final gas attack.[10]

Also on 16 September British wireless posts intercepted a German official statement on the raid, which makes an interesting contrast:

> S.E. of Arras the enemy artillery activity became intense in the afternoon. Under cover of a smoke cloud the British attacked at Chérisy on a front of 1500 metres. Tanks and flame projectors cleared the way for the assaulting troops, but our excellent resistance by artillery and machine guns broke down the attack. In those places where the enemy penetrated into our lines they were ejected in hand-to-hand fighting by our infantry. Towards evening the enemy again attacked at the same point. This undertaking also failed and they were driven back with great loss.[11]

Copies of this circulated rapidly among 50th Division staff. Lieutenant-Colonel Karslake in particular seems to have enjoyed what was a very great compliment to his deception plan.

The Chérisy raid, if unusually large and elaborate, was just one of nineteen undertaken by Third Army in September 1917 alone, and was soon forgotten. Three men of 7th Field Company, seven of 8th Durhams and eighteen of 9th Durhams received the Military Medal for their exploits in the raid, and Captain Williams received the Military Cross for his leadership of C Company. Captain Stevenson also got a bar to his Military Cross for his two flights above Chérisy. Two days after the raid Karslake left 50th Division to become GSO1 of 4th Division. In August 1918 he became GSO1 of the Tank Corps in succession to the celebrated J F C 'Boney' Fuller, and he was to retire between the wars as a lieutenant-general. In October 1917 Brigadier-General Cameron was promoted to command 49th (1st West Yorkshire) Division.

After the war he reverted to his substantive rank of lieutenant-colonel, and fulfilled his lifetime ambition of commanding 1st Cameron Highlanders. He was to retire as a major-general. On 5 October 1917, Lieutenant-Colonel Bradford was promoted to brigadier-general commanding 186th Brigade, 62nd Division, as the youngest general in the British Army. On 30 November a shell hit his headquarters and he was killed.[12]

In the British Army reorganisation of Spring 1918 9th Durhams, without the famous Bradford to protect them, were downgraded to a pioneer battalion. Major-General Wilkinson was relieved of command while on leave in Britain in February, and made Inspector-General of Musketry. William Rebbeck, who commanded the Engineer party on the raid, died in the pneumonia epidemic while still in France on 4 November 1918. Everyone else mentioned is believed to have survived the war, including Stevenson and Webster. The Chérisy raid was too small, and too normal, a part of the Western Front to have any lasting consequences.

Notes

An early version of this paper was written in 1983 while I was employed as a Research Assistant in the Department of Information Retrieval, Imperial War Museum, and delivered to a meeting of the British Commission for Military History at the Museum in January 1984. I would like to thank Michael J Willis of the Department of Photographs for first pointing out to me the existence of the Chérisy photographs, and Roger Smither, Keeper of the Department of Information Retrieval, for granting me the time to conduct the research.

A different version of the paper was delivered in September 1984 at the DLI Museum in Durham. Although there were no records in the archives of a survivor or eyewitness account of the Chérisy raid, I found that sitting in the audience was George Cole, a Signaller from 250 Brigade, 50th Division, who had acted as a messenger between Bradford and the Artillery on 14 and 15 September when twenty years old. I would like to thank Mr Cole for writing a short account of his experiences of the raid, and Stephen Shannon, Military Assistant at the DLI Museum, for providing me with a copy and arranging the original talk.

For this version of the paper certain personal details of the officers involved, all of whom are long since dead, have been provided by the Ministry of Defence Departmental Records. I am most grateful to James Oliver, the Record Officer, and to J E Kelly, the Head of CS(Records)2 for providing this information.

The main sources for the Chérisy raid are the after-action reports written at battalion, brigade and divisional level and all kept in the Public Record Office, Kew, London. The relevant papers can be found in:

WO95 2840 War Diary 9th DLI April 1915–January 1918
WO95 2841 War Diary 8th DLI April 1915–September 1917
WO95 2839 War Diary HQ 151st Brigade September 1917
WO95 2810 War Diary 50th Div GS April–December 1917
WO95 2814 War Diary 50th Div CRA January 1917–June 1919
WO95 2821 War Diary 7th Field Coy RE May 1915–May 1919
WO95 366 War Diary 3rd Army GS September–October 1917
WO95 771 War Diary VI Corps GS June–September 1917
WO95 785 War Diary VI Corps CHA July–September 1917

These files contain several duplicate documents, notably of the comprehensive report on the raid written by Brigadier-General Cameron. Rather than cite them all for each point of fact, I have footnoted below only those facts which come from other sources.

1. Details of 76th Reserve Infantry in summer and autumn 1917 can be found in its regimental history, Gropp, H, *Hanseaten im Kampf*, (Klindworth & Neuenhausen, Hamburg, nd), pp 250–253.

2. PRO WO95 2820 War Diary 250 Bde RFA (50th Div) January 1917–June 1919, entry for the week ending 15/16 September 1917.

3. For the work of the Special Brigade see C H Foulkes, *'Gas!' The Story of the Special Brigade*, (Blackwood, London, 1934). There is no specific reference to the Chérisy raid in this book.

4. Trench Map 1:10,000 51B SW2 Vis-en-Artois, Edition 6A Correct To 30 August 1917. A copy is held by the Department of Printed Books, Imperial War Museum. The area of the Chérisy raid is Square O.

5. Gropp, op cit, p 252.

6. The source for Stevenson and Webster's two flights on 15 September 1917 is PRO AIR1 2240/209/42/9 War Diary III Bde RFC September 1917, and AIR1 1515/204/58/50 III Bde RFC and RAF Recommendations for Honours and Awards II March 1916–1 April 1918.

7. G Cole's personal narrative is the only source for the mention of burning straw to create smoke and flames in the raid.

8. PRO WO95 2815 War Diary Assist Div Medical Services 50th Div April 1915–June 1919, entry for 15 September 1917.

9. For details of the Livens projector and its use see Foulkes, op cit, pp 159–173 and pp 206–207.

10. The London Times, 8C 17 September 1917.

11. This particular translation of the German statement can be found in PRO WO95 2823 War Diary 245 MG Coy 50th Div July 1917–March 1918, 'Intelligence Summary No. 102' by 50th Division staff. A slightly different translation appears in the Papers of Lieutenant-General Henry Karslake, Department of Documents (pending boxes 314–317). This is the only reference to the Chérisy raid in the Karslake papers.

12. Shortly after the end of the First World War the rank of Brigadier-General was downgraded in the British Army first to Colonel-Commandant and then to Brigadier, as the highest of the field ranks rather than the lowest of the general ranks. No other nation observes this convention, but because of it Bradford's record is unlikely ever to be surpassed.

The loss of HMS *Hood*, 24 May 1941

Paul J Kemp

Paul Kemp is Head of Public Services in the Department of Photographs, and was formerly Schools Officer on board HMS *Belfast* 1981–1983.

In the years between the two World Wars the strength of the Royal Navy was symbolised by the battle-cruiser HMS *Hood*. She was built in 1918 by J Brown Ship-builders Clydebank and was certainly one of the finest looking capital ships built by any navy. In 1920 she joined the fleet as flagship of the Battlecruiser Force: a position she would hold for most of her life and from 1923 to 1924 participated in the famous World Cruise, to the Far East, Australia, the United States. She remained with the Home and Atlantic Fleets until 1936 when she joined the Mediterranean Fleet and saw service on the Non-Intervention patrols during the Spanish Civil War. The beginning of the Second World War found *Hood* working with the Home Fleet in the North Sea. She was detached to join Force H at Gibraltar and took part in the tragic action against the French Fleet at Mers-el-Kebir in June 1940 before returning to the UK for a short refit.

HMS *Hood* enjoyed what would now be known as a 'high profile' and the press were fond of endowing *Hood* with superlative qualities not always justified – and thus she was known to the public as the 'Mighty *Hood*'. Small wonder then, that the news of her destruction after an eight minute engagement with the German battleship *Bismarck* on 24 May 1941 was received with shock and disbelief throughout the country.

Her opponent was the 42,000 ton German battle-ship *Bismarck*, built in 1939 by Blohm and Voss: the first of a fleet of capital ships projected under Admiral Raeder's 'Z' plan. Although the brunt of the Battle of the Atlantic was borne by the U-boat arm of the German Navy there was still a role for the heavy units of the surface fleet. The exploits of the *Admiral Scheer*, *Admiral Hipper*, *Scharnhorst* and *Gneisenau* had shown that, under favourable conditions, convoys could be attacked with success. The stumbling block lay in the battleship escorts which the Royal Navy was allocating to convoys. Such an escort, HMS *Ramillies*, had caused *Scharn-horst* and *Gneisenau* to abandon their attack on convoy HX 106 on 8 February 1941. *Bismarck*'s role would be to deal with such escorts while her consorts despatched the merchant ships.

Such was the genesis of Operation 'Rhine': a commerce raiding foray into the North Atlantic in which *Bismarck* would be accompanied by the cruiser *Prinz Eugen* and joined by the *Scharnhorst* and *Gneisenau* which were lying at Brest in occupied France. But it was not to be: *Scharnhorst* was in need of a refit and *Gneisenau* was torpedoed and seriously damaged on 6 April 1941 in a daring attack for which Flying Officer K Campbell of 22 Squadron RAF was posthumously awarded the Victoria Cross. Thus it was *Bismarck* and *Prinz Eugen* alone which set out on operation 'Rhine'.

Bismarck (Kapitän zur See Ernst Lindemann) Admiral Gunther Lutjens, the flagship of and her cruiser escort *Prinz Eugen* (Kapitän zur See Helmuth Brinckmann) had departed from Gdynia on 18 May and on the morning of 24 May both German ships were heading south west through the Denmark Strait between Iceland and Greenland. A report of their departure from the British naval attaché in Sweden was confirmed by RAF air reconnaissance of Bergen in Norway, where Lutjens had stopped to fuel, which showed the two German ships lying at anchor. But the first contact was not made until 23 May when the cruisers *Suffolk* and *Norfolk* on routine patrol in the Denmark Strait sighted the *Bismarck* and, despite being fired on, remained in contact transmitting reports *Bismarck*'s course and speed.

HMS *Hood* (Captain R Kerr CBE RN – flag Vice Admiral Launcelot Holland) and HMS *Prince of Wales* (Captain J C Leach RN) together with six destroyers had left Scapa Flow on 22 May and were speeding north to intercept the *Bismarck*. On the face of it Holland's two ships had an advantage in firepower since *Hood* was armed with eight 15 inch guns and *Prince of Wales* with ten 14 inch guns. *Bismarck* carried eight 38cm guns but was escorted by the *Prinz Eugen* armed with only eight 24cm guns. However, the two German ships were new and had trained extensively together in the Baltic whereas the *Hood* had recently emerged from a refit and had not had the chance to complete a work-up. *Prince of Wales* was in an equally poor condition: she had only recently been handed over by her builders and there were still technicians from Vickers Armstrong onboard making final adjustments to the main armament. It was clear to Holland, on the basis of information coming from *Suffolk* and *Norfolk*, that he was in a good position to be able to intercept the *Bismarck* soon after dawn on 24 May, but during the night of 23/24 May the cruisers lost contact. The Royal Navy's experience of German tactics in the Atlantic had shown that the Germans were masters at the art of evasion and accordingly Holland changed to a northerly course on the assumption that Lutjens might be proceeding south east in order to shake off the shadowing cruisers. In the event Lutjens held on to his westerly course and Holland's manoeuvres had the unfortunate effect of causing him to lose bearing on the enemy or, in less technical terms, to fall behind.[1]

At 0256 contact was regained by *Suffolk* and at 0535 *Bismarck* was sighted by *Prince of Wales* some 17 miles off her starboard bow. At 0537 *Prince of Wales* took station on *Hood*'s starboard quarter and both ships made an alteration to course to starboard. As a result Holland's two ships were now approaching *Bismarck* practically head-on: a decision which has earned Admiral Holland the most savage criticism from professional and armchair historians alike. Yet in reality there was little else he could do. At the range at which

HMS *Hood* at anchor at Spithead in May 1937 for the Coronation Naval Review. This was the image of the ship most familiar to the British public who named her 'The Mighty *Hood*'. DS 595/18

Bismarck works up in Kiel Bay in late 1940 during her acceptance trials. HU 7925

The engagement off Iceland: 24 May 1941. The photograph, taken from *Prinz Eugen*, shows *Bismarck*'s C and D turrets firing at *Hood*. HU 381. Collection of Korvetten Kapitän Paul Schmallenbach.

The last known photograph of HMS *Hood* taken from behind the barbette for B turret onboard HMS *Prince of Wales*. Seconds later HMS *Hood* blew up. HU 50190

the engagement began *Hood* was acutely vulnerable to plunging shellfire from *Bismarck*'s main armament. It was imperative therefore to close the range so that should *Hood* receive a hit it should be on her stoutly protected sides rather than her thinly protected decks. Correct though Holland's decision was, it gave away the tactical advantage which he initially possessed, since the turn to starboard allowed the German ships to pass ahead. Holland was now committed to a stern chase instead of being able to cut them off. Holland was further hampered in that *Hood*'s two after 15 inch turrets and *Prince of Wales*'s after 14 inch turret would not bear on the target because of the angle of approach: he was denied the use of over half his armament.

Holland had ordered fire to be concentrated on the leading German ship assuming that *Bismarck* would be in the lead. Lutjens, however, had ordered the *Prinz Eugen* to go ahead and, while the British ships were firing at her, *Bismarck* was left undisturbed to engage the *Hood*. There is evidence that the mistake was realised in *Hood* and that Holland gave the order to 'shift target right' but it is not known whether or not the order was received by *Hood*'s gunnery team. The mistake was realised almost immediately in *Prince of Wales* which shifted target right to engage *Bismarck*.

Hood was the first to fire at 0552 with *Bismarck*'s first salvo following shortly afterwards. Gunnery conditions were not ideal for the two British ships particularly for the *Hood*. The speed at which the great ship was travelling made accurate ranging difficult and the spray which was sheeting over her bows cannot have made things any easier. *Prince of Wales* was equipped with a Type 284 gunnery radar but Admiral Holland had forbidden its use on the grounds that the transmissions would be picked up by the Germans. *Bismarck* and *Prinz Eugen* were shooting superbly, aided by their excellent stereoscopic rangefinders which made target acquisition very simple. *Bismarck*'s first salvo fell short, the second went over, the third straddled the *Hood* and the fourth was a close short. *Prinz Eugen* was also shooting well and a 24cm shell from her second salvo struck the *Hood* on the boat deck by the mainmast causing a fire among the RU (ready use) 4 inch ammunition and URP rockets stowed there, which burned with a vivid pink glow clearly discernible in the German ships.

At 0555 Holland ordered the first of two turns to port which would allow him to open his A arcs and bring the after turrets to bear. The signal for the second turn was flying when *Bismarck*'s fifth salvo arrived and the *Hood* was rent in two by an enormous explosion. The forward part of the ship reared up to the vertical before sinking while the after part remained afloat for some three minutes shrouded in smoke. Of her ship's company of 95 officers and 1324 men only Midshipman William Dundas, Able Seaman Ted Briggs

Able Seaman Robert Tillburn, one of only three survivors from HMS *Hood*, on leave in England after the battle. HU 50191

Vice Admiral Geoffrey Blake who chaired the first and unsatisfactory Board of Enquiry. A 17048

Rear Admiral H T C Walker who was responsible for the second, more comprehensive report. The photograph was taken in 1945 by which time Walker had been promoted Vice Admiral. A 30995

and Able Seaman Robert Tillburn survived. The three spent nearly two hours in the water before being rescued by HMS *Electra*.

That so few survived was because of the extraordinary violence of the explosion and the speed with which the forward portion of the ship sank: those below decks would not have had time to get out. Of those on the upper deck many would have been killed by the fire and subsequent explosions among the RU 4 inch ammunition. Others may have been able to abandon the sinking ship but may have drowned or succumbed to hypothermia. Of the three survivors Able Seaman Briggs got out of the bridge through the door onto the starboard bridge wing; his last sight was that of Admiral Holland slumped in his chair. Midshipman Dundas, who was also on the bridge, escaped by kicking through one of the windows. Able Seaman Tillburn, who was manning one of the 4 inch guns on the port side, simply walked off the ship's side into the sea: a remarkable escape.[2]

Those who observed *Hood's* apocalyptic end recorded a variety of impressions. Captain Leach in *Prince of Wales* saw *Bismarck's* fifth salvo fall and judged that two of the four shells fell short and one over but that something 'had arrived onboard *Hood'*.[3] He then described the explosion as:

> . . . a very fierce upward rush of flame in the shape of a funnel . . . almost immediately the ship was enveloped in smoke.[4]

Leading Seaman Winston Littlewood in *Suffolk* saw '. . . a huge orange pillar of sparks going up into the air and clouds of black smoke'[5] while Captain Phillips in Norfolk saw 'a ball of fire . . . brilliant yellow'.[6] To others the explosion was surprisingly anticlimactic. Lieutenant Esmond Knight RNVR in one of *Prince of Wales's* air defence positions recalled:

> I remember listening for it and thinking it would be a most tremendous explosion, but I don't remember hearing an explosion at all.[7]

The three survivors did not recall anything in the way of an explosion. All three were aware of the fire on the boat deck and the roar of the exploding ammunition. Briggs then remembered:

> . . . a blinding flash which swept around the outside of the compass platform . . . she listed slowly, almost hesitatingly to starboard. She stopped after ten degrees when I heard the helmsman's voice shouting up the voicepipe to the OOW 'steering's gone, Sir!'[8]

There followed what Briggs later described as 'a sudden, horrifying cant to port'[9] which went on until she reached an angle of 45° by which time it was clear she would not recover.

To Able Seaman Tillburn taking cover on *Hood's* boat deck, the explosion was barely noticeable. He did not recall any blast but rather a noise similar to the main armament being fired.[10] To the German observers in *Bismarck* and *Prinz Eugen* watching through rangefinders and binoculars the explosion was unnerving. *Bismarck's* gunnery officer, Korvetten Kapitän Adalbert Schneider, saw the fifth salvo fall and said, 'Wow! was that a misfire? That really ate into him.'[11] Korvetten Käpitan Wolf Neuendorf, the navigating officer, saw *Hood* 'split in two'.[12] Leutnant zur See Burkhard von Mullenheim-Rechberg in the after gunnery control position recalled:

> At first the *Hood* was nowhere to be seen, in her place was a colossal pillar of black smoke reaching up into the sky . . . I saw the bow of the battlecruiser projecting upwards at an angle.[13]

News of *Hood's* loss stunned the Navy: many officers recalled decoding the Admiralty signal again and again in the sure belief that there had been a mistake. The Admiralty was quick to respond to her loss. A communiqué was issued at 9pm on 24 May which baldly stated that the *Hood* 'had received an unlucky hit in the magazine and blew up' and added that 'it is feared that there will be few survivors from HMS *Hood*.' On 28 May Admiral Sir Dudley Pound, the First Sea Lord, ordered an enquiry to be set up under the chairmanship of Vice Admiral Sir Geoffrey Blake.

The Blake enquiry submitted their report on 2 June – only nine days after *Hood's* loss. The report consisted of two typewritten pages of conclusions which found that:

> . . . a 15 inch shell fired from *Bismarck* at the range and inclination of the fatal fifth salvo could, if lucky, and possessing sufficient delay, reach the after magazines.[14]

The report then appeared to contradict itself by claiming:

> It is extremely difficult to associate the observed fact with the explosion of the 4 inch magazines the forward bulkhead of which is 64′ aft of the mainmast.[15]

Since there was evidently some doubt as to what

HMS *Hood* blows up. A photograph taken from the *Prinz Eugen* shows a vast cloud of black smoke marking where the battlecruiser exploded. The smaller column of smoke on the left of the photograph is from the guns of HMS *Prince of Wales*. HU 385: Collection of Korvetten Kapitän Paul Schmallenbach.

The port side of HMS *Hood* photographed in 1940 showing on the right the doors for the above water torpedo tubes commonly associated with the cause of the explosion. A 180

Three days later the tables were turned: survivors from the *Bismarck* in the water alongside HMS *Dorsetshire* as they wait to be picked up. ZZZ 3130C

had caused the explosion the Board raised the possibility that one of *Hood*'s four 21 inch torpedoes kept on the upper deck might have exploded either as a result of a hit from a 24cm shell fired by *Prinz Eugen* or from one of the 38cm shells in *Bismarck*'s fifth salvo. Such an explosion may have broken the ship's back resulting in 'rapid foundering'.[16]

There was considerable dissatisfaction at the Admiralty with the report. Vice Admiral Tom Phillips, the Vice Chief of the Naval Staff, noted on 18 July:

> . . . the report as rendered by this board does not give me confidence that a searching enquiry has been carried out: in particular the failure to record the evidence of the various witnesses of the event strikes me as quite extraordinary. I also note that of the three survivors from *Hood* only one was interviewed. This strikes me as quite remarkable.[17]

Phillips proposed a second enquiry, under the chairmanship of Rear Admiral H T C Walker, which met in August and presented its report on 12 September 1941. A total of 176 witnesses gave evidence including 71 from HMS *Prince of Wales*, 89 from HMS *Suffolk*, 14 from HMS *Norfolk* and the two survivors from *Hood* who had not given evidence already. The Board also heard evidence from specialist officers in the various technical divisions of the Admiralty with an interest in discovering what had happened.

The findings of the second board were not so very different from the first. The report concluded that:

> The sinking of the *Hood* was due to a hit from *Bismarck*'s 15 inch in or adjacent to *Hood*'s 4″ or 15″ magazines causing them all to explode and wreck the after part of the ship.[18]

The Board rejected the explosion of a 21 inch (53cm) torpedo explosion as a cause of *Hood*'s loss together with fire on the boat deck.

So what had happened to the *Hood*? This article does not set out to provide a definitive answer but rather to take a fresh look at the evidence. There are two theories as to the cause of the explosion: firstly that one or more of *Hood*'s 21 inch torpedoes exploded causing a massive structural failure; secondly that a 38cm shell exploded inside or adjacent to one of the after magazines causing an explosion which tore the ship apart. A number of other theories have also been proposed, namely failure of anti-flash interlocks in the turret trunks, but these can be discounted for lack of corroborative evidence.[19]

Hood carried two above-water torpedo tubes on

each side of the ship. A total of eight 21 inch torpedoes were carried; each torpedo was armed with a warhead containing 500lbs of TNT. The torpedoes were a doubtful feature of the design and many naval officers argued for their removal on the grounds that there would be few tactical situations in which *Hood* could usefully employ these weapons.

That the torpedoes were the cause of the explosion was proposed by members of both Boards but the strongest supporter of this theory was Sir Stanley Goodall, the Director of Naval Construction. In a dissenting opinion to the findings of the second Board Goodall wrote:

> If one or more shells from the fifth salvo burst in this devastated area (where the fire was already burning) where there are eight torpedo warheads, four each side, each containing 500lbs TNT, at the base of the mainmast and if one or more of these warheads detonated the result would be an explosion where it was actually observed. Such an explosion would break the ship's back already weakened in this neighbourhood by the earlier damage.[20]

Yet Goodall was probably wrong. The Board had considered this question in great detail and sought the advice of many torpedo experts. Their conclusions, based on pre-war experience, were that a hit from either a 38cm or a 24cm shell on *Hood*'s side abreast the torpedo tubes would not detonate the warhead. Likewise if a shell struck the torpedo but did not detonate, the torpedo would not explode. The only situation in which one of the torpedoes would have detonated would be if a shell hit the warhead and exploded. Assuming such an event took place the force of the explosion would have been directed along the deck and upwards rather than downwards to tear the ship apart.

Magazine detonation as a result of a 38cm shell penetrating the armour is a more likely cause which raises the vexed subject of the efficiency of *Hood*'s armour protection. While *Hood* was under construction, work was suspended to allow an additional 3450 tons of armour to be worked into her hull as a result of lessons learned at the Battle of Jutland (31 May 1916). The addition represented a substantial improvement but *Hood*'s protection was, at best, marginal. Several schemes existed to improve this state of affairs, but by the time of her loss the ship had served for 21 years without a major refit.

Hood was protected along her sides by an armoured belt in three sections. The upper section was 127mm thick, the middle 178mm and the bottom 305mm thick.[21] Her deck protection was less extensive, ranging from 32mm to 48mm on individual decks but a total thickness of 161mm. The armour scheme gave *Hood* an immune zone – the area from the target inside of which penetration of the belt may occur and outside of which deck penetration is possible – from 22,500 yards to 29,500 yards: ie 7,000 yards. At 0552 when *Hood* opened fire the range was 25,000 yards: just inside the edge of the immune zone.

There were three ways in which a shell could have pierced the armour belt. First by passing over the belt and plunging through the thinly protected deck to explode inside the magazine; secondly by striking the belt itself and penetrating to explode inside the ship and thirdly that a 38cm shell fell slightly short of *Hood*, travelled some distance underwater, penetrated the hull beneath the belt and detonated inside the ship.

The first case can be easily discounted since the angle of fall of the shells in *Bismarck*'s fifth salvo was not steep enough to penetrate the deck: for plunging shellfire to be effective the range would have to be in excess of 29,500 yards. Outright penetration of the belt is possible given the range at which the action took place and *Hood*'s angle of inclination to *Bismarck*. However the angle at which such a shell would have struck the *Hood* would render an outright penetration unlikely. The third case is the most probable.

A 15 inch shell falling at an angle of between 10.5° and 13.9° and landing short, could have penetrated the hull beneath the belt. Providing the fuse was not rendered useless by the impact with the water the point of detonation would have been in the area of the after magazines.[22]

Assuming that such a penetration took place what would have been the result of such a hit? Pre-war experiments showed that 15 inch APC shell were practically immune to sympathetic detonation. However the cordite propellant was not as stable. The Royal Navy used a double-based cordite containing a substantial amount of nitroglycerine which tests had shown was extremely susceptible to ignition in certain circumstances.[23]

If a 38cm shell from *Bismarck*'s fifth salvo was the cause of the explosion then there are certain inconsistencies with what was actually observed of *Hood*'s end. First, most observers recalled that the explosion was essentially noiseless, yet magazine explosions are characterised by a terrific bang.[24] Secondly there was a small delay between the fall of the fatal salvo and the explosion: ammunition explosions are fairly instantaneous. Thirdly the explosion was observed by most witnesses (42% of those interviewed by the second Board of Enquiry) to have occurred around the mainmast. If magazine detonation was the cause of the explosion, and there is no other credible alternative, the problem arises that there is no magazine in this area: the nearest being the 4 inch located some 64′ aft of the mainmast.

These three factors all indicate that it was most

likely the rapid uncontrolled burning of cordite propellant which caused *Hood*'s loss rather than the explosion of her shells or torpedoes. The detonation of a 38cm shell near the two after 15 inch and four 4 inch magazines containing approximately 115 tons of cordite would result in the ignition of the propellant causing a build-up of gas. For a while the gas would have been contained by the magazine structure – hence the delay between the fall of shot and the explosion – but when pressure became too great it would have taken the line of least resistance and burst forward, blowing out the bulkhead into the engine room before venting upwards through the exhaust vents located on the upper deck immediately fore and aft of the mainmast. Although the venting of the gas into the machinery space and out through the exhaust vents would have relieved the pressure somewhat, it would not be sufficient to prevent the cordite fire from tearing the *Hood* apart. To those watching from *Prince of Wales*, *Norfolk*, *Suffolk*, *Bismarck* and *Prince Eugen* the explosion would have been visible as the appearance of spectacular jets of flame around the base of the mainmast.[25]

Three days later, on 27 May, the *Bismarck* was sunk. After being disabled by a 14 inch shell hit from *Prince of Wales* and aircraft torpedoes she was finished off by the big guns of the battleships HMS *King George V* and HMS *Rodney*. Of her ship's company in excess of 2,200 only 115 survived to become prisoners of war. Ernst Lindemann, her one and only commanding officer, was last seen walking on the upturned forecastle of his ship just before she sank. Neither he nor Admiral Lutjens survived.

The true cause of the loss of HMS *Hood* will never be known and this article can be little more than an attempt to supply a possible explanation. It is technically possible for her wreck to be located and filmed using similar means as were employed to find the wreck of the *Titanic*. Such an operation would probably yield little in the way of new knowledge since what was left of her hull could well have broken up on impact with the sea bottom and in any case would be an affront to the relatives of those who lost their lives onboard. One thing, however, is certain: HMS *Hood* and the story of her brief and violent last engagement will continue to fascinate historians for generations to come.

Notes

1. See S W Roskill, *The War at Sea*, vol 1, HMSO, London 1954 for a good general account of the *Bismarck* action.
2. A Coles and Ted Briggs, *Flagship Hood: The Fate of Britain's Mightiest Warship*, Robert Hale, London, 1985, pp 219–220.
3. Evidence of Captain J C Leach RN in PRO ADM116/4351, p 198. Case 6762 the Loss of HMS *Hood* in action with the German battleship in the North Atlantic on 24 May 1941.
4. Ibid.
5. Ibid, Winston Littlewood, p 191.
6. Ibid, Comment on the action by Captain A J Phillips RN of HMS *Norfolk*, p 44.
7. Ludovic Kennedy, *Pursuit: the sinking of the Bismarck*, Collins, 1974, p 87.
8. Coles and Briggs, op cit, pp 215–216.
9. Coles and Briggs, op cit, p 215.
10. PRO ADM116/4351.
11. Baron Burkhard von Mullenheim-Rechberg, *Battleship Bismarck: A Survivor's Story*, USNI Press, 1980, pp 110–111.
12. Ibid, p 109.
13. Ibid, p 109.
14. PRO ADM116/4351 pp 6–7.
15. Ibid, pp 6–7.
16. Ibid, pp 6–7.
17. Minute by VCNS, PRO ADM116/4351, pp 10–11.
18. Ibid, pp 89–108.
19. W J Jurens, 'The Loss of HMS *Hood*: A Technical Re-Examination', *Warship International* No 2, 1987, pp 154–155. This article is required reading for anyone interested in the cause of *Hood*'s loss.
20. A Raven and J Roberts, *British Battleships of WW2*, USNI Press, 1976, pp 350–351.
21. See John Roberts, *Anatomy of the Ship: The Battlecruiser HMS Hood*, USNI Press, 1982 for full details of *Hood*'s armour protection.
22. Jurens, op cit, pp 146–147.
23. Ibid, pp 151–152.
24. HM Ships *Vanguard*, *Bulwark* and *Natal* were all lost during the First World War as a result of magazine explosions. A common factor in the accounts of the various witnesses was the noise of the explosion.
25. Jurens, op cit, pp 155-156.

The Ministry of Information and documentary film, 1939–45

Clive Coultass

Clive Coultass is Senior Keeper and Keeper of Audio-Visual Records. Previous appointments include that of Senior Lecturer in History at James Graham College, Leeds, 1962–1969, Keeper of Film Programming (IWM) 1969–1970 and Keeper of the Department of Film (IWM) 1970–1983.

The 'documentary film movement' has been acclaimed as one of the finest achievements of British cinema by film historians, who see it as having reached its peak during the Second World War. It is perceived to be the model on which the subsequent and peculiarly British tradition of realistic film-making in both cinema and television was based. The term 'documentary' itself was invented by John Grierson for a non-fictional film which would describe (or 'document') some aspect of real life. Moreover, the documentary would be both informative and educational. Grierson first deployed his single-minded and moralistic ideals through the medium of the Empire Marketing Board Film Unit, started in 1928, and then five years later with its successor, the GPO Film Unit. In fact there had been earlier documentaries, the War Office's First World War campaign films and some instructional productions from the twenties, but film historians have tended to neglect these and to identify the British documentary school as beginning with Grierson.

The officially-financed GPO Film Unit soon found imitators in the independent sector: companies like Realist, Strand and Verity, and one notable commercial sponsor, Shell, which created its own film unit for publicity purposes. The diverse aims of these organisations may call into question the designation 'movement' but there was at least a common sense of style and also an attempt, through a body called Film Centre, to coordinate the work of the documentary film-makers. However, by the end of the thirties there had emerged two distinctive kinds of production, especially in the work of the GPO Film Unit: one which was purely narrative and another which was dramatised, with a re-enactment of real events, though without the use of professional actors.[1] This latter development is a significant one (though far from unique in the general history of documentary film[2]) but it was rooted in the same Grierson-inspired precepts of the depiction of actual people in their genuine living and working environments.

It was this well-established group of film-makers which was responsible, under the direction of the Ministry of Information (MOI), for the large body of documentary films produced for propaganda purposes during the war. Film historians have recognised their importance, even if they have concentrated perhaps too narrowly on the work of a few outstanding personalities (Jennings, Watt, Rotha, for example[3]). But conventional historians with media interests have more recently turned away from the documentaries in favour of commercial feature films and newsreels which, they contend, were seen by greater audiences and which more accurately reflected wartime public tastes. The documentary film-makers, the argument goes, were anyway public school-educated élitists who, in spite of holding the left-wing ideological beliefs common to many intellectuals in the thirties, were too distanced from common humanity and did not have that ready perception of the needs of mass audiences which characterised the approach of the entrepreneurs of the commercial film industry. The first head of the MOI's Films Division, Sir Joseph Ball, had been responsible before the war for the Conservative Party's film propaganda and he had no intention, so it is now believed, of employing the documentary film-makers.[4] The GPO Film Unit was to be deliberately excluded, an act of policy which seems also to have impressed some of the film-makers themselves.[5] Moreover, it was only following major changes within the MOI (and the British government) in 1940 that the documentary group was able to establish itself firmly as the centrepiece of film propaganda in the ministry.

It is certainly true that a planning committee of the MOI, set up just before the outbreak of war to provide a scheme for the use of film, had highlighted the newsreel as likely to be the most effective instrument for propaganda. It also expressed the hope that there would be some support for the feature film industry. However, this was not all; clearly there would be accommodation for the documentary and in fact the GPO Film Unit was to form the nucleus of the Films Division's organisation for production and distribution. The committee even set down an idea for a 'reassurance' film – the concept in itself is a first statement of documentary propaganda policy – which might be called *Britain Is Ready*. The suggested content, including nostalgic use of idealised pastoral and urban scenes, was a blueprint for what indeed became some of the principal themes to be exploited by wartime film-makers. Its culmination would be a demonstration of strength, illustrated in particular by sequences of Britain's traditional bulwark, the fleet at sea.[6]

But this film was never made. What people feared the most at this time was an assault from the air. The GPO Film Unit was employed instead by the Home Office to make a film about civilian precautions in the event of mass raids. It was titled *If War Should Come* and it was finished within a week of the start of production. Approximately a third of the planned two thousand prints had been struck when hostilities began. Cinemas were temporarily closed by the government in a panic move to prevent large groups of people assembling in places where they might be bombed. After a few days, though, the MOI, far from ignoring the GPO Film Unit, asked it to continue production of the film but to amend it slightly and retitle it *Do It Now*. All production and distribution costs were paid by the ministry and when the cinemas soon reopened two thousand of them throughout Britain showed the film in the week beginning 18 September 1939.[7]

'Reassurance' propaganda was hastily trans-ferred to Alexander Korda's long commercial film *The Lion Has Wings*. It was convenient to do so because it had been planned before the war as a means of persuading the British people that the RAF could defend them and Korda had already sought official assistance. After the start of hostilities he added a lengthy didactic opening, a eulogy of Britain's democracy and way of life, contrasted with the evils of fascism. Although Ian Dalrymple's script was patronising in manner, the section was more skilfully constructed than much of the rest of this rambling production. The MOI provided no funds for it but gave such general support that Korda's company, London Films, handed over a percentage of profits to the government. Official encouragement also led to the GPO Film Unit supplying footage of armaments factories for inclusion in the film.

The real reason for the GPO Film Unit not being handed over to the MOI in September 1939 was that the Post Office itself wished to keep control of it. It was agreed, though, that the ministry would have first call on its services. A complicated financial arrangement was worked out whereby the GPO would charge against the MOI's Vote the whole cost of the unit's working – salaries, accommodation, materials and so forth.[8] In order to strengthen the relationship, two Post Office officials were transferred to the MOI Films Division: C E G Forbes as Deputy Director with executive responsibility for the film unit, and A G Highet as administrator for documentaries. It was Forbes who pointed out to Ball, five days after the start of the war, that the GPO Film Unit had drawn up a plan for a production about the reactions of Londoners to the new war situation.[9] Ball agreed that such a film might make good propaganda abroad and instantly released the funds for the two-reel project which became titled *The First Days*.[10]

Ball's prejudices did undoubtedly favour the commercial industry but his efforts in that direction had little effect. His main objective, to provide short-term finance for feature film production, came to nothing; it was even opposed in Parliament by Lord Strabolgi who thought that the Board of Trade was the more appropriate body to deal with such affairs. An internal Films Division report in November commented on the 'vacillation and uncertainty throughout the film industry' caused by the government's attitude.[11] Moreover, three 'careless talk' films commissioned from Michael Balcon's Ealing Studios turned out to be almost wholly inept. By contrast, over the winter the GPO Film Unit produced two notable dramatised documentaries, *Squadron 992* and *Men of the Lightship*. The second of these films was directed by David MacDonald who was a product of the commercial industry but who came into line immediately with the documentary movement's principles when Alberto Cavalcanti, head of the GPO Film Unit, stipulated that real seamen, not actors, should be used in this propaganda piece about Nazi atrocities against British lightships. The sinking of the East Dudgeon lightship in February 1940 had prompted the MOI's Policy Committee to make as much out of the incident as possible.[12] Again, there seems to be little substance in the view that the GPO Film Unit was not being employed by the ministry, even though it undoubtedly had the capacity at the time to do more. The competence which it had demonstrated so far was not lost on Balcon, a member of the industry who was most anxious to give support to the war effort.

Ball had been removed and replaced in the New Year by Sir Kenneth Clark, Director of the National Gallery, and the Films Division initiated a new programme for the production of documentaries, not all of which came to fruition. The Treasury, which had found the existing arrangements too cumbersome, suggested that the MOI should now formally take over the GPO Film Unit, a measure which proceeded on 1 April, with the proviso that the unit should be handed back to the Post Office after the war if they wanted it.[13] Another Films Division report gave an outline of proposed propaganda policy, breaking it down into three basic themes: what Britain is fighting for, how Britain fights, and the need for sacrifices if the fight is to be won. There were a number of suggestions for the treatment of these topics in feature films. Even more significantly, there was criticism of the existing arrangements concerning the five competing newsreel companies; it was argued that the MOI should play a stronger role in directing their aims. For documentaries, the primary role would be informational; these films could demonstrate to Britain, to her allies and to the neutrals how the British war effort was working in specific areas, mainly the fighting services and various groups of workers. Overall, the document postulated a considerable degree of interventionism in film affairs, even though it emphasised the need to keep propaganda discreet: 'film propaganda will be most effective when it is least recognisable as such.'[14] One of Clark's major steps was to provide funds for the feature *49th Parallel*, a story of a handful of survivors from a sunken U-boat who try to escape from Canada. The film was meant to influence opinion in the USA against the Nazis.

Nevertheless, continuing criticism of the MOI for what was held to be an absence of a clear and effective policy led to more administrative changes in the spring and summer of 1940 (though it was to be a further year before the only truly successful Minister of Information, Brendan Bracken, was appointed). Clark was succeeded on 22 April by Jack Beddington, Assistant General Manager of Shell, who had been responsible for a vigorous advertising campaign before the war, making use of the company's own film unit. Beddington's authority was to determine the direction of the Films Division for the rest of the war. He made two immediate decisions,

The First Days. Ambulance girl checks her appearance in wing mirror. Made in September 1939, this was the first of many home front films. MH 24288

Balloon Site 568. A woman dressing a shop model is recognised by two of her friends in the WAAF. After the reunion she also resolves to join the service. Films of this kind were produced in order to help recruitment. FLM 1004

Coastal Command. The crew of a Sunderland flying boat display their mascot. The film was one of a number of dramatised longer documentaries produced by the Crown Film Unit. FLM 1332

first to expand a scheme for the non-theatrical distribution of film, to reach audiences which would not normally be able to go to the cinema, and second to inaugurate a programme of 'five-minute films', short informational pieces which could be rapidly made and so retain their topicality in a quickly-changing war situation. (So many of these were needed that most would be commissioned from the independent units.) He had to deal with Balcon's apparent desire to use the GPO Film Unit himself, a move which he resolutely resisted, though Ealing did gain the bonus of having Cavalcanti join their company when Beddington had finished his revisions.[15] Cavalcanti was able to advise the studio about techniques of neo-realism which Balcon hoped to introduce into his wartime features. At the MOI the new head of film production was Sir Arthur Elton, a distinguished producer of documentaries with a particular interest in the area of science and technology. Ian Dalrymple was appointed head of the GPO Film Unit and it was his proposal that the more appropriate name 'Crown Film Unit' be adopted. Pinewood Studios, which had been closed at the beginning of the war, became their home and also that of the production branches of the Army and RAF Film Units.

Before establishing the pattern of the MOI's film production, Beddington had to resist a number of the conclusions made by a report from the Select Committee on National Expenditure, published in August 1940.[16] This drew attention again to the failure of the ministry's policies in the first year of war. The reassurance aim was not enough, it said, mainly because there was no evidence that the public needed a boost to its morale (a questionable statement, and it did not make the obvious inference that people's morale had never actually been tested by the inaction of the Phoney War). The newsreel was still recognised as the most important area of film propaganda but the attention given to features and longer documentaries alike was criticised, because such films were related to 'precise and probably transient needs'. The decision to make five-minute documentaries, however, was applauded. Reservations were expressed about the non-theatrical scheme on the curious grounds that it was 'more in the nature of general education'. No more money should be spent by the MOI on feature films (though it was too late to withdraw the funds given to *49th Parallel*), nor should the Films Division submit possible scripts to producers; instead, it should recognise the individualistic nature of the film trade and allow companies to make their own proposals, confining its role to that of giving general approval.

It would be hardly surprising if Beddington had felt this to be a weak set of recommendations, brought about by bureaucratic concern for conserving expenditure rather than interest in prosecuting an active policy of film publicity and propaganda. The newsreel proposal was not disputed and

in practice the companies were to be made more direct agents of government propaganda, their scripts and visual content subjected to tight censorship by the MOI. Beddington promised to review the non-theatrical scheme after a three month period, but there is no evidence that he ever did so, and it continued to operate as he had planned it. With regard to feature films, he still wanted the Films Division to 'act as a critical clearing house for ideas' and in time he was able to achieve this by setting up a committee on which the officials and the producers were both represented.

It was Beddington's decision to depart from the report's views about documentaries which provoked controversy, not least within the MOI itself. It must be said that had the Films Division gone on to approve the production only of five-minute films, most of the documentaries from the Second World War which have been so admired by film historians would never have existed. For this reason alone one should be grateful for Beddington's stand. His apparent flouting of the Select Committee's advice has been linked to the film-makers' zeal for social reform, in a commentary made by the historian Nicholas Pronay, who has written of Beddington's 'corporatist mentality', backed up by the leftward-leaning sympathies of Sidney Bernstein, founder of the Granada cinema chain and now an adviser on distribution in the Films Division.[17] But the truth is that no deep political motivation was responsible for the change. It had been realised that cinema programmes had been shortened as a result of pressures brought about by the blitz and there was room in them for longer non-fiction films which could be easier to sell than one-reelers. The case was put, neither by 'corporatist' Beddington nor socialist Bernstein, but by Ian Dalrymple, a Conservative Party sympathiser. He had joined the MOI from the commercial industry, about which he had no illusions, and it was his opinion that the Crown Film Unit was better equipped to quickly and efficiently produce documentaries in a climate where the profit motive was not a factor: 'I make this recommendation as one who has always worked in commercial films and has many years' experience of trade psychology'. Moreover, he was opposed to any move towards cutting the staff of the unit, whose salaries had been upgraded by the MOI. His ideas provoked a wrathful response from Frank Pick, the ministry's Director General, who told Beddington that Dalrymple should be 'brought under control'. Beddington made an equally robust defence. Unfortunately the surviving records contain no minutes of the meeting between Pick and Beddington on 11 November 1940 but it is clear that the Films Division emerged as the victor in the argument. An annual budget of £100,000 was now to be set aside for a programme which was designed to produce fifty-two five-minute films and twenty-six longer documentaries.[18] This production policy was not to be seriously challenged again.

The reinvigoration of the documentary programme coincided with the drastically altered war situation from the summer of 1940. After the fall of France and through the Blitz period there was a very obvious need to sustain public morale but the MOI deduced, probably correctly, that too much exhortation would be counter-productive and the provision of direct information was a greater requirement.[19] People had to be educated in the performance of certain simple and mundane duties connected with areas like civil defence, maintaining secrecy, health and so forth. For this task the shorter documentary was admirably suited (the 'five-minute' limitation was not followed literally, one reel length being the true standard) and the MOI went even further by providing informational trailers attached to the newsreels. Most of the work was undertaken by the independent units, the Crown Film Unit tending to concentrate on larger and more intellectually-conceived projects. The direction which Crown took became more that of historical record, with some of its more famous films evoking the mood and spirit of Britain at war, productions of this kind being intended partly for foreign consumption.

It is known that the mass cinema-going public wanted escapism and diversion most of all, qualities found mainly in feature films, of which those from Hollywood greatly outnumbered British productions. A film propaganda campaign intended to influence the people had to be pursued partly by stealth. The rapid-paced newsreels may seem to have had more direct appeal than the leisurely documentaries. Their terse, sharp commentaries were the audio–visual equivalent of the kind of journalism which was projected by the popular newspapers. The documentary method had been evolved by middle-class intellectuals with radical sympathies and sometimes the commentaries betrayed this fact. Crown's *The Heart of Britain*, for example, a film about the regions during the blitz period, used a distinctively Oxbridge-type voice for its narration. Mass-Observation discovered that two other films from the same unit, *Britain at Bay*, where the narration was spoken by J B Priestley, and *Dover-Front Line*, in which citizens of that heavily bombarded town spoke directly to camera, were more popular. Verbal communication therefore was partly the key to acceptance by the public. Mass-Observation's Tom Harrisson thought that people reacted against the newsreels, that the aggressive tones of their narrators created a kind of 'phonetic nausea', and he felt, contrary to the impression cherished now by some historians, that the documentaries were better received[20] (it may be noted that the accents of E V H Emmett of Gaumont-British News and Leslie Mitchell of Movietone News, for example, were also of the upper-middle class, BBC-type).

Mass-Observation is the only major source for a judgement on how particular films were received by the public but one must take account of the fact that its methods of analysis were sometimes rudimentary, often being based on no more than simply listening to people's reactions in a cinema, and also selective, in that only a very small number of films were considered, and even where surveys by interview were conducted they were done only at a tiny minority of cinemas. Evidence about the popularity or otherwise of documentaries is contradictory and inconclusive. It is interesting to discover, for instance, that Crown's much publicised *Target for Tonight*, a fifty-minute re-enactment of an early bombing raid over Germany, directed by Harry Watt, caused disappointment, at least to one group whose responses were collected, after being promoted by the press to the level of a feature film. The public presumably wanted death or glory, not the starkness of such a bare, factual production. On the other hand, a more modest film from the same unit, *Ferry Pilot*, describing the work of the Air Transport Auxiliary, was favourably received. Emphatic persuasion, as in Concanen's *Seaman Frank Goes Back to Sea*, in favour of National Savings, was resented. Dramatisations were often liked – a commercially-produced short, *Miss Grant Goes to the Door*, in which a couple of village ladies manage to thwart a Nazi invader, was one example, fanciful though it looks now – but not when they became so exaggerated that they strained credulity, as in the 'rumour' film *You're Telling Me*, made by Rotha Productions. Films which employed complex techniques, like Realist's *Newspaper Train*, directed by the New Zealand animator Len Lye, puzzled people – even so, Mass-Observation recorded some intelligent comments about it – but a straightforward documentary on a little-known field of the conflict, Shell's *War in the Pacific*, was much appreciated.[21] The non-theatrical scheme used nearly one hundred and fifty units to project 16mm prints in venues like village halls and factory canteens and the MOI's regional Film Officers tried to assess public opinion of the films by distributing questionnaires. Helen Forman remembered especially the enthusiastic reception for *Listen to Britain*, the masterly Crown documentary directed by Humphrey Jennings and edited by Stewart McAllister to present a series of impressionistic visual and aural sketches of British people on the home front.[22]

Overall it is not constructive to generalise too dogmatically about audience responses to different types of films. The public was made up of individuals whose perceptions must have differed widely throughout such a highly regionalised and class-divided society as Britain. Reactions both to newsreels and documentaries probably varied a great deal according to the war situation at any particular moment. What the documentaries do now, arguably more than any other kind of film, is provide evidence for the circumstances of the British people during the Second World War, and for

Kill or Be Killed. A British sergeant tracks a German sniper. This film by Realist is an example of a training and instructional production. MH 24277

Dustbin Parade. Scrap materials are recruited for the nation. Made by Halas-Batchelor Productions, this is one of a number of animated films designed to help the war effort. MH 24289

We Sail at Midnight. The Lend-Lease conference room in Washington. This Crown production is an example of a purely informational film, about Lend-Lease procedures, but in this case one which was intended to strengthen Anglo–American understanding. FLM 1139

historians to ignore them is a limitation which they should not allow if they want to search for a fully rounded portrait of the nation at that time. However, it is necessary to take account of the full range of films, not only those made by the more famous directors which have received sole consideration in a number of cinema histories.[23]

A major part of the MOI's support for film-making was directed towards distributing the documentaries overseas. Through the period 1940–1 much effort was devoted to trying to influence opinion in the USA, where in spite of the sympathetic stance of President Roosevelt, there was a powerful isolationist lobby and some more directly anti-British groups. Alexander Korda had moved to Hollywood and attracted bitter criticism from the isolationists over his patriotically pro-British feature *Lady Hamilton*, implicitly comparing Napoleon's ambitions with those of Hitler. At home though, the completion of *49th Parallel* had proceeded too slowly, owing to production difficulties. The way was open therefore for the commissioning of shorter propaganda films, a need satisfied by the Crown Film Unit's documentaries *London Can Take It* and *Christmas Under Fire*, both with narrations by the American journalist Quentin Reynolds. They were distributed in the USA by Warner Brothers and attracted some attention, including further anger from the isolationists. Net profits of $45,000 were given to a Spitfire Fund.[24] *Target for Tonight* also seems to have been well received in some American circles, but there can be no doubt that films like these reached only a minority and probably they were most influential with the already-converted.[25] After America's entry into the war, the emphasis changed slightly, to try persuading our ally that Britain was keeping up its contribution to the war. Sidney Bernstein crossed the Atlantic to negotiate a distribution deal which was finally signed in the autumn of 1942, whereby British films were to be handed round in a rota between the eight main American distributors.[26]

London Can Take It (with its British-distributed equivalent, *Britain Can Take It*), a collaborative effort between Watt, Jennings and McAllister, has become a classic film of the blitz. However, there are many others, of which only a few examples can be given, which might merit the attention of the historian. Indeed, Crown's *Ordinary People*, also made for overseas distribution, started with the self-conscious caption 'to the future historian'; it depicted a cross-section of the community as they cope with everyday tasks during a typical raid. *Neighbours Under Fire* and *Post 23*, both produced by Strand Films, also dealt with community problems, Realist's *Living With Strangers* and Strand's *Village School* with the evacuee situation, Realist's *They Also Serve* with the role of women at home, while a film like *Machines and Men*, made by the CWS Film Unit, had a northern industrial background. There was a flood of purely informational films which told the public how to tackle current tasks, like providing first aid, making an incendiary bomb harmless, or digging an allotment. The standard of professionalism shown by Crown and by the independent documentary units can be contrasted with the ludicrous results when 20th Century Fox tried to put across a 'blackout' message in *Mr Proudfoot Shows a Light*, a production which did not inspire confidence in the commercial industry's ability to make short films.

It is easy to criticise the blitz documentaries for the restricted view which they gave of events. For an overseas audience they were intended to present an appearance of unified effort, an abandonment of class interests and an absence of panic. They concealed the very real shortcomings of official policy or the muddle and confusion which was suffered by the bombed-out inhabitants of some areas, especially in the East End of London. They built up an image of unity which was soon to disappear. But at least they made an honest attempt to portray real people in real situations and as such they have left a valuable audio–visual legacy of British citizens being mobilised for war. Awkward moments in some of the dramatisations no doubt were a consequence of the gap in understanding between the middle-class film-makers and the working-class people whose lives and circumstances they were trying to capture on the screen. Even so, these documentaries are a more truly representative record than the fantasies of feature films like *Salute John Citizen* or *The Bells Go Down*, played by West End actors and actresses (in the latter film the wisecracking comedian Tommy Trinder takes a cockney role).

When the Crown Film Unit returned to the subject of the blitz it did so with its most extended film to date, *Fires Were Started*, released in 1943 but looking back at the events of 1940–1. Definition of 'feature documentary' is difficult but the term is generally applied to a film with the dramatic structure of a feature and the strict authenticity of detail characteristic of the documentary. In this case the players were all AFS firemen and in spite of some moments of poetic licence in Jennings's dialogue the film comes across as a convincing and definitive historical record. Pat Jackson directed for Crown the even longer feature documentary *Western Approaches*, a story of merchant seamen adrift in a lifeboat, made in colour and finished late in 1944. This movement by the documentary school towards the feature was paralleled by an attempt by the commercial industry, notably Ealing, to introduce a higher degree of realism. Harry Watt had left Crown, following disagreements with Ian Dalrymple, to join Balcon's studio and for them he made the short feature *Nine Men*, about a patrol in the Libyan desert, a work which employed lesser-known actors and was very much moulded by the documentary tradition. This new neo-realistic style was also apparent in Ealing's *San Demetrio-London*, directly based on an incident in the Battle of the Atlantic, but it was an example not to be repeated in a climate where audiences required more basic entertainment from their cinema-going.

The longer documentary which was most successful with the public (and which won a Hollywood Oscar) was the Army Film Unit's *Desert Victory*. The War Office had recruited the staff for this unit mostly from the commercial industry and at first they had difficulty in adapting to the documentary method; early attempts were unimpressive and they had to call in Crown to assist them with a film about the Lofoten raid. But the head of the unit, David MacDonald, did have documentary experience and it was the combination of him as producer and Roy Boulting as director which turned *Desert Victory* into a triumph, helped by its timely release when the Eighth Army's victory in North Africa was still hot news.[27] The hallmarks of the AFU's style were precise attention to military and campaign details with swift narration, eschewing political and social content, and the formula was further developed in the Anglo–American *The True Glory* (another Oscar-winner), about the campaign in North-West Europe, and in *Burma Victory*.

The Blitz was followed by a period when the attention of the MOI and its documentaries turned towards the theme of production in industry. This was the time now of the mass enrolment of women for factory labour, and encouraging pieces, like Verity's *Jane Brown Changes Her Job*, were produced to persuade women that life in industry was not too depressing; many of these were shown non-theatrically to women's audiences. They were another type of reassurance film, especially in an environment where many workers did not feel that the outcome of the war might be an enrichment of their social conditions and where the employment of women inevitably caused much disruption to family life. Indeed a short film like *Essential Jobs*, from Rotha Productions, a dramatised way of explaining how a particularly mundane task was indispensable to the war effort, betrays a recognition that cynicism and lassitude were becoming elements of the post-Blitz mentality. The same company's *Night Shift*, the most accomplished of the factory documentaries about women, suffered from patches of halting dialogue but in general its impressions of the shop floor and the canteen, with genuine Welsh workers, were well conceived and more authentic than comparable scenes in the feature *Millions Like Us*, again cast mainly from the West End pool of players.[28]

From the summer of 1940 *Documentary News Letter*, published by Film Centre, had campaigned for the documentary not only to deal with current events but also to project expectations of a better world after the war. Initially the MOI had been unenthusiastic about their screen propaganda moving in that direction. Roy Boulting recalled that his dramatised short film *Dawn Guard*, in which two members of the Home Guard exchange ideas about the post-war situation, had been coolly received by the Films Division, and another project, Realist's *Goodbye Yesterday*, was suppressed altogether.[29] It is possible that Brendan Bracken allowed more latitude to the film-makers when he saw that the public mood was turning in favour of social reform.[30] Whatever the reason, the theme became more common from 1941 to the end of the war. But it was not a dominant one; the impression which Nicholas Pronay gives when he writes about 'a committedly single-party and partisan group of film-makers' is misleading.[31] In fact only a small proportion of films introduced the subject at all. Humphrey Jennings, the best known of the documentary film-makers, only touched on the aftermath of the conflict in his final wartime film, *A Diary for Timothy*, and even this provoked complaint from the Films Division's officials.[32] Where social criticism did occur it was a part of that tide of public opinion which produced the Beveridge Report and which was to lead to the Labour Party's election victory in 1945. It is of course no accident that films like Spectator's *Tyneside Story* and Strand's *Wales, Green Mountain – Black Mountain* were set in areas which had suffered pre-war depression. The first was acted by a local theatre company and the second had a script by Dylan Thomas; both gave the view that circumstances after the war should be better, a proposition which the average working-class audience would be unlikely to reject. The documentary film-makers were liberal-minded people searching for a post-war consensus; to see their movement as a kind of left-wing conspiracy is overstating the case.

Paul Rotha was the most radical of them and he used both his production company and his own newsreel series to present his ideas.[33] Two of his films, *World of Plenty* and *USA – the Land and its People*, written by Eric Knight who had emigrated to America from England before the First World War, were disliked by Sidney Bernstein who saw them as straining Anglo–American relations at a time when Bracken and the government were anxious above all to maintain amity between London and Washington. The idealistic, and no doubt impractical, scheme for organising food resources put forward in *World of Plenty* was accompanied by statistics of pre-war nutritional levels which were seen by the US Department of Agriculture as reflecting badly on them, even though Rotha quickly asserted that he was attacking no government in particular. In Britain, too, the Minister of Agriculture described the scenario as 'dangerous'. Beddington and Elton both wished the film to be completed and its successful reception at a world food conference in 1943 was some vindication of their views.[34] However, *USA – the Land and its People* had a rougher passage; Knight's intention to expose the darker sides of American life, though consistent with New Deal objec-

tives, was again opposed from New York by Bernstein and the film appeared only in a modified form in 1945.[35] The proposition of social change, outlined in this modest way by the documentary group, hardly appeared at all in the commercial feature film, only one director – John Baxter – making any real effort to come to terms with it.[36]

Paul Rotha was an especially militant film-maker and there is no doubt that the subsequent history of British documentary was a disappointment to him. Ian Dalrymple, for his part, would have liked the Crown Film Unit to have progressed further in the direction of historical record but his failure to persuade the MOI that unissued film material should be preserved was a contribution to his decision to resign and rejoin Korda who had returned from America to set up a new company.[37] Basil Wright succeeded to the leadership of Crown in January 1945; both he and Beddington left the MOI (which would shortly become the Central Office of Information) as soon as the war was finished. Beddington's guidance had been helpful to the documentary film-makers and it had been totally non-political; there is no evidence of 'corporatism' in his outlook. Indeed, writing three years after the war, he chastised the documentary movement for its political bias and regretted that many of its original founders had not moved onwards in their ideas:

> The old gang twelve or fifteen years ago were pioneers with new ideas, great enthusiasms, courage and honesty. They are now middle-aged, much fatter or thinner than they were, and no longer potential geniuses. I cannot see that they have made any advance in the last five years. Humour they do not understand; criticism they resent. This is no state of mind with which to startle, tickle or impress the world.[38]

In fact the Crown Film Unit was to be dissolved by the Conservatives in 1951: the great Grierson-inspired movement was terminated at last.

A general study of Second World War British cinema is a valuable source for the historian searching for a comprehensive outlook on British society. It has been commonly accepted that, in spite of the contraction of the industry, the war brought about a renaissance of British films. There is some truth in this, but the thesis ignores a number of factors: the existence of a few commendable films before the war, the fact that a number of prominent directors who had started in the thirties coincidentally happened to reach maturity during the war, the recognition that the bulk of British films remained as mediocre as ever, and the circumstances that the growth in the cinema audience was not caused by any improved quality in the films themselves but by the simple need to escape from the war for an afternoon or an evening (and preferably to see Hollywood movies). The best British features were not necessarily the most realistic and indeed often were the most off-beat ones. Documentaries were more firmly grounded in reality and, while one must take account of the attitudes both of their official sponsors and their makers, they provide now a wide-ranging guide to the appearances, the speech, the living conditions and the actions of British people during the Second World War.

Notes

1. *Industrial Britain* and *North Sea* were respectively good examples of these two genres.
2. Consider, for example, the Soviet films of the twenties or Robert Flaherty's documentaries.
3. Roger Manvell, *Films and the Second World War*, New York and London, 1974, is more comprehensive than most cinema histories.
4. See the Introduction to Frances Thorpe and Nicholas Pronay, *British Official Films in the Second World War*, Oxford and Santa Barbara, 1980, pp 1–40.
5. Paul Rotha, *Documentary Diary*, London, 1973, p 233.
6. PRO INF 1/762, Report of 2 June, 1939. The chairman of the committee was J G Hughes-Roberts, Government Cinematography Adviser, who at the time was responsible for the Imperial War Museum's collection of First World War films, deposited in the War Office.
7. INF 6/349.
8. INF 1/56.
9. INF 1/30.
10. There is no substance in the story related by the director Harry Watt that the film was made without the knowledge of the MOI officials. See Harry Watt, *Don't Look at the Camera*, London, 1974, pp 128–9.
11. INF 1/196.
12. INF 1/848.
13. INF 1/56.
14. INF 1/57.
15. INF 1/867.
16. 13th Report of the Select Committee on National Expenditure, INF 1/59.
17. Nicholas Pronay, ' "The Land of Promise": The Projection of Peace Aims in Britain', in K R M Short (ed), *Film and Radio Propaganda in World War II*, London and Canberra, 1983, p 58.
18. INF 1/81.
19. See Marion Yass, *This Is Your War : Home Front Propaganda in the Second World War*, London, 1983, for a concise account which includes consideration of film policy.
20. Tom Harrisson, 'Films and the Home Front – the evaluation of their effectiveness by "Mass-Observation" ', in Nicholas Pronay, and D W Spring (eds), *Propaganda, Politics and Film 1918–45*, London, 1982, p 239.
21. Various reports in the files of the Mass-Observation Archive, University of Sussex.
22. Helen Forman, 'The non-theatrical distribution of films by the Ministry of Information', in Pronay and Spring, *Propaganda, Politics and Film*, p 230.
23. Thorpe and Pronay, *British Official Films*, catalogue all films produced and distributed by the MOI in 1939–45. For more detailed consideration of individual documentaries, see Clive Coultass, *Images for Battle : British Film and the Second World War 1939–45*, London and Toronto, 1989.
24. INF 1/600.
25. American public opinion was more strongly swayed in favour of Britain by Hollywood's own *Mrs. Miniver*.
26. INF 1/632.
27. See Anthony Aldgate, 'Creative Tensions: *Desert Victory*, the Army Film Unit and Anglo–American Rivalry, 1943–5', in Philip M Taylor (ed), *Britain and the Cinema in the Second World War*, London, 1988, pp 144–167.
28. *Millions Like Us* did at least employ amongst its players a Yorkshireman (Eric Portman), a Welshwoman (Megs Jenkins) and a Scot (Gordon Jackson).
29. See Roy Boulting, IWM Department of Sound Records interview no 4627/06, transcript pp 3–7, and Basil Wright, IWM interview no 6231/08, pp 42–4.
30. Yass, *This Is Your War*, op cit, pp 57–60.
31. Pronay, 'The Land of Promise', in Short, *Film and Radio Propaganda*, p 60.
32. Wright, IWM interview, op cit, pp 55–8.
33. *Worker and Warfront*. See Thorpe and Pronay, op cit, pp 262–3.
34. INF 1/214, 6/561.
35. INF 1/217.
36. Baxter's films *Love on the Dole* (1941), *The Common Touch* (1941), *Let The People Sing* (1942) and *The Shipbuilders* (1943) were socially progressive but not sufficiently well made to have much effect.
37. Elizabeth Sussex, *The Rise and Fall of British Documentary*, Berkeley and Los Angeles, 1975, pp 151–2.
38. *Documentary Film News*, July 1948, p 77.

Explore an extraordinary era of art history through the pages of
The Journal of Decorative and Propaganda Arts.

Our international quarterly, founded in 1986 by the Wolfson Foundation of
Decorative and Propaganda Arts, promotes scholarship in the pivotal years 1875 to 1945.

Acclaimed for uncommon content, radiant illustrations, and distinctive design,
the Journal boasts awards from Print Magazine, Mead Paper, the Art Libraries Society
of North America, and the American Institute of Graphic Arts.

Among many eminent contributors are Isabelle Anscombe, Rossana Bossaglia,
John E. Bowlt, David Brett, Alastair Duncan, David Gebhard, Nicola Gordon Bowe,
Henry Hawley, Karal Ann Marling, Peyton Skipwith, Colin White, and Gabriel P. Weisberg.

Subscriptions $30 for individuals, $50 for institutions, $8 for overseas airmail.

The Journal of Decorative and Propaganda Arts 2399 N.E. Second Avenue Miami, Florida 33137-9956 USA (305) 573-9170.